Varieties of realism,

GEOMETRIES OF REPRESENTATIONAL ART

MARGARET A. HAGEN
Boston University

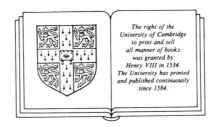

The right of the
University of Cambridge
to print and sell
all manner of books
was granted by
Henry VIII in 1534.
The University has printed
and published continuously
since 1584.

CAMBRIDGE UNIVERSITY PRESS
CAMBRIDGE
LONDON   NEW YORK   NEW ROCHELLE
MELBOURNE   SYDNEY

Published by the Press Syndicate of the University of Cambridge
The Pitt Building, Trumpington Street, Cambridge CB2 1RP
32 East 57th Street, New York, NY 10022, USA
10 Stamford Road, Oakleigh, Melbourne 3166, Australia

First published in 1986

Printed in the United States of America

Library of Congress Cataloging in Publication Data
Hagen, Margaret A.
Varieties of realism.
Bibliography; p.
Includes index.
1. Visual perception.   2. Art–Psychology.
3. Geometry.   I. Title.
N7430.5.H33   1986   760'.1'9   85–10982
ISBN 0 521 25313 6 hard covers
ISBN 0 521 31329 5 paperback

This book is dedicated to
MADELEINE BRUHN
MARIE OWEN
HELEN BEE
ANNE PICK
From a grateful student.

Contents

Preface

The history of a book is arbitrarily truncated by its publication. This book sprang from the simple ground of a single assumption about the nature of representational pictures, and was fertilized by indignation over the writings of others who did not accept the assumption, or, worse yet, adopted its opposite. The assumption was that all successful representational pictures make available to the beholder the same kind of visual information as does the ordinary environment. Years spent toiling in the empirical vineyards led not to the rejection of the original assumption but to the consideration and adoption of additional variables – resulting in the elaboration of a theory of representational art that seemed at times in danger of falling under its own weight.

This book represents a distillation of the findings from those years of research on pictorial information. It is based not only on conventional psychophysical exploration of traditional Western art (and what passes for art in perceptual research), but also on comparisons between Western efforts and the art styles of many non-Western cultures. It was exposure to the complexity and diversity of the world's art styles that eroded my own ethoncentrism; it is my earnest hope that examination of this book will do likewise for its readers. Western thought has long been distorted by the putative wisdom of the aphorism, "Westerners draw what they see while all others draw what they know." It is time for Western thinkers to relinquish their dubious hold on the secret of visual information and acknowledge its common ownership by all makers of successful representational art. An open-minded exploration of the world's art styles, extant and past, illuminates not only the complex character of representation, but also the nature of visual perception itself. That is the thesis of this book, and its goal.

Acknowledgments

This book was begun when I was on sabbatical leave granted by Boston University, and I am deeply grateful for the time afforded me. I owe gratitude to so many people for so many things that is simply not possible to thank them all here. The people and institutions who gave me permission to reproduce works they own are acknowledged in the figure captions, but some are deserving of very special thanks. These are the people (nearly all women) who work in the photoservices departments (nearly all windowless) of museums: in particular, the Seattle Art Museum, the Museum of Fine Arts in Boston, and the Metropolitan Museum in New York. Their kindness, helpfulness, patience, and efficiency were truly impressive, and I could never have finished the book without them. I am grateful to many people who read the manuscript at different stages of its development, especially Jim Todd, Julian Hochberg, and Rudolf Arnheim. It should be understood that all remaining errors and misconceptions are my own. Indeed, it is my fervent hope that Professor Arnheim can forgive me for holding what is for him a completely untenable viewpoint. I owe him a great deal. I thank my friends who encouraged me when progress seemed unbearably slow, and my editor, Susan Milmoe, as well as the helpful people at Cambridge Unviversity Press.

My intellectual debts are too numerous to list, but two must be briefly noted: Harold Jacobs, who reintroduced me to geometry after many years, and James R. Newman, whose tremendous achievement in collecting and editing the four-volume *World of Mathematics* can never be sufficiently praised. For mathematician and lay person alike, it is an invaluable tool and a joy to read. I owe an incalculable amount to Robert Shaw and Herb Pick; I hope they like the book.

James J. Gibson died before I began to write this book. I would like to believe he would have appreciated this application of his theory to the world of art, but I would not count on it. He himself at several different times in his career examined pictures for what they could tell us about perception, and perception for what it could tell us about pictures, but was never satisfied with the results. Neither was I. I am better pleased with the formulation offered in this volume, which is not to say that Gibson would be. Nevertheless, this book is unavoidably a tribute to him and his work, and it should be read as such.

Margaret A. Hagen
Boston, Massachusetts
February 1985

1 Introduction

*Any and every representation of the universe necessarily is
based on a selection of significant elements. Even
hypothetically there cannot exist a total vision outside of
human perspectives nor outside the perspectives of man at a
given stage in his history. . . . Every art is selective.*

P. Francastel, *Medieval Painting* (1967)

Purpose of the book

The world's many cultures have embraced an astonishing
variety of representational art styles, some still in the process of development and others existing only in specialty
wings of museums. In this book I intend to analyze and
explain some of the critical similarities and differences
among the myriad art styles in terms of their perceptual
and geometrical foundations. Art is subject to laws and
these laws can be expressed in the language of mathematics.
The thesis that geometry, perception, and art are closely
related is not entirely new. Many writers on the history
of mathematics have argued that the artists of the Italian
Renaissance played a critical role in the development of
projective geometry. These same artists, especially Leonardo da Vinci, also figure largely in the history of visual
perception. The novelty of my argument is the claim that
all art, not just that of the West, is governed by geometric
principles. Although Western art is generally acknowledged to be primarily geometric, the "primitive" art of
Egypt, South Africa, the Northwest Coast – indeed, all
nonperspective art – is often characterized as a form of

symbolic representation, more akin to written text than t
geometry.

My contention is that Western art exploits only a sma
subset of the options allowed in geometry. Consideratio
of other options within the geometrical concepts of trans
formation, invariant, and group can point the way to
new understanding of the varieties of realism in represen
tational art.

Structure of the argument

To formulate this argument, I shall examine the histor
of the concept of natural perspective, the geometrical struc
ture of light to the eye as a stimulus for visual perception
Then I shall attempt to clarify for the nonmathematica
reader some of the most useful concepts from moder
geometry for the study of vision and art. By presentin
recent research, which applies these concepts to the prob
lems of perception, I hope to illuminate their relevance an
their promise. The body of the book presents a categori
zation system that analyzes representational art using term
of the modern geometry of image generation.

I am a perceptual psychologist. It is with much trepi
dation that the perceptionist ventures into the domain o
the art historian, or worse, into that of the artist. It is on
thing to write about the perception of pictures and to con
duct empirical research on the topic; it is altogether anothe
to attempt a statement on the psychology of representa
tional art. Thus I wish to be as clear here as possible abou
my domain of discourse: what I mean by *representationa*
and *art*. It would be foolhardy to attempt to state particula
definitions of these difficult terms, but it is necessary a
least to limit the areas of the discussion to follow.

What is meant by *Art*

Characterizations of Art (with a capital *A*) abound in ever
field from anthropology to mathematics. The art historia
George Kubler, (1962) once suggested that the idea of Ar
could be expanded to embrace the whole range of man
made things, making the universe of manmade things co

incide with the content of art. But such an all-embracing expansion is far beyond the scope of meaning intended here. How shall I specify the boundaries of what to include? The perceptual psychologist surely cannot do it on the basis of intention of the artist, function of the piece, or aesthetic appeal to the viewer. In a perceptual analysis it does not matter whether the purpose of a work was to promote instruction and reverence in Christians, to capture or generate magic in ancient rituals, to guarantee the comforts of the present life in the next, to picture to the king the visage of his intended lady, or to create an object of beauty. What matters perceptually is the nature of the product, and in specifying relevant characteristics of artistic creations themselves it is possible to arrive at the circumscription of the domain of art. This is accomplished more easily by exclusion of artistic products than by enumeration.

By art I do not mean sculpture, crafts, artifacts, or the elegancies of rhetorical forms. I mean the two-dimensional creations of skilled people, whether painted, drawn, etched, engraved, photographed, or even programmed. I do not mean the startlingly beautiful patterns of nature, or the happy accidents of chance construction, or the uncontrolled expressions of children. This is not to suggest that the drawings and paintings of children may not show developing artistic expression, but only that they are not yet art in the sense intended here. Two-dimensional art in this book is always skilled labor, the end product of developed technique; even, and perhaps especially, as it occurs in the Ice Age caves of Spain and France. This delimitation of art excludes, in addition to the unskilled drawings of children, a great many snapshots of summer camp and family picnics. These products are certainly pictures, and undoubtedly subject to some of the same criteria of analysis that I will present, but they are not art.

What is meant by *representational*

Representational is another word that in meaning everything means nothing. For human beings, and for many other organisms as well, almost any *A* can represent almost any *B*. It is quite possible to establish, by repeated couplings in space and time, an arbitrary association between almost any two things. In this sense, any painting can be considered to be representational if that is the will of either artist or viewer.

In a more limited sense, and one less outrageous to the contemporary artist, a painting could be considered to be representational only if that is the intent of the artist. Using the artist's intention as the criterion for representational status would allow at least for the division of art into creations whose contents are intended to depict something else, however abstractly or obscurely, and creations whose contents are intended to point only to themselves. This latter category is not relevant to my treatment of representational art; and the first category is much too large. This prescription also ignores the frustrated cry of the layman who wishes to be told what the picture is intended to be when it does not look clearly like anything.

In order to cut the category of representational art down to a manageable size, I shall exclude from it all arbitrary and completely idiosyncratic representations, and retain only those creations for which the representational basis is not only nonarbitrary but also common to all. By common to all, I do not mean that the character of the representation is necessarily obvious at first glance to the uneducated eye, but only that a brief direction of attention must produce an "Ah ha!" response from the viewer. A limited guidance to the features of the depicted contents must produce identification or recognition at least of general character. It may take years of training to appreciate the subleties of the rendition of the contents, but if it takes years to see the subject matter at all, then a picture is not representational art in the sense I intend.

This point of view is not shared by all writers on the subject of representation, and may indeed be the minority view at present. Nevertheless, it is a criterion for representational art that will determine the scope of my analysis. That the boundaries have not been arbitrarily selected will be supported by a review in Chapter 10 of the large body of literature on developmental picture making. The interested reader is also referred to the cross-cultural literature reviews in Hagen and Jones (1978) and Jones and Hagen (1980b).

Problem of style

Because the main focus of this book is to generate a perceptual, geometrical system of categorizing representational art styles, we are led immediately to the problem of style in art. But *style*, of course, is another of those carpetbag words. Perhaps an anecdote will illustrate what I do not mean by style. I once attended an art history lecture for college freshmen, in which the professor showed a dozen slides of Picasso's work, from earliest to latest periods, in fairly rapid succession. He asserted at the end of the slide show that despite the changing techniques and idioms in Picasso's work, one could always see the same persistent style and signature of the artist across it all. I do not mean by *style* anything so subtle as the concept illustrated by this art historian. I mean the coherent system of depiction embraced not by an individual artist, but by a people, or by their artists, at a more or less specifiable place and time in history. Thus, whereas I know that it will do violence to the distinctions observed by the educated eye, I shall write conventionally, if simplistically, of the style of painting in ancient Egypt, contrasting New Kingdom style with Old, or of the style of Roman mural painting, or of pre–seventeenth–century Japanese painting. Such usage is not intended to indicate insensitivity to the complexity of the problems of style, but rather simple inadequacy of vocabulary. Perhaps *uniform mode of rendering* is a better phrase than *style of depiction*, if only because it is less familiar. On the other hand, *mode* doesn't really mean much of anything either, and *style* at least has the appeal of familiarity to the nonspecialist.

The conventional designation of styles to be used in the argument assumes that freshmen in an art history class could, on the first day of class, reliably sort into piles a half dozen exemplars of each of the styles to be analyzed. It assumes that traditional Japanese art looks sufficiently unlike Western Gothic art to elicit relatively reliable cat-

egories from people who are naive about art. It does n
assume the impossibility of categorical overlap or of m
sorting relative to conventional lines. Indeed, it should
noted that different styles often contain many works th
would confuse the naive as to their respective conventior
stylistic designations. However, I hope that the perce
tually based system of categorization can account both f
missortings and for overlapping categories.

What is meant by *perception*

Presenting a perceptually based analysis of representatior
art styles also requires explaining what is meant by t
perceptual basis to be used in that analysis. By *perceptior*
mean the active picking up of information about the e
vironment, the functioning of the organism in terms
environmental affordances and constraints. To interact
to perceive; to experience is to perceive; to respond is
perceive. To grow, to develop, to learn, even to exist
all, presupposes an environment with which the organis
interacts. One can go so far as to argue that the conce
of organism means nothing without the complementa
concept of environment, and conversely that environme
has no meaning except as a behavioral interface for .
organism. This idea is not a new one, but recent write
have stated it most strongly and clearly. James Gibs
(1979), in his last book, *The Ecological Approach to Visu*
Perception, asserted what he called the principle of m
tuality: "An organism, by definition, requires an enviror
ment surrounding it and, conversely, an environme
requires organism(s) to surround." This principle stat
that to specify or describe the environment of the organis
is to characterize, in general terms, the organism itself;
describe the organism is to outline the general character .
its environment.

There is not much agreement on the issue of which
the most fruitful or valid approach to the study of perce
tion. My own preference is to characterize the hypothetic
environment as precisely as possible, and then to chec
empirically the validity of the interface. If a particular "er
vironmental" variable does not result in covarying pe

ceptions by the relevant organism, then it does not belong, at that time, to the environment of the organism. Of course, as the organism develops, the environment with which it interacts becomes more complex.

Perception, however, is not simply undifferentiated responsiveness. The demarcation of areas of responsiveness to be called perceptual will vary with the biases of the psychologist. By human perception, I mean the pickup of specific information about the relatively persistent properties of the human environment: the objects, surface layout, and events that exist in relation to human behavior, to which human beings are capable of responding. By relatively persistent properties, I mean the size, shape, distance, slant, color, and composition of the objects and surfaces in a cluttered and changing environment, as well as the form and sequence of events that occur within it. Some of these properties, like size, seem more persistent than others, like distance, but each property is persistent across certain specifiable changes and is destroyed by others. In this sense, all perceptual properties are relative to context, just as they are relative to the perceiving organism.

Specific visual information for the objects and events in the environment is carried in the light to the eye, in the stimulus for vision. It is here, particularly, that geometry has been most useful in furthering our understanding of visual perception. In Appendix D, I trace the historical development of the application of geometrical concepts to vision, but one thorny issue in the field of representational art remains to be discussed: the source and role of realism in art.

Role of realism

Representational pictures, like other objects, provide optical information about their relatively persistent properties, about themselves and their depicted contents. The optical information provided by a picture about *itself* as an object is necessarily the same kind of information provided by any object about its own properties. However, the information a representational picture provides about its depicted *contents*, its subject matter, may or may not be the

same as the visual information for that content in the or
dinary environment. In the specification of the nature o
pictorial information lies the heart of one's position on th
role of realism in representational art.

My position is that representational pictures, *all* repr
sentational pictures from any culture or period in histor
exploit the fact of *natural perspective*, the geometry of th
light that strikes the eye. They succeed as representatio
because they provide structured visual information equi
alent to that provided by the real scene represented. Th
equivalence of ordinary and pictorial information can b
understood by examining the concepts of invariant, tran
formation, and group from modern geometry. By appl
ing these concepts both to real world and to pictori
information, to natural and to artificial perspective, I hop
to make clear the geometrical basis underlying the varieti
of realism in representational art. Modern geometry giv
us a framework for establishing a system of categorizatic
of representational art that will allow for the placement o
any coherent style, and for its analysis in terms of sim
larities and differences relative to other styles. It also w
permit precise specification of the degree of kinship b
tween any two art styles, both perceptually and geo
metrically.

2 Information and invariants

An individual who explores a strange place by locomotion produces transformations of the optic array for the very purpose of isolating what remains invariant during those transformations. It is not that he has to remember a series of forms but that the space emerges from these optical motions. What went out of sight as he moved one way comes into view as he returns; it does not vanish like smoke, but disappears by being hidden.

James J. Gibson, *The Senses Considered As Perceptual Systems* (1966)

Structure and information

It is my contention that all representational pictures succeed as representations because they carry the same kind of visual information as the scenes they represent; representational pictures exploit natural perspective geometry to carry that information. But what is "visual information" and what is "natural perspective geometry"? And what do they have to do with each other?

In Chapter 1, I wrote that perception is the pickup of information about such relatively persistent properties of the human environment as size, shape, or distance of an object. Where does this information come from? It is useless to speculate on its origins in representational pictures without a firm grasp of its sources in the ordinary, everyday environment.

There has always been considerable controversy surrounding the nature of information, of perception, of vi-

sion itself. It is my opinion that the ecological approac
developed over many years by James J. Gibson of Corn
University, is the clearest, most accessible and basica
useful for the study of visual perception. Because it star
in opposition to most of the traditional analyses of p
ception and may indeed seem surprising even to the su
posedly naive, an historical perspective on the terms a
issues in the study of vision is provided in Appendix
A quasi-historical outline of Gibson's theory is present
here.

Gibson's theory

Gibson began his analysis of optical structure as inf
mation for perception in his book *The Perception of
Visual World* (1950). He revitalized the geometrical co
ception of the angles of the visual field, ascribing to the
sufficient, mathematically specifiable information to affc
a direct perception of the distance, size, shape, and sl
of objects in the visual world. Perception owes to Gibs
the explicit statement of the ecological assumptions n
essary to anchor visual experience in the real world.
basic tenet of Gibsonian thinking is that the human en
ronment almost always includes a ground surface with s
above, that most objects of interest to humans, includi
the observer himself, are located on this surface, and tl
surfaces in the environment like grassy meadows, pebb
beaches, and concrete streets are more or less regular
their makeup. The surfaces of the world structure the lig
reflected from them in such a way that that optical structu
then serves as information for those surfaces.

Gibson clarified the distinction between *structure* and
formation in *The Senses Considered as Perceptual Systems* (196
Structure means an arrangement or *array* of light. Info
mation means *information* about or specification of son
thing, so that some aspect of light is related by physi
laws in a one-to-one way to some aspect or property
the object reflecting it. A specific aspect of structure in t
light may or may not function as information abou
component of the environment.

Sources of structure in the light

Understanding the Gibsonian concepts of structure and information in the light requires a context of certain other Gibsonian notions, namely, the *ambient optic array* and the *station point of observation*, in the framework of Gibson's theory of *ecological optics*. As Gibson (1966) explains:

A habitat consists of an arrangement of surfaces, that is, a layout of planes at various angles to one another. Call them faces or facets, depending on whether they are large or small. If this layout is illuminated, the reflecting planes will generate the dense interlocking network of rays. At every point in the illuminated medium there will be a sheaf or "pencil" of rays converging from all directions. This ray-sheaf is simply an abstract mathematical statement of what is meant by ambient light. The fact to be noted here is that there is no limit to the number of possible convergence points in the medium. Each of these can be called a *station point*. (p. 15)

The surfaces of the ordinary environment are not radiant in themselves; they reflect the light from other radiant sources like the sun. Thus the steady-state ambient light, bouncing off the surfaces of an illuminated environment ad infinitum, or until the sun goes down, is structured by the reflectance properties of the surfaces off of which it bounces. Surfaces of different colors (and textural composition) reflect light in different ways, as do surfaces varying in angle of inclination relative to the light source and to the observer. Finally, reflectance of light is affected by the shadows and shading occasioned by the positioning of objects relative to the light source and to each other. All of these sources of surface and reflectance variation in the world cause the light to a point of observation to be structured in a particular way unique to that point of observation, projectively. Each of these differences in reflectance among faces or facets of objects in the world determines discontinuities or borders in the light to the eye. Thus, each of these borders in the light is specific to some change in surface color, composition, slant, or relative orientation, even on the tiny scale of facets of a single surface like the bumps in coarse fabric (Figure 2.1). These borders or structures in the light, then, are *potential* information for aspects

Figure 2.1. An extremely close photograph of a piece of coarse fabric. (Photograph supplied by the author.)

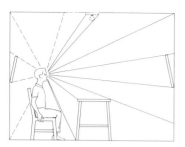

Figure 2.2. Edges of surfaces and forms of solid angles. (From James J. Gibson, The Senses Considered As Perceptual Systems, p. 195. © 1966 by Houghton Mifflin Company. Reprinted by permission of the publishers.)

of structure and layout of surfaces in the ordin environment.

Visual solid angle analysis

This analysis of the whole *optic array* of visual solid ang bounded by the edges of surfaces grew directly out Euclid's theories and the work of the Renaissance painte with certain important differences both in analysis and consequences assumed for perception. The forms of visual solid angles of the optic array are determined, a Euclid, by the relations of the surfaces to the point observation. Light reflecting from objects travels in strai lines, more or less, from the visible surfaces of the obj to the eye, forming an array or arrangement of solid ang as in Renaissance painting, with their apexes at the eye their bases at the visible surfaces of the objects. The dra ing in Figure 2.2 illustrates a section through solid vis cones or pyramids. Such an array is present at every po of space that could be occupied by an eye, and is differ at every point in space.

The optic array of visual angles is known more familia as the *natural perspective* to a point. It is generally assun that the space of natural perspective is bounded by w actually can be seen by an observer standing at a particu place, looking in a particular direction, at a particular of objects. This bounded space is called the *visual field* is rather different from the Renaissance window of vie The binocular visual field is roughly oval in shape extends about 180° to the side and about 150° verticall Each visible surface within this visual field subtends own solid visual angle of slightly different size and sh; for every eye position (Figure 2.3). It is generally assun that the visual solid angles of the optic array are subtenc at the surface of the retina on the opposite side of the no point of the lens. Figure 2.4 illustrates the diverging lig reflected from two points in the world, bent and gathe to points of focus at the back of the eyeball. Specifyi characteristics of the retinal image leads into controve over what aspects of structure in the light to the eye

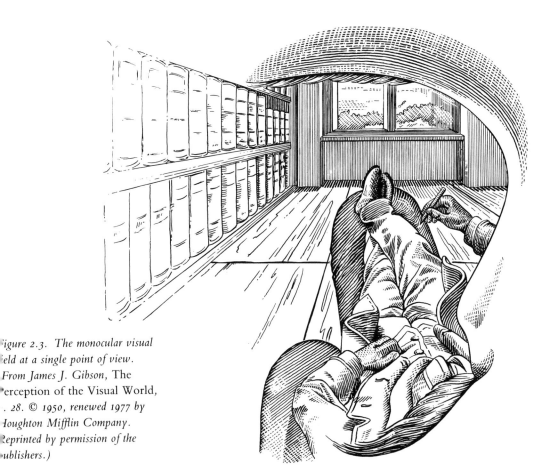

Figure 2.3. The monocular visual field at a single point of view. From James J. Gibson, The Perception of the Visual World, *. 28. © 1950, renewed 1977 by Houghton Mifflin Company. Reprinted by permission of the publishers.)*

potentially informative for perception. For our purposes, it is only important to note that all of the boundaries in the optic array on one side of the projection to the point of observation are also present on the other side of that point, with minor modifications due to lens distortion. What is significant, as Gibson has repeatedly pointed out, is that the structure is *available* in the light, not that it necessarily is used on all occasions by all organisms.

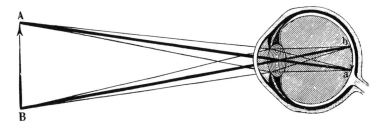

Figure 2.4. The retinal images of world points A and B. (From M.H. Pirenne, Optics, Painting and Photography, *1970, p. 3 top.)*

Figure 2.5. *Changes in visual angle size with increase in distance.* Θ¹ *and* Θ² = *angles formed by the eye and the front edge of each square.* D = *distance.*

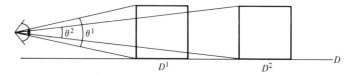

Visual information I: gradients and occlusion

A particularly important set of structures in Gibson's ear work was that of *gradients* in the visual field. The wo gradient means nothing more complex then an increase decrease of something along a given axis or dimensio More precisely, a gradient is the rate at which some mension of the optical stimulus, such as the size of t angle subtended by an object, varies with respect to sor other dimension of the optical stimulus, such as the di tance of the object from the observer. This change in ang size is not linear but exponential, as can be seen in Figu 2.6. As distance is doubled, angle size is halved, whimeans that the size of the solid angle intercepted by a squa at four feet is twice as great as at eight feet; at eighty fec the angle is half as large as at forty feet. (Fig.2.5)

Visual angle size changes much more rapidly at ne distances than far ones, a point that will be of considerab importance in my analysis of style in art. A gradient angle size diminution is illustrated in Figure 2.6. The pi mary monocular gradients are those of textural, linear, ai size perspective. Textural perspective is a gradual increa in the density of the fine structure, the spots and gaps, the extended pattern of either a single surface or all of tl surfaces in the visual field (Figure 2.7).

Figure 2.7 illustrates both a drawn and a naturally o curring textural gradient from a continuously receding lor gitudinal surface. Size perspective is a decrease in the si of the figures in the visual field; it presupposes contou or figures on a background, each of which may have i own textural perspective. Linear perspective is illustrate in Figure 2.8. All of these perspective gradients can d crease to a zero limit of size or spacing, or to a maximu density of texture. The horizon in the visual field is, i trospectively, a line at which these limits are reached.

Conceptualizing gradients as information derives fro

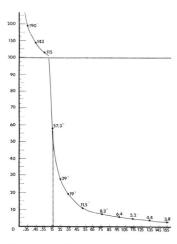

Figure 2.6. *Visual angle curve.*

the Euclidean assumption that visual-angle relations determine appearance, and the horizon limit reminds one forcibly of Euclid's "limit of vision." But as demonstrated in Appendix D, Euclid did not analyze appearance in terms of nested complexes of visual angles and by limit of vision he did not mean angular differences too small to see. Gibson's early work was much closer to that of the Renaissance painters than to Euclid's.

Gibson's argument that gradient structures in the light could provide direct information for various aspects of the visual world was formalized mathematically by his student, W. C. Purdy. Gibson and Purdy argued that the monocular gradients provide sufficient information to specify relative distance, the flatness or curvature of surfaces, the slant of surfaces relative to the viewer and to the earth, and size to within a scale factor. Gibson also argued that the relative size of objects was given directly in the light to the eye by the number of surface textural elements of the ground covered by a given object resting on it, independently of the distance of the object from the observer. That is, a three-inch object will cover, or occlude, three one-inch squares on a checked tablecloth, no matter how near or far from the observer, as can be seen in Figure 2.9.

Visual information II: motion

Gradients are not present only in single views; they also persist as a person moves around. As the observer *moves* through a cluttered environment, certain gradients in the light to the eye stay the same and specify the relatively persistent properties of size, shape, composition, slant, distance, and color of objects. For example, the slant of each of the surfaces depicted in Figure 2.2 is specified by the *continuous gradient* of the *flow velocities* of its optical texture (its motion parallax), with a different gradient for each different degree of slant. When a surface is slanted farther and farther away from a person's vantage point, then the angular *size* of the surface grows smaller and smaller in a lawful progression; at the same time, when a person moves around in the world, the *shapes* of the visual solid angles

Figure 2.8. Linear perspective: the
Borromini arcade in Palazzo Spada,
Rome. (From M.H. Pirenne,
Optics, Painting, and
Photography, 1970, p. 153.)

Figure 2.9. The six-inch triangle
on the right covers six units of
texture and the seven-inch triangle
on the left covers seven units of
texture despite varying distances.
(Photograph supplied by the
author.)

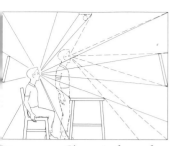

Figure 2.10. Change in forms of visual solid angles with shift in station point. (From James J. Gibson The Senses Considered as Perceptual Systems, p. 196. © 1966 by Houghton Mifflin Company. Reprinted by permission of the publishers.)

projected from the surface are changed continuously. For example, if the observer stands up in front of a square surface, then the shape of the visual solid angle determined by the square will change as a regular series of trapezoids, as is shown in Figure 2.10. These systematic changes in the sizes and shapes of the visual angles as the person moves around the environment generally are called *motion perspective*. Air Force researchers try to recreate these flowing changes in visual angle in their flight simulators to teach people to land airplanes without sending them up in the air in expensive aircraft.

Visual information III: invariants

One particular aspect common to the work on gradients and occlusion and on perspective and parallax served as the basis of Gibson's most radical reformulation of the specification of visual-angle information in the light to the eye. He argued that the occlusion of texture elements by objects, the gradients of size, line, texture, and parallax, and various aspects of perspective shape are all *invariant* across certain situations of observer motion. With the shift in emphasis from the static to the motion gradients, Gibson essentially dispensed with the concept of the visual field of nested angles and argued instead that *perception is primarily dependent on pickup not of static single structures in the light, but of structural invariances across views changing with motion.*

The idea of invariant information in the light, persistent across retinal changes, contrasts sharply with the assumption that the stimulus for perception is a series of still pictures or images on the retina that must be integrated across time to give holistic perceptions of the three-dimensional environment. This assumption implies that the visual system operates essentially as a movie camera, shooting still images and storing them for comparison. In contrast, Gibson argues that perception does not depend on the structure of a single set of nested visual angles, but on invariant information revealed and picked up as the person moves through the environment, or as movement takes place in the environment itself. A concrete example

will help to make this assertion sound less abstract. W
saw that a surface at a constant slant projects a particul
gradient of texture compression to an observer. That i
the surface texture will grow projectively smaller at a pa
ticular, albeit changing, rate as long as the surface stays
the same slant. If that surface is, for example, the groun
then the gradient will stay the same as the observer wal
along it. If the ground rises or falls, the gradient chang
and the observer perceives a hill or a valley. Of cours
this texture gradient, like all the other information in tl
light, is invariant only across some situations and not others

Classes of invariants

Gibson's concept of mathematically specifiable invarianc
of structure in the light is the single most significant a
vance in geometrical analysis of optical information sin
Euclid. Euclid described the problems of geometrical
determined appearance through exposition of the relatio
between one or two visual angles and distance, bequeat
ing us the problem of reconstructing the visual constanci
of size and shape. The Renaissance painters extended E
clid's ideas into scene analysis of nested visual angles throu
their awareness of the need for certain ecological elemen
in a scene, like the ground plane and other continuo
surfaces, on which to base the visual angles in the "re
world." Despite, or perhaps in part because of, these ec
logical additions designed to make pictures unambiguou
later thinkers dismissed the informative qualities of pi
torial and retinal images and the geometrical analysis
visual images. It was assumed that visual stimulation gain
meaning only through nonvisual experience. Gibson's ra
ical reformulation of geometrically determined appearan
through exposition of the concept of invariance show
that visual information can determine alone the perceptic
of the constant or persistent properties of objects, as w
as the layout of surfaces and the structure of discriminab
events. In his last book, *The Ecological Approach to Visu
Perception*, published before his death in 1979, Gibson pr
posed four general classes of invariant information. T
first class includes the invariants described above.

1. *Invariants of optical structure under change of the point of observation*. Gibson wrote that the flow of the optic array with movement does not destroy the structure beneath the flow. Some of the changes of the optic array with movement are transformations of its nested forms, but the major changes are increments and decrements of structure as surfaces undergo occlusion. Invariants of proportions, ratios, cross-ratios, and gradients underlie these transformations and increments/decrements.

2. *Invariants of optical structure under changing illumination*. Gibson argued that illumination can change in amount, in spectral composition, in direction and because sunlight, moonlight, and lamplight can fluctuate in intensity, differ in color, and alter the direction from which they come to a layout of surfaces. With change in the medium, some features of the optic array will change accordingly. Gibson argued that there must be invariants for perceiving the layout and relative reflectances of the surfaces, but that they are not yet known; they almost certainly involve ratios of intensity and color among parts of the optical array.

3. *Invariants across the sampling of the ambient optic array*. Sampling involves the reversible sweeping of the field of view over the whole optic array, back and forth, with continuous successive overlap. The common structure in the sliding sample is invariant.

4. *Local invariants of the ambient array under local disturbances of its structure*. By local events, Gibson meant displacements and rotations of rigid detached bodies, deformations of rubbery surfaces, and other disturbances, like growing and smiling that are difficult to categorize. According to Gibson, all these local disturbances are seen to be continuations of themselves by virtue of certain nondisturbances of optical structure (1979: 310–311).

Are these invariants all geometrical? Are they all rooted in the concept of visual angle developed since the time of Euclid? Concerning the geometrical character of these four classes of invariants, Gibson wrote:

It would simplify matters if all these kinds of change in the optic array could be understood as transformations in the sense of *mappings*, borrowing the term from projective geometry and topology. The invariants under transformation have been work out. Moreover it is easy to visualize a form being transpose inverted, reversed, enlarged, reduced, or foreshortened by slar and we can imagine it being deformed in various ways. Bu unhappily, some of these changes *cannot* be understood as on to-one mappings, either projective or topological. (1979:31 Gibson's italics)

While Gibson's concern that the complexity of potenti optical information not be overlooked in geometrical sim plifications is no doubt justified, it is also premature. W have by no means exhausted, in Gibson's formulation c any of those preceding, the specification or utility of gec metrical invariants as optical structure and information fc perception. It is my contention that the development c the concept of invariants in modern geometry was invalu able for the understanding of the structures available in tl light as potential information for visual perception. Tl concept of invariants helps us to understand how percep tion of the relatively persistent properties of the enviror ment is possible, how the perception of pictures is possibl and what the relationship is between the ordinary env ronment and pictures that represent it. To make this thes clear, I'll present the concepts of invariant and transfor mation, first as they are developed in geometry and applic to perception, and then as they are usefully applied to th problems posed by depiction in representational art.

Perceptual objects and events

The geometrical concepts of invariant and transformatio will be enormously valuable explanatory tools only if w can get a handle on what they are to help explain. Definin perception as the pickup of information about the relativel persistent properties of the human environment – the *ol jects*, *layouts* of surfaces, and *events* that exist in relation to human behavior – gives us a very large domain to brea down. Traditional categories exist for the relatively per sistent properties of objects and their layouts that simplif their organization: objects and surfaces have size, shape distance, textural composition, slant, and tilt. Perceptua

Figure 2.11. Metric transformations in ordinary space: translation, rotation, and reflection.

events are much harder to categorize even in a preliminary way.

Types of events

Movements of the body and motions of objects in the world are the primary types of events of interest to vision. In the little perceptual world of the self, objects move left or right, toward or away, up or down, and in all combinations of these directions. Object motions include people walking, birds flying, water falling, and cars rushing toward one's person. The basic motions of rotation, translation, and reflection are the primary events involving rigid bodies in the ordinary environment. Figure 2.11 illustrates the primary events in ordinary space. The number of possible combinations of these motions is unlimited. However, it is sufficient to consider only the simplest cases because what is true of them is also true of the more complex motions.

While the motions are the primary perceptual events in

the ordinary environment, they are by no means the on
ones. For living things, there are also the events of grow
and aging. For all things there is the class of destructi
events: They explode and implode, burn up, and unders
chemical changes like wilting and corrosion. Objects c:
be disassembled, or broken up, or bent out of shape. Peop
get wrinkles. All objects project shadows. We are a lon
way from a full classification matrix for all of the chang
that can and do take place in the world, even on the lev
of ordinary perception.

Let us for now consider types of events or changes witl
out worrying too much about classifying them. We wa
around things, objects move back and forth, spin arour
and flip over, approach, and recede from us. Change
transformations, are "global" or "local" depending c
whether they involve movements of the observer relati
to surfaces like the ground plane or motions of objec
relative to the observer. A global transformation takes pla
when the observer moves; the entire section of the optic
array projected to the observer changes as the observ
moves head and body around through space. A local trar
formation takes place when an object (or part of the ol
server's body, like a hand) moves while the perceiv
remains in one place. And, of course, global and loc
transformations can take place at the same time, as whc
a perceiver walks while watching a bird fly past, or wall
toward another person who is approaching the perceive

All of these transformations can be understood mor
easily if we think about them in geometrical terms an
geometry gives us, not incidentally, a preliminary classi
fication scheme for transformations as well. But first, t
understand transformations in geometry, we must tack]
the mathematical notion of "mapping."

Geometrical mappings

The idea of "mapping," of what is called "functional think
ing," is one of the most fundamental concepts in mathe
matics. As Herman Weyl remarked in 1940, "The importar
thing which the average educated man should have learne
in his mathematics classes, so the reformers (of mathe

matics) claimed, is thinking in terms of variables and functions." What the average educated person more likely retains from those mathematics classes of long ago is not, however, a habit of thought but a vague memory of figures and equations. Because this idea of a mathematical function is one of the simplest keys to understanding the geometrical concept of transformation, I will outline it very simply as an entrée to the idea of transformation.

Mathematical functions

A mathematical function is an explicit, specifiable, determinate relationship between two sets of values; a function "maps" one set of values onto another. More precisely, a function is a pairing of two number sequences in which any term of the first sequence determines exactly one term of the second. An example of a function spoofed by Weyl is that relating income level and income tax, a "clumsy" function created by "pasting several linear functions together, each valid in another interval or bracket of income" (1940). A function relating two variables can be represented by a table as for example by a recent U.S. tax-rate schedule (Table 2.1). However, given the strong and highly variable responses of individuals when confronted with this table, it probably serves poorly as an illustration of a function. Indeed, Weyl (1940) remarked that "an archaeologist who, five thousand years from now, shall unearth some of our income tax returns together with relics of engineering works and mathematical books, will probably date them a couple of centuries earlier."

A more useful example is the straight–line function graphed in a coordinate system. The coordinate system was invented by Descartes; an example is given in Figure 2.12. The two axes of the graph are called the axis of the abscissa, or x–axis, and the axis of the ordinate, or y–axis. The point where they cross is called the origin. In the simplest case, the axes are perpendicular to one another, and the distances along them are evenly spaced and equally sized, that is, a single unit is used for the scales on the two axes and for measuring distance in all directions. Any point in a coordinate system can be located by a pair of numbers

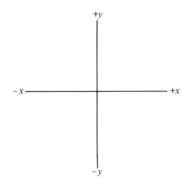

+y

-x ─────────┼───────── +x

-y

Figure 2.12. Cartesian coordinate system with perpendicular coordinates.

Table 2.1. *Tax rate schedule for 1984*[a]

If the amount on Form 1040, line 37 is:			
Over—	But not over—	Enter on Form 1040, line 38	of the amount over—
$0	$2,300	—0—	$2,300
2,300	3,400	...11%	3,400
3,400	4,400	$121 + 12%	4,400
4,400	6,500	241 + 14%	6,500
6,500	8,500	535 + 15%	8,500
8,500	10,800	835 + 16%	10,800
10,800	12,900	1,203 + 18%	12,900
12,900	15,000	1,581 + 20%	15,000
15,000	18,200	2,001 + 23%	18,200
18,200	23,500	2,737 + 26%	23,500
23,500	28,800	4,115 + 30%	28,800
28,800	34,100	5,705 + 34%	34,100
34,100	41,500	7,507 + 38%	41,500
41,500	55,300	10,319 + 42%	55,300
55,300	81,800	16,115 + 48%	81,800
81,800	...	28,835 + 50%	

[a] Schedule X for single taxpayers.

called its coordinates. These numbers represent the distances of the point from the x– and y–axes. Because any point can be represented in the coordinate system, so can any figure that is a collection of points, such as a line or a circle. Figure 2.13 shows two coordinate systems: One is a line graph and the other, a circle. These graphs show one way in which the function relating the x's and y's can be illustrated. The relationship between x and y can also be illustrated by a table of the related values. A partial table of related x and y values for the line is shown in Table 2.2.

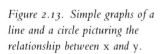

Figure 2.13. Simple graphs of a line and a circle picturing the relationship between x and y.

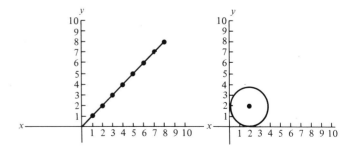

Table 2.2 X and Y values
for line

$y = 1X + 0$	
X	Y
	1
	2
	3
	4
	5
	6
	7

In addition to the graphs and the tables, the functional relationship between x's and y's also can be illustrated by a formula or equation. For example, the general equation for a straight line is $y = ax + b$. The specific formula that describes the line in Figure 2.12 is $x = 1x + 0$. The general formula for a circle is $(x - h)^2 + (y - k)^2 = r^2$, where h and k are the coordinates of the center of the circle and r is the radius (see Figure 2.12). For the specific circle graphed in Figure 2.13, the formula is $(x - 2)^2 + (y - 2)^2 = 2^2$, which means that at the point on the circle where $x = 2$, y equals 0 or 4, and where $y = 2$, $x = 0$ or 4. Similarly, one may "plug in" values to the equation and obtain values of y from x, and vice versa.

Thus we have three ways — the graph, the table and the formula — in which the mapping of the values of y onto x can be demonstrated. The three ways are equivalent and, generally speaking, any function can be exemplified in all three ways. At least any graph, any figure, can be expressed as an equation and as a table of values of the points that make up the figure. Some equations cannot be graphed and some produce very strange graphs. For example, if r in the equation for the circle is equal to 0, then the "circle" is only a point because it has no radius. If r^2 is negative, then the circle is called imaginary because the square root of $-r^2$ gives imaginary values for r. In any case, the only functions of interest to this exposition are "graphable" functions, equations whose values can be located clearly in coordinate space.

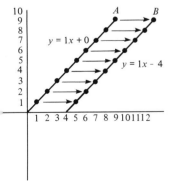

Figure 2.14. Translation of line A onto line B.

Geometrical transformations

The type of mapping of principal importance to the geometers is not the simple function illustrated above; it is not the simple mapping of one set of values of y onto another set of values of x. Geometrical mappings relate a set of mapped values to another set of mapped values, or an entire plane of points to another plane. For example, in Figure 2.14, line A is mapped onto, or transformed into, line B. This particular transformation is called *translation*, because the line is translated, or moved across, the plane. The general function that describes line A, and all other straight

Table 2.3 *X and Y values for untransformed and transformed line segments*

Transformed		Untransformed	
$Y = 1X + 0$		$Y = 1X - 4$	
X	Y	X	Y
1	1	1	-3
2	2	2	-2
3	3	3	-1
4	4	4	0
5	5	5	1
6	6	6	2
7	7	7	3
8	8	8	4
9	9	9	5
10	10	10	6

lines, is $y = Ax + B$, while the particular formula for lir A is $y = 1x + 0$. The line that is the product of tl transformation, line B, has the same general function, $= Ax + B$, but the specific equation is, of course, differer from that for line A. The equation for line B is $y = 1x$ 4. Table 2.3 gives the two tables of x's and y's for bo the untransformed and the transformed lines. It is easy see that although the specific values of x and y for the tw lines are different, the general equations are not. A simp translation transformation does not affect straightness (i general, the degree of an equation).

Consider the two circles pictured in Figure 2.15. We sa that circle A is transformed into circle B. Circle B is small in radius than circle A but has the same center, that is, has not been translated across the plane. This "shrinking of the circle is a *Similarity* transformation, so called becau the shapes of the two figures, untransformed and tran formed, are similar, or unaffected by the transformatio The general form of the equation for a circle is not affecte by this similarity transformation, but specific values variables are. With other types of transformations even th general equation is changed. The properties of a geometr figure that remain unchanged, the invariants, are directl related to the specific transformation used, and there a no clear limits to the types of transformations that may b

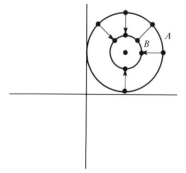

Figure 2.15. Similarity transformation of circle A *onto circle* B.

applied. James Newman, in *The World of Mathematics* (1950), writes: "A geometric figure is transformed by changing its co-ordinates, by mapping one space on another, by moving the figure pursuant to a procedural rule, e.g., projection, rotation, translation. More generally, any object of thought may be transformed by associating it with or converting it into another object of thought" (pp. 1535–6). In this spirit, of course, even the simple changes of algebraic functions can be thought of as transformations. However, for clarity, I will continue to refer to changes in mathematical expressions in general as *mappings*, to mappings of one series of variables (x) on to another series (y) as *functions*, and to mappings of figures onto figures or of planes onto planes as *transformations*.

The idea of *invariant* is the complement of the idea of transformation. The properties of figures (and of algebraic expressions) that are left unchanged by a transformation are referred to as "invariant under that transformation." Some transformations leave nearly the whole figure in all of its particulars invariant, and some change nearly every property. Geometric transformations of figures can be grouped according to the properties of figures that they leave invariant. In fact, geometry itself is divided and classified by certain sets of transformations. High school geometry, which usually deals with what is called the geometry of *Motions*, or *Metric geometry*, is only one geometry among many possible geometries. In Metric geometry figures are moved about the plane in a variety of ways not affecting the size or the shape, the metric properties, of the figure. Other geometries, such as Similarity geometry, which would be used in discussing my earlier example of the circle shrinking, allow more tranformations of the figure but leave fewer figural properties invariant. For example, "shrinking" of the figure clearly does not leave its size invariant. As one adds transformations, one loses invariants; the more it is possible to do to a figure, the less remains of the original. Since the invention or discovery of non–Euclidean geometry, the number of geometries as consistent logical systems based on axioms similar in kind but different from the Euclidean axioms has proliferated. In 1872 Felix Klein showed that many of

Table 2.4 *Hierarchy of geometries*

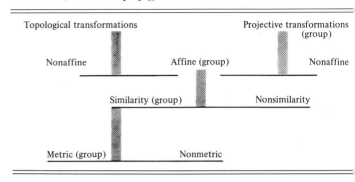

these geometries can be organized in terms of groups
transformations preserving specifiable invariants, and th
this organization comprises a hierarchy of geometries.
Table 2.4, the four geometries of greatest interest to pe
ception and to representational art are shown in their h
erarchical arrangement. They are Metric, Similarity, Affin
and Projective geometry. Each of these geometries is cha
acterized by the types of transformations proper to it, at
is defined as a *group* of transformations.

Groups of transformations

I have been using the term *group* of transformations in
very informal and nonmathematical way. However,
mathematics, *group* has a specific meaning. It is necessa
to understand that meaning because the existence of grou
has important consequences for perception. Understan
ing the concept of groups also makes it a great deal easi
to understand the hierarchy of geometries.

What is a "group"? A group is a system consisting of
class of things along with a rule for combining membe
of the class and satisfying four conditions. One might sa
that the system must have four properties to be a grou
These four properties are closure, associativity, identit
and reversibility. The example most frequently used
illustrate the concept of group is the set of whole number
all the positive and all the negative numbers plus zer
with addition as the rule of combination. It is easy
understand the four necessary properties with this example

1. *Closure.* A system is said to exhibit closure if the *product* (result) of combining two members of the set is also, always, a member of the set. In the example of the set of whole numbers, it is clear that adding any two whole numbers together always gives another whole number, e.g., $2 + 3 = 5$ or $6 + (-4) = 2$. (In the set $a + b = c$, a, b, and c are members of the class.)

2. *Associativity.* A system exhibits associativity in its operation if the result of combining three or more members of the class is the same, however they are grouped, as long as the order of the members is constant; generally $a + b + c = a + (b + c) = (a + b) + c$, that is, $(2 + 3) + 5 = 10 = 2 + (3 + 5) = 10$.

3. *Identity.* A system has the identity characteristic if the class of things making up the system possesses a member, known as the identity element, such that the combining of this element with any other member of the class leaves that second element identical to itself, unchanged by the operation. Generally, $a + i = a$, that is $3 + 0 = 3$, $-4 + 0 = -4$. Without zero, the set of whole numbers would not have this property.

4. *Reversibility.* A system has reversibility if, for each member of the class of things in the system, there exists another member, called its reciprocal, such that combining the two gives the identity element. Generally, $a + (-a) = 0$, that is, $3 + (-3) = 0$, $-(10) + 10 = 0$. Reversibility can be considered the "untransformation" of the system, just as identity is "nontransformation" in a practical if not mathematical sense.

In many treatments of the concept of group, it is only the first property, closure, that is considered to be the essential group property. Some groups are distinguished by an additional property, *commutativity*. A group is commutative if the order in which operations are performed does not affect the outcome. For example, in the whole number group above, $a + b + c = a + c + b$, or $1 + 2 + 3 = 3 + 2 + 1 = 1 + 3 + 2$, and so forth.

In perception, all of the group properties are important. Another example of a group more central to geometry will

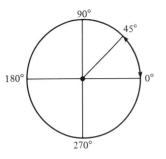

Figure 2.16. *Group of rotations around a circle:* $45° + 360° = 45°$; $45° + 0° = 45°$; $45° + (360 - 45) = 0°$; $45 - 45° = 0$.

suggest why this is so. Consider a circle marked into 360° In this system the class of things consists of all possibl rotations of a radian around the circle and the rule of com bination is simply the execution of a rotation. It is clea that this system is closed because any combination of turn produces a degree of rotation that could be effected by single rotation, that is, a 45° turn plus a 15° turn is equiv alent to a single 60° turn. The system has an identity ele ment, in fact two equivalent ones, the rotations of 0° an of 360°. Thus, a rotation of 170° plus a rotation of 360 gives a resulting rotation of 170° (Fig. 2.16). The syster is also reversible, again in two ways, because any degre of rotation can be cancelled by a reverse turn or by a additional rotation of 360° minus the original rotation. Fo example, 45° plus −45° gives 0° of rotation, and 45° plu (360° − 45°) also gives 0°, the identity element. The lav of combination is both associative and commutative be cause neither the grouping nor the order of the rotation affects the result. Thus we see that one can transform member of the class and then recapture identity of th element by reversing the transformation. One can effect transformation of an element that leaves the identity of th element intact, and the performance of these transforma tions is entirely within the confines of the system; all resul obtained are described within the system.

When a set of "things" to be considered is as large a the infinitely large set of all possible rotations, there enormous descriptive economy in consideration of the s as part of a group system. There is no need to enumerat the infinitely large number of members of the set in ord to examine their properties; what is true of one membe is true of all. The system as such can be considered rath than the individual elements because the performance operations within the system does not lead one outside i Thus we can consider great classes of things like rotatior around the plane or movements through space with el gance and economy. I will try to show that this econom of group analysis is also instrumental in the process perception itself as well as in the analysis of representation art.

The utility of the concept of group also will be apparer

in the description of the four geometries of major importance for the analysis of visual information. Metric, Similarity, Affine, and Projective geometry will be discussed in Chapter 3 in terms of their most important transformations and invariants. There is one very important point to keep in mind when applying the concept of group to the hierarchy of geometries. In the classic example of a group that I have just given – the set of whole numbers plus the rule of addition – the elements can easily be distinguished from the rule of combination. But in considering geometries as groups, one must realize that the elements are themselves transformations, like the set of all motions in the plane, and the rule of combination is simply the performance of a transformation. So in a group of transformations a mapping of, for example, one figure onto another, followed by another mapping of that figure onto still a third is equivalent to yet another single mapping, because a group is "closed." Any mapping can be "unmapped," if you will, by a reverse mapping. There is always a mapping of a figure or a plane, for example, onto itself that does not affect identity, and the grouping of the mappings does not affect the outcome, (but the order often does). In geometry, the mappings, the transformations themselves, are the elements of the group. Do not be led to believe otherwise by the classic whole–number system example of group.

Geometrical hierarchy of transformations

All of the transformations discussed in this chapter are Projective, as can be seen from Klein's hierarchy. But, in some cases, the transformations of ordinary perception are also Metric, or Similarity, or Affine, as well as Projective. In collapsing all of the groups of transformations into projectivities, we lose important distinctions among them that are important both to geometry and to perception. Each group of transformations preserves some invariants and not others. Metric transformations preserve all properties of figures transformed except locale and orientation; the Similarities are the same except that size is lost. Under the Affinities, angularity is lost but parallelism is still invariant.

Under the Projectivities, nearly all of the simple figur[e] properties are no longer invariant except straightness, b[e]tweenness, and other primitives. This is not to say, how[w]ever, that the Projective invariants are not significant an[d] indeed, critically important for perception, only that t[he] figural invariants of the other geometries also have i[m]portant perceptual roles to play, and must not be ove[r] looked under the assumption that all visual information [is] *only* Projective. I'll begin the explanation of the hierarch[y] with Metric geometry and work up, trying to show ho[w] each level is important to perception.

3

The hierarchy of geometry in visual perception

Only the relations of time, of space, of equality, and those which are derived from them, of number, size, regularity of coexistence and of sequence — "mathematical relations," in short – are common to the outer and the inner world, and here we may indeed look for a complete correspondence between our conceptions and the objects which excite them.

Hermann von Helmholtz, *The Recent Progress of the Theory of Vision (1868)*

Metric geometry

The most basic and familiar of the geometries is defined by the group of rigid motions. This geometry is what most of us learned in school as Euclidean geometry; it is sometimes also called Orthogonal or Metric geometry. I will use the term Metric because it is the least confusing and the most apt. The defining characteristic of this geometry is that metric dimensional properties of figures – size, distance, and angles – are preserved across the transformations. There are only three possible transformations in Metric geometry:

1. *Translation*, which is the displacement of the figure in the plane – up, down, or sideways
2. *Rotation*, which is the spinning of a figure in a plane around some fixed point called the center of the rotation
3. *Reflection*, which is flipping a figure over in a plane, through a line or a point

Figure 3.1 shows examples of each of the three types of transformations in a more formal way than the cartoon in Figure 2.11.

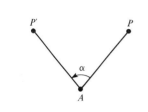

(a)

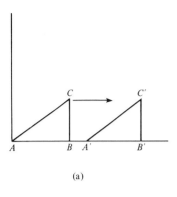

(b)

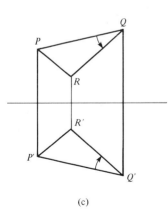

(c)

Figure 3.1. Metric transformations: (a) translation, (b) rotation, (c) reflection.

Although reasoning from figures is a dangerous, albe time-honored, business in geometry, it can be seen that three types of transformations send each figure into a *co gruent* figure. Congruent figures, defined in a rough-an ready fashion, are figures whose outlines match at eve point. The principal difference among the three transfo mations is that reflections can change the "sense," or o1 entation, of the figure so that it is no longer possible simp to "slide" an original figure over its image to check co gruence. Generally, then, Metric transformations c. change either position or orientation or both when tran formations are combined. Any sequence of motion tran formations simply creates another motion transformatio This property of the set of transformations called closu is a defining characteristic of a group. If a sequence Metric transformations of a figure produced a result n possibly caused by some other motion, then the set motions would not constitute a group. Since only positi and orientation of a figure can be changed by motions, is obvious that all of the other familiar properties of figu are left *invariant* by Metric transformations. These invaria properties include size, shape, distance, angle size, straigl ness, parallelism, length, ratio of division of lengths segments, collinearity, betweenness, area, and certain i tios among the points of a line. *Distance* is the fundamen invariant preserved in Metric geometry.

Concept of Equivalence Class

One useful way of illustrating what is meant by a set invariants specific to a group of transformations is to co sider the *Equivalence Class* for the group. An Equivalen Class is the set of objects all considered to be the same the criteria of a particular geometry. The Equivalence Cl for the group of Motions is the class of all figures of t same size and shape whether they are moved about in t plane or flipped over. Thus, in Metric geometry, figu1 are considered to be equivalent, regardless of position orientation, as long as they are of the same size and shaț Although this sounds like a very large set of figures, it really the smallest Equivalence Class of all the geometri

Since motions send each figure into a congruent figure, almost any change in a figure destroys equivalence. The image of a segment, ray, angle, or triangle is the same as the original. Motions leave the absolute value of every angle invariant and thus preserve perpendicularity; they send a parabola into a parabola, a hyperbola into a hyperbola, and a square into a square. Any transformations that do not do this are not Metric.

Metric transformations in perceptions

In Chapter 2, we saw that light is structured by the surfaces off of which it bounces and that these structures can serve as information for perception. Traditionally, the structures in the light to the eye have been described only by Projective geometry. But there are a variety of cases where the Metric structures in the light are important to perception. For example, it is frequently argued that congruence of images at the eye almost never occurs in perception, but this is clearly not the case. Gunnar Johansson, the famous Swedish perceptionist, wrote: "In everyday life of animal and man, transformations of the retinal patterns satisfying the demands for congruence must be regarded as rare exceptions. Ordinarily, transformations in the projections from rigid objects in motion (Euclidean form change) or motion of the eye relative to the environment result in form and size change when described in Euclidean terms but as invariant figures when described within the framework of projective geometry" (1978, p. 266).

Congruent projections may be a very small subset of all possible projections of any object, but they are most certainly not rare. Every simple repeated motion, like moving the head from side to side while gazing at a stationary object, results in congruencies of images. Rotation of an object, or of an observer around an object, results in as many congruent images as are specified by the object's period of symmetry. For example, a cube rotating has a congruent image, a symmetry, every quarter rotation. The more axes of symmetry are present, the more congruent images exist. Consider the snowflake (Fig. 3.2.) rotating on its central axis like a pinwheel; even in such a simple

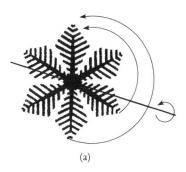

(a)

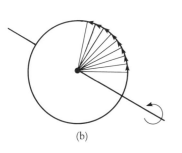

(b)

Figure 3.2. (a) Snowflake rotating on central axis like a pinwheel; (b) rotating circle.

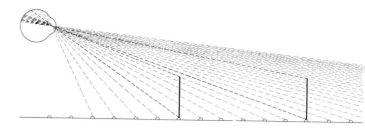

case, there are six congruent images. In the case of a rotating circle or sphere there is an infinitely large number of symmetry axes and thus an infinitude of congruent images. The congruent subset of any family of projection preserves the metric properties of the figure – its qualities of shape and absolute size.

A tradition of perceptual theory stresses the similarity of shapes under certain conditions of observation and deemphasizes differences under other conditions. Figure 3.3 shows a standard textbook illustration of the *size constancy* problem: How do we distinguish the sizes of two shapes that are projectively equal? It is seldom noted that this congruence depends upon very particular conditions of observation: The observer must be at two exactly compensating distances and angles from the two objects in order to offset size and shape differences and produce projective equality. This very special condition is rare outside of psychological laboratories, as is the experience of two projections of similar shape and different size. People are very acute at distinguishing exact optical size differences although as a perceptual task this rarely is necessary to any behavior. It is generally only in perceptual laboratories that images of objects without any background or layout in space are made available. In the ordinary environment *backgrounds* and *adjacencies* of objects nearly always differ with objects usually resting on textured surfaces in a cluttered environment. Also, in the ordinary case, angle of view changes with distance so it is rare that the projected shapes of two objects at two different distances would ever be identical. Figure 3.3 shows the ordinary case of viewing two similarly shaped objects resting on the ground at two different distances. This should be contrasted with the situation pictured in the traditional illustration (Fig. 3.4).

Outside of laboratories so many sources of information

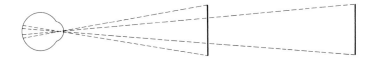

co–occur and covary that projective metric congruence of two different objects is indeed rare. But projectively congruent images from the same object are commonplace in ordinary inspection of the environment because the observer repeats simple motions like moving from side to side, and because so many regular objects have periods of symmetry that produce several congruencies, even in a nonrepeated observer movement, like a single walk around the object. It must not be forgotten that these congruencies are not between the object and its projection, but between the projection at one point in time or space and at others. At the risk of sounding absurd, I must note that objects are big and the eye is small. Objects can be "flat," but the eye is always curved. Trying to make a case for exact figural equivalence, congruence, between surfaces in the world and images on the retina is foolish. The exact character of any visual projection is a function of the shape and composition of the lens and cornea, the degree of curvature of the retina, the state of accommodation and convergence of the eye, deformations and imperfections, individual differences in these factors, and more. The point I wish to establish is that congruent *projections* are common in perception under certain conditions, whatever the nature of so-called retinal *images* in those situations.

Similarities

In ordinary perception, more common still than the Metric congruencies are the Similarities, the next geometry up the hierarchy. Similarity geometry has a larger equivalence class of figures than Metric geometry because it has more transformations and fewer invariants, as do all the geometries as we ascend the hierarchy. The Similarity group of transformations contains all three of the fundamental Motion transformations plus an additional one, known as the *radial* transformation. Every Similarity transformation is a one-to-one mapping of the plane onto itself or another

37   SIMILARITIES

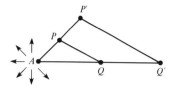

Figure 3.5. Radial similarity transformation.

plane in which each distance is multiplied by the sam positive number called the similarity ratio. If the similarit ratio is greater than one, then the plane, or figure, is ex panded by the ratio times all distances; if the ratio is le than one, then the plane or figure is contracted or shrun by the same factor. When the ratio equals one, the tran formation is simply Metric; finally, when the ratio is negative number, the transformation is considered to b the product of a positive radial transformation plus a Metr reflection. Figure 3.5 shows an example of a radial Sim larity transformation in which the similarity ratio is tw and the origin of the expansion is at *A*. In Metric trans formations, everything about figures was preserved excep position and orientation. Under Similarity transforma tions, we lose the invariants of length and area, but retai shape and angle size, and all their correlated component like parallelism, perpendicularity, ratio of division, collin earity, and betweenness. Essentially, the equivalence clas of figures for the Similarity transformations consists of a figures of the same *shape*, regardless of size, orientatior or position. Thus, from the perspective of the Similarit group, all of the figures in Figure 3.6 are equivalent, one to-one mappings of each other.

Similarity transformations in perception

In ordinary perception, every time an object is approache at a constant frontal angle, the pattern of optical expansio at the eye is a continuous Similarity transformation, a di lation of projected texture of the surfaces. When the ob server or surface recedes at a constant frontal angle, the

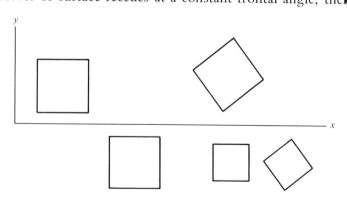

Figure 3.6. Members of a similarity equivalence class.

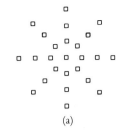

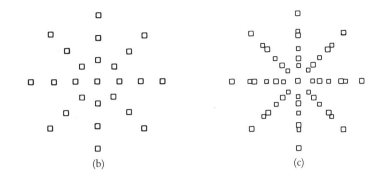

(a)

(b)

(c)

the pattern of contraction of the projected optical texture is also a continuous Similarity transformation. The symmetrical Similarity transformation occurs only when the observer is directly, frontally approaching or leaving a surface or vice versa. If the surface is very large relative to the observer, like a wall approached while staring straight ahead, then the pattern of expansion is one of unbounded texture, as in Figure 3.7. This is a radial transformation with the center fixed at the center of the gaze. If the approached surface is small relative to the observer, as, for example, a rectangular mirror hung on the wall with the center at eye level, then the optical expansion pattern has a bounded shape as well as texture (Fig. 3.8). This transformation is *reversible* with the pattern on the retina growing and shrinking as the observer moves toward and away from the surface. The varying rate of expansion or contraction is a function of the distance of the surface from the observer. The nearer the surface, the more rapid the rate of change, a phenomenon that was illustrated by the graph of the change of visual angle with distance in Figure 2.6. Thus both distance and time to impact are specified by the rate of expansion of the optical pattern.

The transformation is symmetrical and a Similarity only when the perceiver is directly approaching a visually unbounded surface like a wall or frontally approaching the center of a visually bounded surface like the mirror on the wall (or, of course, approaching or being approached by a sphere at any angle). If the observer walks toward a small object centered above or below eye level, then the pattern of optical expansion is not symmetrical and is not a Similarity transformation. Examples of nonsymmetrical pat-

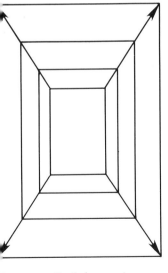

Figure 3.8. Optical expansion pattern of bounded surface.

39 SIMILARITIES

terns of optical expansion and contraction will be discus
in the section on Affinities. That people are responsive
the difference between symmetrical and nonsymmetri
expansion patterns was shown by Gibson, Olum, a
Rosenblatt in 1955. A symmetrical expansion pattern
information that some surface is going to hit the obser
in the face; a nonsymmetrical pattern means a path of a
proach to one side or the other depending on the directi
of the asymmetry. Bower, Broughton, and Moore in 19
showed that babies as young as 6 days of age were a
capable of discriminating a symmetrical hit pattern fr
an asymmetrical miss path.

Similarity and the horizon

In addition to the studies of perceptual approach and avo
ance, peoples' sensitivity to the information carried
Similarity transformations was also the subject of F
Sedgwick's work on the information for perception carri
by the visual horizon. Sedgwick (1973) argued that t
horizon is unique in one very important respect: It ne
changes its projective location. Every other location in t
optic array is transformed when the observer moves, t
the horizon is not. The horizon is always "horizontal" a
always at eye level. These invariant projective charact
istics mean that the horizon is a stable reference in the op
array, making available a whole class of information abc
spatial layout. "The size, distance, and orientation of o
jects resting on the ground plane are geometrically spe
fied by a set of invariant relations between the projectio
of those objects and the projection of the horizon" (p.
Sedgwick gives the horizon–ratio relation as an examp
Figure 3.9 shows an object resting on the ground at sor
distance from the observer. The observer's line of sight
the horizon is "parallel" to the ground "plane" at a distan
from it equal to the height of the point of observatio
This means that the horizon necessarily intersects the obj
at a height that is equal to the height of the point of o
servation. Thus, no matter how distant an object is, t
portion of the object below the horizon is exactly equal
the height of the point of observation. "The total heig

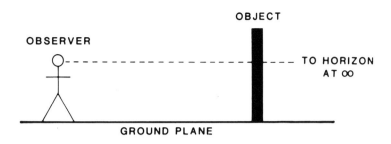

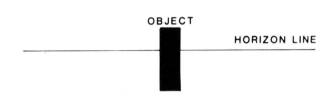

Figure 3.10. Illustration of various horizon–ratio relations. (From H.A. Sedgwick, in J. Beck, B. Hope, and A. Rosenfeld, eds.: Human and Machine Vision, 1983, p. 453.)

of the object is then specified by the relation between the total visual angle subtended by the object and the visual angle subtended by the portion of the object below the horizon" (p. 4).

Figure 3.10 shows a clear example of this information for size as given by Sedgwick (1983). He points out that the total visual angle subtended by the tree from top to bottom is about three times as large as the visual angle subtended by the part of the tree that is below the horizon. The horizon–ratio relation says that the tree then is about three times as high as the height of the point of observation. If one considers that point to be approximately five feet high, at eye height, then the tree should be about fifteen feet tall. The small bush to the right of the tree subtends a visual angle only about half that between the ground at that point and the horizon, so the bush is about half eye height, or two and one-half feet tall. For the telephone poles, that ratio of total visual angle to visual subtended by the poles below the horizon is about 4 to 1; thus the height of each pole is about twenty feet. The case of the telephone poles illustrates the Similarity property of this invariant most clearly. Despite whatever Projective transformations may take place in the overall shape of the object, the vertical dimension, or height of the object, undergoes only a Similarity transformation. The relation between total visual angle and visual angle below the horizon is in-

variant across all telephone poles, always specifying t
relation between height of pole and height of observe
irrespective of distance. This invariant proportionality i
Similarity invariant. Approximate similarities are also n
ticeable across the overall shapes of the poles in the seri
because these are objects whose essential, most characte
istic dimension is the vertical. Projective alterations in t
shapes are certainly present, but they are not importar
and may be omitted in pictures.

Summary

Empirical study of Similarity information in the light
only in its infancy. The primary emphasis in geometric
thinking about optical information has been on Projecti
alterations in the bounded shapes in the light to the e
and not on the persistent Similarities. Even the work (
approach that has enjoyed a considerable degree of en
pirical investigation has tended to concentrate on rate
expansion of the optical pattern rather than on symmet
of sequences of shapes. Indeed the whole complex area
perceptual responsiveness to symmetries awaits systemat
investigation.

Affinities

The family of geometry known as the Affinities produc
equivalent figures that strain the limits of intuitive perce
tual categorization. An Affine transformation is a one-to
one mapping of the plane onto itself or an image plane,
which the images of any three points on the same line a
themselves on a second same line. Affine transformatio
preserve collinearity (the property of being on the san

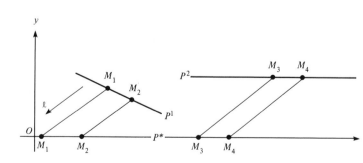

*Figure 3.11. Parallel projection of
P onto P★ in the direction of line ℓ.*

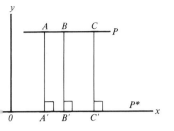

Figure 3.12. Metric parallel projection.

line) and parallelism, but not, in general, lengths of line segments, sizes of angles, or areas. On first glance, Affine mappings include some pretty exotic-looking transformations, but first glances can be deceptive. The most fundamental of the Affine transformation is *parallel projection.* Several of the other main Affine transformations are presented in Appendix A.

Parallel projection

Let P and $P^\star$ be any two planes, and l a line *not* parallel to either of them. For each point M of the plane P we will make the point $M^\star$ of the plane $P^\star$ correspond so that the line $MM^\star$ is *parallel* to the line l (Fig. 3.11). This mapping is called a *parallel projection* of P onto $P^\star$ in the direction of the line l, because all of the lines of the projection are parallel to l. If the planes intersect on the line l, then every point of this line is invariant under the mapping.

A special kind of parallel projection is illustrated in Figure 3.12: *orthogonal* projection, in which the direction of the parallel projection lines is perpendicular to the image plane. When the two planes themselves are parallel as well as the lines, then the mapping is Metric, or just a spatial displacement with size and shape preserved. When the two planes intersect in line l, the transformation is equivalent to either a *compression* against l or a compression followed by a reflection both with axis l.

Compression

In order to illustrate Compression, we will assume the plane, P, and let k be a positive number and l a given line of the plane, as shown in Figure 3.13. Let M be any point of the plane, and MP the *perpendicular* from the point, M, down to the line, l. The image point, M', is the point such that $M'P = kMP$. Thus both M and M' lie on MP, on the same side of the line l. If M lies on the line l, then $M' = M$. This transformation is called the Compression with coefficient k and axis l. The transformation is called a proper compression if $k < 1$, because every point not on the line l is moved closer to it, and figures in the plane are thus

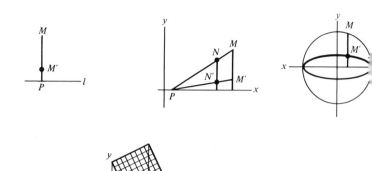

Figure 3.13. Perpendicular
compressions down to the line ℓ or x.

"compressed." The transformation is called a stretching
$k > 1$, because every point not on the line l is mov
farther away from it and figures are thus "stretched." Thu
as shown in the example, an ellipse is a compressed circ
with the diameter of the circle as the axis l of the compre
sion, and the ratio of the axes, minor to major, of th
ellipse as the coefficient of the compression.

Fundamental character of parallel projection

Parallel projection, like all the Affine transformations, mu
tiplies all distances in the same direction by a consta
factor, and preserves the ratio of division, betweennes
and parallelism. Every Affine transformation of the plan
including the Motions and Similarities, is the resultant
parallel projections. According to the geometer David Ga
(1969), not more than six parallel projections are require
to generate any Affine transformation. Even the nongeom
eter can demonstrate with a straightedge and pencil that
Metric reflection is the product of two parallel projection
and a Metric rotation or translation can be generated b
four projections at most, usually two. A Similarity tran
formation of a triangle is the resultant of only four parall
projections.

It is fairly easy to demonstrate that the other Affin
transformations presented in Appendix A are also the prod

ucts of repeated parallel projections. (A hint for proving this is that a simple compression can be shown to be a parallel projection, and transformations like hyperbolic rotation, which appear quite complex, are really the product of two compressions, and are therefore the resultant of a series of parallel projections.) Thus, all of the transformations of the three geometries discussed so far – Metric, Similarity, and Affine – can be seen simply as different expressions of a single transformation, parallel projection, repeated a specifiable number of times.

Equivalence classes

In Affine geometry, any two triangles are equivalent because the Affine group contains a transformation that maps any one triangle onto another. Also, any two line segments, angles, parallelograms, parabolas, ellipses, or hyperbolas are affinely equivalent. To understand this type of equivalence, which is not always intuitively apparent, consider the Affine classification of the conics. In analytic geometry, the general equation in the second degree in x and y is proved to represent a curve of one of the nine following forms.

1. Ellipse★
2. Hyperbola★
3. Two intersecting lines★
4. Parabola★
5. Two parallel lines★
6. Single point (two coincident lines)★
7. Imaginary ellipse (empty curve with no points)
8. Two imaginary intersecting lines
9. Two imaginary parallel lines

Each one of these is called a conic section because a double cone can be cut, or sectioned, to give these results. The sectioning of a cone is shown in Figure 3.14. Each of these conic sections is described by a form of the equation, $ax^2 + bxy + cy^2 + dx + ey + f = 0$, solved nine different ways. These nine forms are sometimes called *canonical forms*, an idea we will return to later. Although all nine forms are of interest to the mathematicians, only those marked

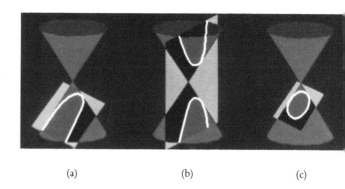

(a) (b) (c)

Figure 3.14. Conic sections. (a) Parabola, (b) Hyperbola, (c) Ellipse. (Courtesy David Kamins, Computer Graphics Laboratory, Boston University.)

with an asterisk are germane to the purpose of this bc as they constitute *equivalence classes* of figures in Af geometry. Each of two curves of the same conic type be taken into the other by some Affine transformation. quadratic equation is Affinely equivalent to one and c one of the nine conics listed.) No Affine transforma can take a curve of one type into a curve of another ty Thus, two curves of the same conic type are Affinely equ alent and two curves of different types are not, with result that all ellipses and circles (which are a special k of ellipse) are Affinely equivalent to each other beca there is always an Affine transformation that will take ellipse into another. In the same way, all triangles are finely equivalent to each other.

It is interesting to note that there are also subclasse equivalence. For example, all circles are, of course, equ alent to each other as Similarities because there is a Si larity transformation to take any circle into another. T is also true of pairs of parallel lines and pairs of parabo Any two figures are considered to be equivalent to e other or not within the context of a particular geome and not across them. We are most accustomed to con ering equivalence of figures only within the usual cont of Metric or Similarity geometry. Thus we refer to t circles as the same as each other but certainly different fr noncircular ellipses. It will be useful to keep in mind t equivalence really depends on set, on the context of c cussion, on the relevant set of transformations, and not simple appearance. Classification of figures on the basi appearance may turn out to be more a matter of habit t of fundamental "likeness." This flexibility in the notior equivalence will become even more apparent once we have considered transformations and invariants in Projective geometry.

Affine invariants

The invariant that distinguishes an Affine from a non-Affine transformation is, of course, parallelism. Angles change size under Affine transformations, but parallel lines stay parallel. In ordinary perception, Affine structures in the light most frequently occur when objects or surfaces are viewed at distances that are very great relative to the size of the surface or object. At these distances the light reflected from a surface is effectively parallel to the viewer. The classic example of parallel light is the light from the sun, but we need not go nearly that far to approximate parallelism. Very great distance viewing takes place in all naturally occurring "telephoto" conditions, such as looking at a scene through a window that cuts off the near, or foreground, part of the view. Very great distance viewing also takes place from tall buildings and aircraft. The great perceptionist Hermann von Helmholtz reported the loss of size perspective he experienced as a child when viewing human figures high up in a steeple. Many people are familiar today with the long-distance, patchwork-quilt effect of viewing people, buildings, automobiles, and fields from 30,000 feet, and even higher. At such great distances, the edges of houses and the border of fields appear to be parallel; the projection lines of the light to the eye are effectively parallel. This distance is called optical infinity and its magnitude is a function of the size of the surface being viewed. Perceptual parallelism is a function of a very slow rate of change in visual angle.

Although the preservation of parallelism most clearly distinguishes Affine from Projective transformations, Affine transformations in the light to the eye also carry information for which points are on the same line or edge and for which edges are straight, in addition to carrying information for which edges are parallel to each other. (Topographical invariants specify which edges meet and the theorem of projective uniqueness specifies that two

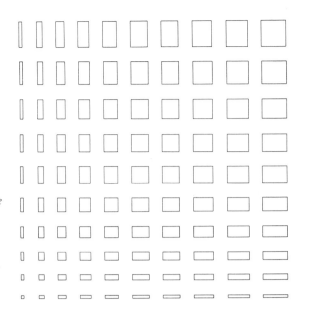

Figure 3.15. Continuous perspective transformations. (From James J. Gibson, The Perception of the Visual World, *p. 194. © 1950, renewed 1977 by Houghton Mifflin. Reprinted by permission of the publishers.)*

images of the same surface *are* of the same surface, as t section on projective geometry later in this chapter w explain.) People are very sensitive to the information Affine transformations, particularly when the transfc mations are continuous. One example would be a rig object moving around in space that casts a family of sha ows that provides information about the movements the object. People "see" the movements of the object its even when they are only allowed to view the shadov The set of shapes in Figure 3.15 illustrates continuous *A* fine projection, or projection at a "very great distance These figures were generated in a laboratory by Jan Gibson using a point-source projector. Both the rigid and the specific motions of the surface are clearly specific (Wallach and O'Connell 1953; Gibson and Cornsweet 1952.

Just how sensitive people are to the specificity of Affine projection was demonstrated by David Perki (1973a,b). He showed adults 128 drawings of boxes, h of which were projections of rectangular boxes and h of nonrectangular boxes. Examples are shown in Figu 3.16. The subjects' task was to judge which were whid judgments over three different conditions of presentati were very accurate. Viewers were quite capable of usi Affine information in their categorizations. In a follow-study, Perkins substantially replicated this finding ev

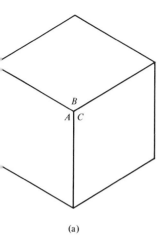

(a)

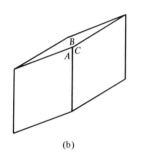

(b)

Figure 3.16. Projections of boxes possibly rectangular (a) and not possibly rectangular (b). (From D. N. Perkins and R.G. Cooper, in M. A. Hagen, ed.: The Perception of Pictures, vol. II, 1981.)

when the drawings were viewed obliquely at 41° and 26° to the picture plane. At these angles the projections to the eye were no longer Affine, but Projective, and in many cases these oblique projections no longer specified possibly rectangular boxes. Yet despite the oblique angle, viewers continued to categorize the Affine correctly and were not confused by retinal projections.

In a replication of Perkins's study by Robert Cooper (1977) with young children, this behavior on side view did not take place. Cooper's three-year-old subjects categorized the boxes as rectangular and nonrectangular just as adults did when their line of sight was perpendicular to the picture plane. But when viewing the drawings obliquely, these young children responded to the retinal Projective information and not to the Affine information carried by the drawings themselves. I found the same tendency in young children to treat the light reflected from pictures as if it came from the actual objects themselves in a study of shadows and shading in pictures (Hagen 1976a) and in one of perspective preference (Hagen and Jones 1978). This finding has interesting implications for the development of the ability to use information from pictures.

Growth and aging

Perhaps the most exciting example of the importance of Affine information in the light for visual perception is the use of Affine invariants to specify growth and aging in the human face. People grow older; their faces change. Yet we recognize the same person across this aging transformation while perceiving that aging itself is taking place. What visual information or structure in the light affords these perceptions? Robert Shaw and John Pittenger (1977, 1978) and Leonard Mark (1979) used the Affine transformations of compression and shear to analyze the changes that take place in the shape of the head with aging. (See Appendix A for the shear transformation.)

They subjected baby faces to both transformations independently and together and found that "91% of the relative age judgments made by subjects agreed with the hypothesis that the strain (compression) transformation

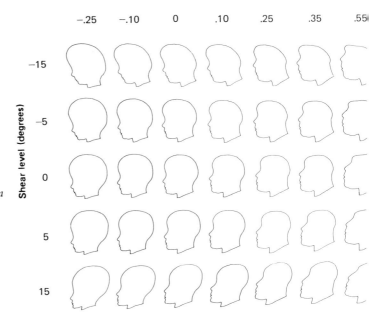

Strain level (k)

| | −.25 | −.10 | 0 | .10 | .25 | .35 | .55 |

Shear level (degrees)

−15

−5

0

5

15

Figure 3.17. Transformations of a facial profile by shear and strain (untransformed profile is at 0.0). (From R.E. Shaw and J.E. Pittenger, in R. Shaw and J. Bransford, eds.: Perceiving, Acting and Knowing, *1977, p. 121.)*

produced monotonic perceived age changes in the stand.
profile. On the other hand, using the shear transformati
to predict their judgments produced only 65% agreemer
(1977: 125). Although Shaw and his colleagues began w
a simple Affine compression (strain) transformation, th
soon found through suggestions from D'arcy Thomps
(1917), the biologist, that the most descriptive strain tra.
formation was Topological, not Affine. Topology is
geometry of elastic, or nonrigid, things. In an ordin.
strain or compression transformation the transformat
is one dimensional, operating only on *x* or only on *y*, a
k is a simple rational number. If *k* is greater than one,
figure is stretched in one direction; if *k* is less than o
the figure is compressed. However, Shaw and his
workers discovered that the appropriate coefficient
compression, *k*, for the age shape changes of the head v
not a simple number but a trigonometric function, av
further, that the strain operates on both the *x* and th
dimensions simultaneously. Thus this transformation ta
straight lines into curves and is no longer Affine. Fig
3.17 shows this Topological transformation combined w
the affine shear transformation applied to a standard profil

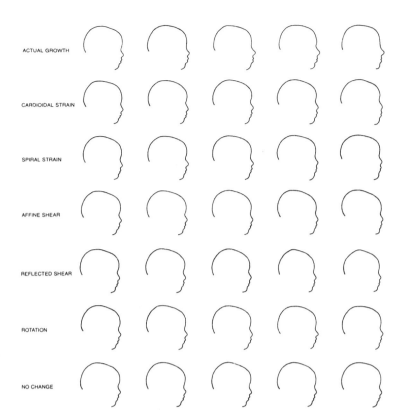

ACTUAL GROWTH

CARDIOIDAL STRAIN

SPIRAL STRAIN

AFFINE SHEAR

REFLECTED SHEAR

ROTATION

NO CHANGE

Figure 3.18. Profile sequences resulting from prospective growth transformations, actual growth, rotation and no change. (From Mark 1979: 63.)

A study by Leonard Mark in 1979 continued this comparative analysis of different types of transformation in order to specify as completely as possible the geometrical information for growth in the light to the eye. Figure 3.18 shows several sequences of prospective candidates for growth transformations and Figure 3.19 graphs the percentage of time each sequence was labeled "growth" by subjects. In this later study, Affine shear was less predictive than in earlier work and it is clear that the nonaffine strain transformation, what these workers call "cardioidal," accounts for most of the change perceived as growth. What is important, of course, is not that there are cases in which nonaffine transformations specify for observers certain phenomena better than do Affine structures, but that the converse is true as well. Most perceptibly animate or "stretchy" events are probably best specified by Topological transformations. Different kinds of events observed under various conditions are specified variously by transformations and invariants that are Affine and Nonaffine,

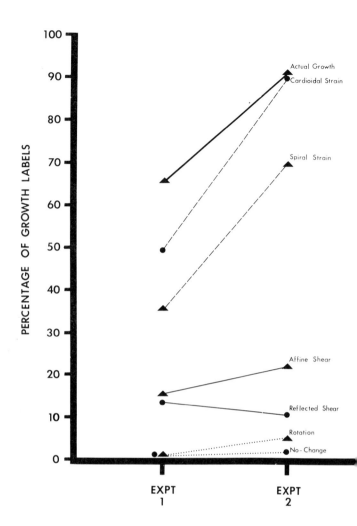

Figure 3.19. Percentage of growth labels as a function of transformation. (From Mark 1979: 64.)

Similarity and Metric. And some kinds of events and la
outs are specified only by uniquely Projective transfo
mations. In the next section, I will discuss what makes
transformation uniquely, or only, Projective and not A
fine, Similarity, or Metric as well.

Projective geometry

The Projective transformations of a plane consist of all t
Affine transformations that we have discussed includi
parallel and orthogonal parallel projections, and also
certain transformations that are not Affine, namely, t
central projections. There are four types of central proje
tions: a line onto a parallel line, a line onto an intersecti

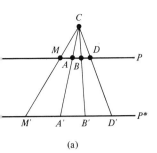

(a)

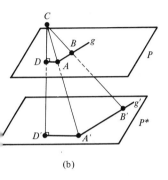

(b)

Figure 3.20. Central projection of P onto a parallel plane P★ with center of projection at C.

line, a plane onto a parallel plane, and a plane onto an intersecting plane. I shall describe only the spatial cases here since everything true for three-space will be true of transformations of the plane into itself.

Central projection of a plane onto a parallel plane

Assume two planes, P and $P^\star$, parallel to each other, and a point, C, not in either. If M is any point of P, and the line, MC, intersects the plane, $P^\star$, in M', then the transformation in which M' is the image of M is called the central projection of P onto $P^\star$ with center of projection C. A central projection of a plane onto a *parallel* plane is a one-to-one mapping that preserves parallelism, concurrence, ratio of division, and betweenness, and multiplies all distances by the same constant, K (Fig. 3.20). $K = 1$ when the center of the projection is immediately between the two planes. The fact that distance is multiplied by a constant factor in all directions in a central projection of two parallel planes means that this type of projection is also a Similarity transformation (as long as the center of projection is on the normal to the center of the original figure). It should be recalled here that a Similarity is also the resultant of parallel projections, so it is quite possible to convert central projections of parallel planes to parallel projections among nonparallel planes. Thus, this type of central projection is very closely related to the types of transformations discussed in the previous section on Affinities. The second type of central projection, however, is quite radically different since it cannot be generated by any finite series of parallel projections.

Central projection of a plane onto an intersecting plane

Perceptually the Projective transformation of greatest significance is the central projection of a plane onto an intersecting plane. This transformation is both uniquely projective and commonplace in ordinary vision.

Again, assume two planes, P and $P^\star$, this time *not* parallel to each other. Thus, they intersect somewhere in a line. We also will assume a point, C, not on either of the

53 PROJECTIVE GEOMETRY

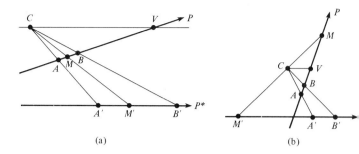

Figure 3.21. Central projection of a
plane onto an intersecting plane.

(a)

(b)

planes. If M is any point of P, and the line, CM, intersec[]
$P\star$ in M', then the transformation in which M' is the ima[]
of M is called the central projection of P onto $P\star$ w[]
center of projection, C (Fig. 3.21).

Central projection between two intersecting planes d[]
fers from that between two parallel planes in one func[]
mental respect: It is *not* a one-to-one mapping of origir[]
to image plane. There is a line in the image plane that lac[]
unique original points, and a line in the original pla[]
whose points have no images. In the example in Figu[]
3.22, the two planes are perpendicular to each other, b[]
the two exceptional lines will occur with any two inte[]
secting planes. The line, v, in the original plane who[]
points have no images is the line formed by the intersecti[]
of the plane parallel to the image plane that passes throu[]
the center of the projection, C, and the original plane itse[]
The line, v', in the image plane, which lacks unique ori[]

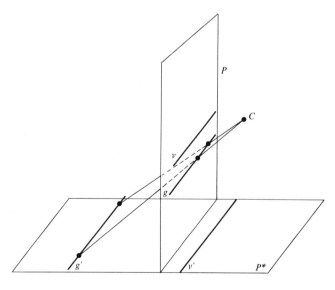

Figure 3.22. Vanishing lines in
central projection of two
perpendicular planes.

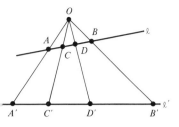

Figure 3.23. Invariant cross-ratio of points.

inals, is the line formed by the intersection of the image plane with the plane passing through *C* parallel to the original plane. Then there is really only an incomplete correspondence between the points of the image and the original planes because two lines are lacking. In these limiting cases, where an entire plane is projected into a line, no figural properties to speak of are preserved.

Projective invariants

Overall, even in transformations where the two exceptional lines are not present, not many figural properties are left invariant by central projection and therefore by Projective geometry as a whole. Properties preserved are collinearity or straightness, the property of being a degenerate or nondegenerate conic, the harmonic properties, some topological properties, and the cross-ratios of points and lines. There are many transformations, including all those so far described, and a huge equivalence class of figures, but very few invariants. Those properties that are invariant are not only not obvious perceptually, but remain tricky to visualize even with examples. The best known invariant property is the cross-ratio of points and lines.

Cross-ratio. The cross-ratio of points is shown in the example in Figure 3.23. Given line *l* and line *l'* and the center of projection, *C*, then the following is true projectively. If *A,B,C* and *D* are distinct collinear points on line *l* with *C* and *D* lying between *A* and *B,* then the quantity *AC/ CB* over *AD/DB* is called the cross-ratio in which the points *C* and *D* divide the line segment *AB.* This quantity is invariant across a projective transformation so the cross-ratio of the image points equals that of the originals, for any four collinear points and their images. This invariance also holds for the cross-ratio of lines, a figural property of even greater obscurity, explained briefly in Appendix B. (The cross-ratio of lines is the cross-ratio in which two intersecting lines divide two other lines when all are concurrent.) If the four points that determine the cross-ratio are all on a transversal cutting the four concurrent lines, then the cross-ratio of points equals the cross-ratio of lines

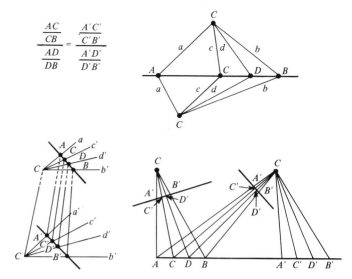

$$\frac{\dfrac{AC}{CB}}{\dfrac{AD}{DB}} = \frac{\dfrac{A'C'}{C'B'}}{\dfrac{A'D'}{D'B'}}$$

Figure 3.24. Invariance of equality of cross-ratios of points and lines for all positions of the center of projection.

and is invariant for all positions of the center of intersection of the lines. In a projection of one plane onto another, the cross-ratio of the original points equals the cross-ratio of the original lines, and both equal the cross-ratio of points and lines in the image plane (see Fig. 3.24).

Cross-ratio and the gradients. The invariance of the cross-ratios is the most important Projective property and has significant implications for perception. Consider the case in which the center of projection is the point of observation as an observer moves around an object (Fig. 3.25). If the four points, *A,B,C,D,* are four points of, for example, an edge of that object, then, if the cross-ratios of those points (and of the "lines" of sight to the moving point of observation) remain the same, then it must be the case that the four points are collinear, on a *straight* edge of the object.

The picture in Figure 3.25 shows invariant cross-ratios for two of the four edges of a tabletop. If we cover that top with a checkered tablecloth, we can see that the cross-ratios of the rows in the fabric also remain invariant and specify *straight* lines. Because the checks, or "points," are evenly spaced, the cross-ratio of the first four checks in a row equals the cross-ratio of the next four checks and the next four and so on ad infinitum. Although this may sound excessively abstract, it is quite familiar to us from walking around tabletops and from looking at innumerable pictures

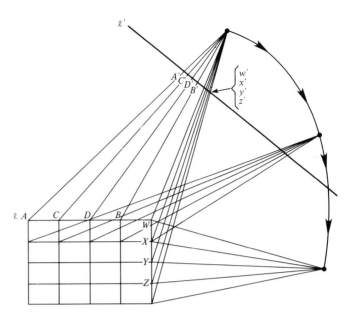

Figure 3.25. Invariant cross-ratios in the light reflected from the top of a table.

of railroad tracks and highways shrinking in the distance to a point on the horizon. As long as the units of the pattern on the surface – or on the edges of the surface or between the ties on the railroad track – project the same cross-ratio, those lines or edges are *straight*, and the surface of the object is *rigid* or flat. The cross-ratios of all rigid surfaces are identical if the same four points are chosen for comparison, *and* if we accept the statement that all surfaces have textures that are more or less regular across the whole expanse of the surface.

But how does the information for rigidity help us to find perspective or gradient information for the slant and distance of objects? We saw in Chapter 2 that a gradient is the rate of change of visual angle, or the slope of the visual angle/distance function. Figure 3.26, demonstrates that the "slope" of this function depends on what distance interval or point on the curve is being considered. "Slope" is how much visual angle changes with each increase in distance. Close to the face, the slope is very large. As the surface being viewed is moved farther and farther away, the slope becomes smaller and smaller, approaching zero when perspective changes are too small to be seen. So the "slope," the rate of change, itself changes. This changing slope is the first derivative of the curve. The values it takes

57 PROJECTIVE GEOMETRY

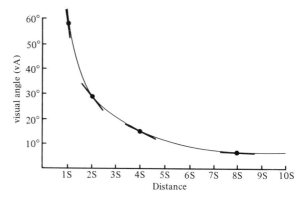

Figure 3.26. Changing "slopes" of the visual angle curve defined by the tangent lines at different points along the curve.

depend not only on the distance of the surface from th viewer, but also on the slant.

The visual angle graph shown in Figure 3.27 can b thought of as consisting of the projected images of lino leum squares on a floor stretching away from the observe in all directions. The graph just plots the projection of th floor along one line of squares. If the floor slants up o down, the first derivative changes. If the surface is slante down away from the observer, then the (changing) rate o change is faster than for a horizontal surface. If the surfac is slanted up toward the observer, then the change is les rapid. The gradients are the *ratios* themselves between on projected texture unit (or railroad tie) and the next one Each subsequent ratio is different from the preceding one just how different is a function of the slant of the surfac relative to the observer.

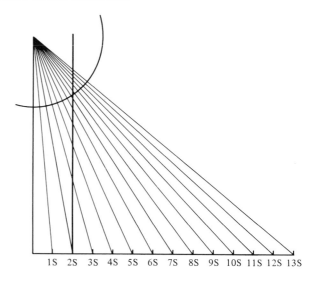

Figure 3.27. The visual angle projection of squares on a linoleum floor.

For a surface slanted just a little bit off the vertical, the size of the closest projected texture unit is only a little greater than the projected size of the next one, because it is only a little closer. Projected size, visual angle, is strictly a function of distance. That a surface is slanted away from the person looking at it simply means that adjacent portions of the surface are farther and farther away from the face. How much farther determines the changing size ratios among the projected texture units. Whereas the ratios change in different amounts with every change in surface slant, the *cross-ratios* do not change – *unless* the surface curves, bends, or stretches. The cross-ratios among four points on a rigid surface will be invariant across all changes in slant while the changing ratios themselves – the gradients – are specific to particular slants. Changing the slant compresses or expands the visual angle curve, changing the shape of the curve itself.

Gradients and cross-ratios deal with adjacent units of texture, all of the same size, all in a row or in a "line." If we consider for a moment three other "points" on a surface in the world, three points that are *not* in a line, another very interesting Projective property appears. In Projective geometry there is the theorem of uniqueness, which states that there cannot be two Projective transformations that send three noncollinear points into three given image points. So, if the three points in question are three of the corners of the table picture (Fig. 3.25) and the three "image" points are considered to be on that hypothetical plane tangent to the fovea, then there is a unique central projection (to the nodal point of the lens) that relates the two sets of images. If the original surface and the image plane are parallel, then *four* points and their images uniquely determine the projection. This property, together with the cross-ratio and the gradients, makes the pickup of Projective information for slant and relative distance possible. It makes perspective feasible.

Gradients and information. A particular gradient or degree of perspective is information for a surface at a particular slant. We have seen that the projected cross-ratio of points across a flat surface of uniform texture remains constant.

section by adjacent section, as the observer scans the surface. Any discontinuity of points in the cross–ratio specifies a change in the surface slant, like a bend or a fold, or another surface altogether. The flat ground plane provides a reference surface of horizontal slant, or 90° slant, and a vertical surface frontally viewed provides another reference surface of zero slant. All other degrees of slant fall between these two cases.

That people are quite sensitive to the information for different degrees of slant carried by different gradients has been known ever since the early 1950s when Gibson and his co-workers conducted a variety of studies of gradients. In an early (1950) study, Gibson photographed abstract wallpaper patterns at different slants and presented them to observers as projected slides. The observers' task was to adjust the slant of a board with the palm of the hand to match the slant of the visible surface. Success depended on the accurate pickup of the texture gradient information. The results indicated a high degree of correspondence between the predicted degree of slant specified by the texture density gradient and the judged slant. In a follow-up study with Janet Cornsweet (1952), Gibson again found good correspondence between degree of slant specified in the light and degree judged by observers to be present. He found that observers were quite accurate in judging both optical slant – the slant of the surface relative to the eye and geographical slant – the slant of the surface relative to the ground plane.

The perception of slant is, of course, a special case of distance perception since a surface with a nonzero slant necessarily has some parts closer to the observer and some farther away. But the gradient analysis applies not just to the relative distances of different parts of the same surface but also to the relative distances from the observer of different surfaces or of different sections of the ground plane. In 1955, E. J. Gibson and her student J. Purdy tested the ability of observers to judge when a great expanse of field was bisected and trisected. Observers stationed at one end of a long field watched as a bicyclist rode down its length. When the rider reached the halfway or one-third point depending on the task, the observer called out. The authors reported that the average error was only 3.1%.

In these early studies and in his book, *The Perception of the Visual World* (1950), Gibson more or less intuitvely defined and mechanically determined the concept of gradient. If the experimenter desired a gradient specific to a surface slanted 45°, he or she simply slanted a surface 45° degrees and showed it to an observer, or photographed and then showed it. But in his thesis at Cornell in 1959, Purdy finally formulated the visual gradients in mathematical terms, thereby laying the foundations for the analysis of gradient information as a derivative of the projective invariants, an achievement of considerable importance to the thesis of my book. Purdy's exposition of the gradients is presented in Appendix B.

Workers following Purdy's mathematical specification of the optical gradients generally ignored his contribution and descended into an acrimonious wrangle over the relative information value of perspective *outline* and receding *texture* for the specification of slant of surfaces – sources of information that are equivalent in Purdy's formulation. Until recently, no attempt at all was made to test explicitly Purdy's predictions regarding relative distance on surfaces or various size dimensions or shapes of objects. However, in 1966, John Hay presented an analysis of linear perspective that was directly related to Purdy's work. Hay discussed the information potentially available in the relations among an object's vanishing points. His analysis is closely related mathematically to the analysis of horizon information for directions and slants which was given by Sedgwick (1973).

In 1981, Martha Teghtsoonian and I, in a direct test of Purdy's predictions for static gradient information in distance perception, found that observers monocularly viewing a regularly checked surface made distance judgments that were at least relatively in accord with the distances actually present. The smallest distance was judged indeed to be the smallest, and the largest to be the largest, with the increases in between being proportional. The linear function relating "real" and perceived distances was

$y = .7x + 0$. Viewers were not permitted to move their heads. When they viewed the surface *binocularly*, viewers judgments accorded with the distances actually present objectively as well as relatively. Under binocular view again with no head motion, the linear function relating real and perceived distance approached $y = 1.0x + 0$.

The literature is not vast, and more work is needed, but it is clear that perspective or gradient information is meaningful to observers in static situations, such as looking at a scene with one eye or viewing a picture or shadow screen. There is also a fairly extensive literature on the importance of the *motion*-generated gradients – the gradients in the patterns and velocities of optical flow in the light to the eye – as information for perception. I will not review it here, as my major interest in this book is in the static case, or those situations most relevant to the pick up of invariant information in pictures.

Geometry and vision

Each of the invariants discussed in this chapter is specific to a particular environmental property or situation. This specificity permits us to say that the various geometrical invariants in the structure of the light to the eye are *informative* for visual perception. The invariants in the light vary in a specific one-to-one way with the persistent properties of the environment. Of course, the specificity of the relationship between structures and the light does not mean that all observers at all times will use the information. The information is potential or available to the perceiver. There is ample research showing that perceivers can and do use invariant information in the light for perception, but the research effort is rather young. Not all the invariants have been investigated for their usefulness in perception, and we do not know what determines in particular situations the actual use of potential information. We do know, however, a good deal about the important role played by the transformations in the process of perceiving invariants, and are aware already of the limits and dangers of a narrowly geometrical analysis of visual information for the ordinary environment. These are the topics of the next chapter, as they must be confronted before we begin in earnest the analysis of geometrical information in static, representational pictures.

4

The appearance of things in the world

"In that way the painting is superior to the photograph. I think that for figures it would be better not to use photograph There's far more information if you have the person sitting there. You really don't know what a person looks like from a photograph. The reason I take a lot of photographs is to make up for the fact that one photograph really doesn't give me all the information I need."

Richard Estes, in *Richard Este The Urban Landscape* (197

Ecological information and rigidity

The invariants in each class or geometry occur in situation of ordinary perception; they are reflected in the light from everyday events. We have seen that these invariants an transformations are not only available in the light to the eye; they are actually informative for perception as wel We thus can form several conclusions about invariants:

1. Invariants in each geometry are *structures* in the light.
2. They are *physically* invariant.
3. They are *perceived* as invariant.
4. They are *informative* for perception.

But if perception is the pickup *across transformation* invariant information in the light to the eye, then how perception possible in the absence of visible transforma tion? When the observer has not witnessed a transforma tion from one member of a set to another, when there wa no opportunity to detect the invariants across the tran formation, what kind of relations among members of class can an observer perceive? This is a major proble for a theory of depiction based on the representation of invariants. A representational picture of an object, in whatever style, is a single product of a transformation, not a whole family of transforming members. How is it possible to recognize anything in the picture, to pick up an invariant without witnessing a transformation? How can we detect what does not change without observing what does?

The answer probably lies in the principle of mutuality between organisms and their environments. Just as the very muscles and bones of our bodies are structured generally and particularly by operation in the human environment – by such factors as the pull of gravity and the generally level terrain relative to a human scale – so is it probably also the case that an organism that depends on a rigid surface for locomotion will exhibit a bias to perceive rigidity in the absence of information specifying nonrigidity. Usually we continue to see in the present what we have seen in the past unless we have specific information that something has changed. In more general terms, this rule probably applies to ecological experience as well. We assume that a single slice-of-life snapshot, in a laboratory experiment or a painting, shows us a cluttered world of rigid objects – because that is the world in which we live. If we are to perceive something different, then there must be information in the light to specify it – invariant information, that is.

To perceive that an object is rigid is to perceive that it can participate in all of the Projective transformations: Affinity, Similarity, and Metric. It is essentially the property of rigidity that defines a Projective figure or solid object. The fundamental Projective invariant of cross-ratio – specifying a straight edge – will not be preserved when a stretchy rubber band is being pulled out, rotated, and projected to another plane. So when we perceive that an object is rigid, we perceive the kinds of transformations that it can undergo.

Transformations and equivalence classes

Ordinary visual experience, however, is of constant change. To perceive invariants is, in many ways, the same thing

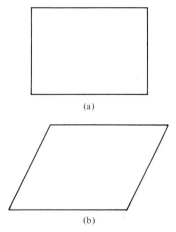

(a)

(b)

Figure 4.1. Affinely equivalent parallogram and rectangle: An Affine transformation will take part (a) into part (b).

as to perceive transformations. To see that an object rigid is to see that it will not bend. To perceive that object is elastic is to see that it will stretch. We percei the transformations as directly as we perceive the inva iants. (See the discussion of growth and aging in Chapt 3.)

Pictures are static images of objects, like brief glimps of the world or an artificial partitioning and freezing visual experience. When we are confronted with an u natural "still" image, we can see in it the potential f change, the possibilities for change themselves. Becau we can perceive the structure of objects directly, we c also see the kinds of changes those structures can underg

We can also perceive invariants and Equivalence class directly – both membership in a class and the nature of t class itself. Not only can we pick up the cross-ratio i variant of a real table and see that the table edges are straig but we also can "see" that an Affine transformation w take the parallelogram "tabletop," shown on the left Figure 4.1, into the rectangular tabletop on the right. V can see that a Projective transformation will take our "pe spective" tabletop into the rectangular top shown in Figu 4.2. Of course, people are not at all likely to say that o table is a central projection of another, but they are qui likely to say that one picture shows a different view o table than another, or that if one were to look at a tab

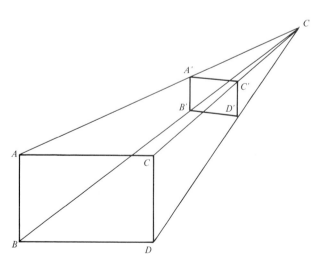

Figure 4.2. Two Projectively equivalent tabletops: A Projective transformation will transform either tabletop into the other.

from straight overhead, it would look so. The perceptual knowledge of transformational equivalence is tacit for most people. They see how things are related, but the knowledge is not formal.

If people see how things are related, do they also see the degree of the relationship? I believe that they do, and that their knowledge influences not only ordinary perception, but their evaluation of art as well. I believe that if people were given a large variety of objects to order in terms of similarity to each other, their order would be determined by the number of geometric invariants shared. The greater the number of shared invariants, the greater the degree of perceived similarity, even when the invariants are too abstract for naive expression. Two objects will be judged most similar to each other when they share the Metric invariants in addition to all the other more abstract ones. A group of ten adults was asked to arrange forms according to degree of similarity; most of them produced the ordering shown in Figure 4.3. They are quite capable of perceiving resemblance based on shared invariants, although they cannot state those invariants explicitly.

Invariants in the light specify the relatively constant, relatively persistent properties of objects and events. But just as the information that specifies those properties depends on transformational context, so the properties themselves depend on the perceptual task or behavior at hand. Any single object affords a variety of behaviors for the

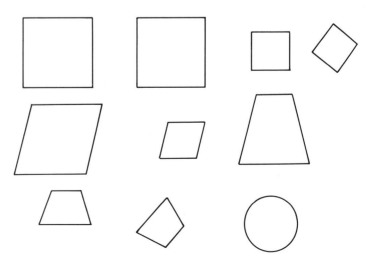

Figure 4.3. The ordering of objects by judged degree of similarity is determined by the number of shared invariants.

organism interacting with it. It is usually said that an object has many meanings or can be categorized or thoug about in many ways. However, this formulation of the problem removes the meaning from the interaction between the organism and the environment. It is of great heuristic value to think of the "problem of meaning" terms of the specific task a person is performing. A person will attend to different aspects of objects in service of various behaviors. What the object means to the organism depends on what the organism is doing at the time. An object is graspable or throwable or bashable as one wishe to grasp, throw, or bash it. Similarly one object is more or less like another depending on the behavior of the organism at that time. In one context of behavior, two object may be very similar; in another, they may have very littl in common. Degree of similarity is a function of contex The easiest way to understand this is to consider the question, When do two objects have the same shape? This lead us immediately to the general issue of equivalence.

The concept of shape

In Metric geometry, figures must have the same exact si and shape to be considered equivalent to each other. The must literally be physically congruent; if one were to c out one of the figures, it could be laid directly on top the other in a perfect fit. At the beginning of Chapter I wrote that although Metric congruencies might be a ve small subset of all possible projections of any object, the are certainly not rare. I argued that such congruencies occu with every simple repeated motion of the observer un dertaken while gazing at an object, and across more com plex motions and movements in accord with the numb of axes of symmetry possessed by an object. "Congru ence," as I am using it here, is a strictly Metric concep It is a concept of exact equivalence of shape. We kno from the preceding section, however, that equivalence figures is entirely a function of the geometry that serve as the context of definition. According to the perceptionis Robert Shaw and John Pittenger (1977), the shape of a object in Metric geometry is identical to the property *rigidity* because the fixed distance between any pair of points remains invariant under the Motions, the most basic of all the Projective transformations. So rigidity is defined as the preservation of all of the fixed distances between object points as the object moves through space. An object that rigidly holds its "shape" can undergo all other Projective transformations in ways quite distinct from those of elastic, or stretchy, objects.

In Similarity geometry, figures need no longer be congruent to be considered equivalent. They must have the same "shape," but need not have the same size. The "shape" invariant in Similarity geometry is the *ratio of similitude*, where distance between any two image points is multiplied by some constant relative to their originals. In Affine geometry, the shape invariant is more abstract. Any two curves of the same conic type (ellipses or hyperbolas or parabolas or two intersecting lines or two parallel lines) are Affinely equivalent; they have the same "shape." Shaw and Pittenger (1977) explain this concept of shape by noting: "A table remains the same table if a leaf is inserted so as to extend its length. A man on stilts is still recognizable as the same person in spite of his elongated height. A cube of clay is still the same mass if compressed or stretched into a rectangular shape. All these transformations in the shape of an object, whether accompanied by size transformations or not, do not destroy completely the aspects of shape by which they may be recognized as a transformed object rather than a new object" (p. 114). They point out that although the simple invariants of shape of the Metric and Similarity geometries are no longer present, Affine geometry has its own invariant of shape: the *ratio of division*, or the distance between two points, $x1$ and $x2$, divided by the distance between the points $x2$ and $x3$. This ratio is invariant under all the Affine transformations.

In Affine geometry, as in all the other geometries, equivalence is determined by transformations. Two curves of the same conic type are Affinely equivalent because some Affine transformations can take one into the other. In like manner, some Metric transformation of translation, rotation, or reflection can take every figure into every congruent figure, and some Similarity transformation will take

figures of the same shape into each other. In Projecti
geometry, the equivalence class is huge because the Pr
jective invariants are so few. *Any* two nondegenerate co
ics are Projectively equivalent and can be transformed o
into another even across type. However, they cannot
transformed into the degenerate conics of parallel and i
tersecting lines. Most important, a straight line cannot
taken into a curve or vice versa. What is straight sta
straight in Projection. Little is preserved in Projective g
ometry to count as shape except such properties as straigl
ness and betweenness, but Shaw and Pittenger argue th
the shape invariant is the cross-ratio (see Chapter 3). Th
summarize the trend in which the "shape invariant" b
comes increasingly complex and abstract as the hierarcl
of geometries is ascended:

1. Euclidean space	$x1 - x2$	Distance invaria
2. Similarity space	$k\,(x1 - x2)$	Ratio of Similitude
3. Affine space	$\dfrac{x1 - x2}{x2 - x3}$	Ratio of Divisic
4. Projective space	$\dfrac{(x1 - x4)\,(x3 - x2)}{(x1 - x3)\,(x3 - x4)}$	Cross-ratio

What we see, what we perceive, what we attend to
always a function of the task in which we are engage
Perceptual equivalence, the recognition of "sameness,"
a function of task. Two figures, two projections of objec
two points of observation and attendant images will
considered equivalent in various terms. That is, two figur
may be Metrically equivalent, perceptually, if the observ
is seeking two identical objects. Two figures will be pe
ceptually equivalent in Similarity terms if the observer
selecting, for example, all the equilateral triangles. A
two parallelograms will be considered perceptually equi
alent, this time in Affine terms, if the observer seeks on
to separate parallel-sided figures from nonparallel figure
If the observer's task is to separate all four-sided figur
from all three-sided ones, then perceptually, in Projecti
terms, all the four-sided figures are equivalent (and all t
three-sided ones). The pictorial analysis in this book w
demonstrate that in art, as well as in perception, the ta

determines the appropriate level of analysis of optical structures.

Shaw and Pittenger argue that our intuitive concept of shape possesses many "natural ambiguities," and that these are given much clearer expression through the description of equivalence classes in geometries. Obviously I agree. But it is important to remember that the four geometries presented here are only a subset of all the possible geometries, yet already they offer considerably more license to the concept of shape, or "identity" really, than one might wish. When do we *actually* say that two objects have the same shape? Only when they are Metrically equivalent? When we say that two objects do *not* have the same shape but that these two are more similar to each other than two other objects, what do we mean? That is, when we say that a square and a rectangle are more like one another than a square and a circle, on what basis do we say that? From the empirically obtained ordering shown in Figure 4.3, it would seem that our tacit knowledge of what must be done to one object or figure to change it into another, of how things are related, also includes understanding how many steps would be involved in effecting the transformation. Of course, if the perception of rigidity is basic, then the perception of a major dichotomy between Projective and non-Projective transformations must also be basic. To perceive invariants is to perceive groups of transformations; to perceive groups of transformations is to perceive classes of objects with the classification changing from one context to the next.

Canonical form

Does this tacit knowledge of degree of relationship among different objects apply as well to degree of similarity among pictures? The so-called objects above were, in fact, pictures, although I referred to them as if they were as solid as bricks. The "square" and the "rectangle" implied the tabletop they modified. But what if there were no tabletop, but only representations of one? Surely the same kinds of images as those in Figure 4.3 could be drawn – as they

were – but how do people see the relationships am[ong]
these image options? What kind of picture is the best [pic]
ture? What kind of picture is most like that tabletop imp[ression]
in the array of images? This question has led various [au]
thors to speculate on the nature of what is often ca[lled]
perceptual "canonical form." The canonical form o[f an]
object is, supposedly, a prototype or representation [pos]
sessing all feature relations distinctive to the object [but]
lacking those that are ambiguous, shared, irrelevant, [or]
noninformative. Defined thus, such a representatio[n is]
probably nonexistent. What kind of object shares featu[res]
with no other object? Most things are not unique in s[uch]
a strict sense of the word.

It might be argued that a picture or an image shoul[d be]
most like the original object when it captures or car[ries]
Metric invariants. But is this true for the pictures o[f all]
cultures? It is not terribly easy to get many Metric inv[ar]
iants in an ordinary Western photograph. Of course, [the]
provision that a picture be a single vantage point, "sn[ap]
shot," composition does not obtain except in certain [cul]
tures like that of the relatively modern West. [A]
representation of an object may contain Metric charac[ter]
istics *not* neccessarily all visible in a single glance, bu[t]
combined into a single image. Is such a composite im[age]
more like the table than a single image? Which is close[r to]
capturing canonical form? It would be tempting to tr[y to]
argue that canonical form as it derives from the conic [sec]
tions may be perceptually relevant if it could be sho[wn]
that the conic types really comprised categories for o[rdi]
nary, nonmathematical people asked to sort examples, [but]
this is probably a red herring, a misleading use of a c[om]
mon term. It seems to me most likely that the canon[ical]
form of an object is a representation that depicts as m[any]
Metric relations as possible *within the conventions of the [cul]
ture's picture-making system*. To see that this assertion is t[rue]
it would be helpful to obtain from half-a-dozen frie[nds]
drawings of a house and of a chair. These pictures sho[uld]
dispel immediately any idea that the canonical form o[f an]
object is simply the view most commonly seen, and [will]
prove useful in the remainder of the book for the evalua[tion]

of different styles of picture making. Making successful representational pictures certainly depends on reproducing the optical information from the ordinary environment, but, as we shall see, it is by no means simply a matter of mechanical reproduction of objects frequently seen.

Caveats and constraints

Ordinary environment

"Perception of the ordinary environment" means just that. When I write of the ordinary environment I do not mean the barren, minimalized environment of the perceptual research laboratory with textureless, two-dimensional cut-outs floating against a featureless background. By ordinary environment, I mean an "ecologically valid" environment, which is stable and cluttered with objects. The environment as a whole is densely structured in nested layers from the microstructure of surface textures to the macrostructure of ground and sky. Light comes from above; light is reflected in all directions and is structured by the surfaces that reflect it; the ground plane is relatively flat, stretching in all directions; the textures of surfaces are distinctive and regular, that is, notably similar across the whole surface. The horizontal direction is given by the horizon itself, everywhere available to view either implicitly or explicitly. The vertical is given by the effect of gravity both on the objects of the environment like trees and waterfalls and on the observer. The unit of analysis relevant to perception is the textured surface, and objects are particular assemblages of surfaces. Objects ordinarily rest on the ground plane, or on other surfaces resting on the ground plane.

Geometry and the "real world"

Perception is the pickup of information about the ordinary environment; it is the pickup of invariants and transformations in the light reflected from the objects and events of the *real* world. Geometry deals with the *ideal* world of dimensionless points, widthless lines, and boundless planes. Perception deals with units of texture, junctions between

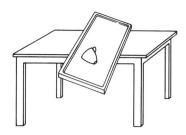

Figure 4.4. We see the coffee cup "translating" across the tray while we perceive its invariant size and shape.

and edges of surfaces, and the surfaces themselves. Surf relevant to perception are stochastically regular in text a sophisticated concept meaning, in perception, "mor less" regular. Likewise, "optical infinity" is a very l translation of the geometrical concept of infinity. Op infinity is not just a theoretical construct in perceptio is an empirically determinable distance beyond which servers, on the average (more or less), see parallel e in the world as reflecting parallel light to the eye. T are real distances, not ideal ones.

The geometrical concepts of transformation and in iant must also be modified, or at least limited, when are applied to perception of the real world. Percei transformations is not only perceiving the kinds of cha objects of different types can undergo, it is also seeing actually is going on, what event is taking place, how so thing is changing. Perceiving environmental invarian seeing what is not changing; it is seeing the propertie environment that are persistent relative to the percep task at hand. For example, we perceive the event of coffee cup sliding off, translating across, the tray and see at the same time that the size and shape of the remain invariant across this transformation (Fig. 4.4). do not perceive formal geometric abstractions although perceive by means of structures in the light best descri geometrically. What we perceive are the objects and ev of the world; how we perceive them involves the g metrical level of analysis.

Concept of group in perception

I do not intend to limit the number of geometries us to a comprehensive description of optical structures to four described in this book. Certainly the existence perception of living "stretchy" things invites analysi optical structures in terms of topology – the geometr which rubber-sheet figures are the unit of analysis. But Metric, Similarity, Affine, and Projective geometries h a history of empirical work supporting their usefulnes an understanding of vision, and they are the geomet most relevant to an understanding of representational a a primarily Projective phenomenon. As we have seen, each of these four geometries is properly considered a "group" of transformations. The existence of groups has important consequences for understanding both perception and the coherence of art styles. A quick reminder of group properties might be useful. In a group, one can transform a member of the class and then recapture identity of the element by reversing the transformation; one can effect a transformation of an element that leaves identity of the element unchanged; the grouping, and sometimes the order, of transformations can be varied without affecting the result, and all products of transformations in the group are also elements in the group. What is the importance of these properties for perception and art?

A primary benefit of group analysis is its great descriptive economy. There is no need to itemize and analyze each member of a very large set that constitutes a group, because whatever is true of one member of the set is true of all. Because the performance of operations within the system does not lead outside it, the system as such can be considered instead of the individual elements. The economy achieved is obvious when one considers that there exists an infinitely large number of possible translations, rotations, or central projections of figures; each operation would have to be observed separately did not various of these include groups and subgroups. Descriptive economy is one obvious benefit of group analysis, important to perception insofar as transformations themselves are relevant to perception. But group properties are important to the behavior of perceiving as well as to an abstract description of how perception takes place.

The perceptual behavior of "sampling," of looking around the environment, is basic to the business of picking up transformations and invariants. The concept of "group" can help us understand what is involved in sampling. During sampling of the optical array, as one walks around an object or moves the head from side to side, both the perceptual behavior itself and the resultant structures in the light exhibit group properties. The observer's head moves to the left and then to the right, reversing the operation: right before left, left before right. It makes no difference–

Figure 4.5. Baby experiencing reversibility, identity, associativity, and closure with physical motions.

all the rigid motions the observer can make are part of set, and rest·can be considered the limiting case of moti the identity element.

Jean Piaget, the famous Swiss child psychologist, ployed this description of human movements in his a ysis of sensory-motor development in the first eight months of life. He argued that reversibility, identity, sure, and associativity were *abstracted* in development fr a body-movement context and *reflected* later in the esser structure of human cognition (Fig. 4.5). Certainly the sa process of "reflecting abstraction" can be applied to behaviors and structures of vision. Just as the sampl behaviors of the perceiver can be subjected to group scription, so too can the structures in the light made av able by those movements. Closed, reversible, associat and always with a limiting case occasioned by no char the set of structures in the light to the eye attendant motion and movements also contains the groups subgroups of transformations. Depending on which gr has pride of place in the observer's attention at the mom Metric, Similarity, Affine or Projective invariants wil revealed and the persistent properties in the world t specify perceived.

Ernst Cassirer, the philosopher, carried this idea of gr as related to perception even a bit further, making gr structure a fundamental rule governing the generatior the objects of perception at various perceptual and g metrical levels. Cassirer observed in 1944 that it is possible to realize a perceptual object in consciousness a mere image; an object of perception cannot be represer except by a rule. He wrote that the concept of group mits us to define more precisely what is meant by a that renders both geometrical and perceptual concepts u versal. "The rule may, in simple and exact terms, be fined as that *group of transformations* with regard to wl the variation of the particular image is considered" (p. Instead of having to *construct* the abstract figures of squ triangle, or circle from a myriad of individual images, geometer and the perceiver need only understand in a gi concrete figure "the totality of possible transformatio (p. 23).

The point of critical importance in Cassirer's (1944) treatment of groups and perception is his stress on the *generative* nature of group-structured apperception of objects:

Geometrical figures are no longer regarded as fundamental, as data of perception or immediate intuition. The "nature" or "essence" of a figure is defined in terms of the operations which may be said to *generate* the figure. Lie and Klein have shown that the characteristic properties of an aggregate are determined only by the group and not by the elements out of which the aggregate is constructed. The figures that belong to a given group constitute a unity, no matter whether and how they be represented in an intuitive way. (p. 24)

He goes on to ask what else indeed is the identity of a perceptual form but what, in a much higher degree of precision, exists as identity in the domain of *geometrical concepts.*

What we find in both cases are invariances with respect to variations undergone by the primitive elements out of which a form is constructed. The peculiar kind of "identity" that is attributed to apparently altogether heterogeneous figures in virtue of their being transformable into one another by means of certain operations defining a group, is thus seen to exist also in the domain of perception. This identity permits us not only to single out elements but also to grasp "structure" in perception. (p. 24).

This concept of identity is of course exactly what Shaw and Pittenger (1977) explored in their discussion of the problem of equivalence and the concept of shape. Yet, interestingly enough, Cassirer denied that perception had direct access to the different levels of the systems of geometry. Cassirer was too much the constructivist, a believer that the mind must construct the meaning of the visual cues or stimuli. At the time of his writing, perceptual theory had not progressed much beyond the Gestalt revolt against the sensationists, although information-based perceptual theory was certainly in the wings. Cassirer believed that each invariant of perception was in fact a schema toward which particular sense experiences are oriented and with reference to which they are interpreted. But he could not see the invariants as informative structures in the light

and he did not quite explicitly write that the different le
of the concept of identity were directly available to
ception. Still, it is he more than any other writer, with
possible exception of Helmholtz, who saw the beauty
utility of the concept of group applied to perception.

This is not a book about the perception of the ordi
environment, but about the perception of pictures of
environment. In the perception of pictures, the concep
group in mathematics as applied to visual structure
extremely illuminating for an understanding of how
resentation of the environment is effected in art. At s
very basic level, representational art re-presents on can
natural perspective, the structures in natural light avail
as information for visual perception. Geometrical gro
applied to natural perspective allow us to consider the
ferent levels or aspects of perspective available to the a
for representation.

In art as in perception, it is possible for the major inte
of the artist to be in representing Metric properties of
world—its sizes, shapes, angles, and proportions—rather
the creations of an architect for use by the builder.
an artist may wish to represent the world as seen f
some particular point of view. Yet even while showi
specific angle, the artist may respect and wish to retain
integrity, the separateness, of the pictured world from
viewer's surround and so retains certain environmenta
variants, like Affine parallelism, in the representation.
an artist may wish instead to create a representation
is essentially a continuation of the viewer's environm
a framed segment or window in a seamless personal sp
In such a rendition, very little is invariant except so
fundamental world properties like rigidity and straight
specified by the Projective invariants, while all other
pects of the scene depend upon and vary with view.
this last type of art, Western post-Renaissance art, tha
many writers take to be the pinnacle of successful re
sentation when it is only the most subjective. Art st
tend to be evaluated according to their position on
geometrical hierarchy so that the number of positions a
from the strictly Projective Western perspective style

termines the degree of "primitiveness." In the next chapter, we shall consider briefly traditional theories of pictorial representation and then see how group analysis can clear up many traditional problems.

5

Pictorial perspective: structure in the light reflected from pictures

It is sufficient that images resemble their objects in some few respects (i.e., in respect of extension, shape, and size); and often, indeed, their perfection depends on their not resembling them as much as they might have done . . . and thus it comes about that often, precisely in order to be more perfect in their quality as images, i.e., the better to represent an object, they ought not to resemble it.

Descartes, *Dioptric* (16

"Truths" of artistic vision

Although consideration of the myriad functions of pictu is outside the scope of this book, we must examine wl pictures give us perceptually. It is sometimes said tl paintings teach us to perceive new or previously unnotic aspects of nature. A function of a good painting, the would be to open our vision, to discover for us a n visual reality. It is very hard to think of examples in whi this is clearly true, and easy to think of examples in whi it is not. Van Gogh's *Starry Night*, for example, did r by any means reveal for the first time the apparently whi ing constellations of the night to the generations of st gazers who preceded him. Yet the night sky, and inde any natural scene, confronts the viewer with innumeral possibilities for the direction of visual attention. So wl *Starry Night*, and any other representational picture, d for the viewer is delimit the range of possible attentio deployment by selecting only a subset of possibilities fr the real scene for depiction. It is this delimitation, selectic and highlighting of visual experience in creative comp sition that gives us the sense of seeing in the picture what we have not seen before in the world. The ordinary observer "has seen it all"; the artist, through breakdown and analysis of substructures within that "all," gives the ordinary observer what is really, in a limited sense, a new experience of seeing. This creative selection among the possibilities of vision makes up one-half of an artist; the skill to depict that selection successfully makes up the other.

What looks lifelike?

It is also sometimes said (by Philistines) that the perceptual function of representational pictures is to depict their subjects realistically. In a provocative discussion, "What Looks Lifelike?" (1954), Rudolf Arnheim, the psychologist of art, demonstrated that the attribution of "lifelikeness" to paintings has a long, and to the modern Western eye, surprising, history. Citing historical documents, he showed that Greeks, Chinese, and pre-Renaissance Europeans all saw in some of the pictures of contemporary artists an astonishing degree of realistic resemblance to their subjects. Arnheim argued that pictures seen as very lifelike, such as those of Giotto, were judged from a context of familiarity with the pictures that had preceded them within the culture. He wrote that it was the deviation from the prevailing norm of pictorial representation that produced the astonishing effect of lifelikeness in Giotto's pictures. It is difficult to argue this case without becoming involved in an implicit developmental thesis. After all, is it the case that *any* randomly selected deviation from the norm will surprise viewers with its advancing lifelike character? For much of Western art, which, like it or not, can be seen to a great extent as an advance toward photographic realism, the argument can be made that any stylistic change in the photographic direction necessarily would produce an impression of realism, to the extent that photographic fidelity provides the criterion of realism. For cultural styles in which development toward photographic realism is not a determining influence, the direction that a lifelike deviation from the norm must take is not as obvious.

An understanding of successful "lifelike" deviations does

not really depend on the thesis of developmental progre
sion within a style toward a particular goal. Because t
range of possibilities of visual experience is indefinite
large, the number of directions that may be taken by su
cessful lifelike deviations from the norm is also indefinite
large. Artistic creation of an impression of realism is r
really very different from the creation of novel visual e
perience in the sense of selection and delimitation. If t
artist's selection of a visual structure to depict is valid
terms of its actual existence in nature, then that selecti
is necessarily "lifelike." If it is novel in terms of paintir
within the culture, then it will be seen as "astonishing
lifelike. Again, the process is one of directing the viewe
attention.

An important distinction must be observed here. T
artistic education of attention takes place primarily with
the world of pictures, not within the ordinary enviro
ment. This is not to say that pictures cannot teach
observer to attend to usually unnoted aspects of the ever
day visual world, but only that this is not their prim.
heuristic function. Pictures – good pictures, successful p
tures – educate in terms of the *pictorial* possibilities of p
ception. Progressive pictures point out perceptual realit
new to the *pictures* of a culture, not new to its people. T
changes take place from artist to artist, and occasiona
result in dramatic change in depiction style, in the creati
of a very different framework for the further explorati
of "realistic" deviations. Such a major change accompan
the adoption of a consistent perspective system in the W
during the Renaissance. Of course, this example must
be taken as evidence that an implicit developmental p
gression toward a particular end is a prerequisite to s
cessful lifelike changes in style. As Arnheim wrote in 19
"In fact, it seems safe to assert that every successful wc
of [representational] art, no matter how stylized and
mote from mechanical correctness, conveys the full natu
flavor of the object it represents." Arnheim assumed t
the "full natural flavor" must be conveyed within the cc
straints of the medium and the prevailing cultural mc
of depiction. Changes in style, whether they are progr
sive or not, take place within a context of prevailing st

and are judged accordingly by members of the culture in which they occur.

Role of cultural convention

In an unusual exploration of the role of cultural convention in the evaluation of contemporary art, the philosopher, Marx Wartofsky (1980), assumed and argued for an intimate connection between a culture's theory of representation and its theory of vision. He contended that existing conceptualizations of pictures and pictorial perception determine the cultural assumptions about the nature of perception itself. Thus, theories both of vision and of pictures are inherently culturally artifactual, and it is a culture's theory about the nature of pictures that determines its theory of vision.

While there well may be an intimate connection between what a culture says about picture making and what it says about the experience of seeing, the connection, both theoretically and practically, is necessarily nonartifactual. My goal is to show that general and specific pictorial perceptual content and, indeed, all representational art styles, are based on certain commonalities of visual experience, generally describable by the different levels of geometrical structure available in natural perspective. The selection from among the representational options of natural perspective in terms of bias, preference, value, or function is determined by cultural convention, but not the set of options itself. The role of cultural context and convention in relation to the geometric; of natural perspective will be clarified in this chapter.

Consequences of cultural style for the consumer

That representational art is created and evaluated within a specific cultural context has far-reaching consequences for the perceptions of the consumer, both artist and nonartist alike. The selection, direction, and education of attention performed by the artist means that paintings teach us to perceive paintings. This is not to argue that we must learn to read paintings as we do prose, but simply that we be-

come habituated to culturally common modes of depicti
by which I mean everything from the criteria for the
pearance of reality to the canons of good taste. The
historian Ernst Gombrich (1972a) gave an excellent
ample of the broad-ranging effects of stylistic context
his presentation of the French Academy's response to
Impressionist exhibition. Because the Impressionist
parture from prevailing style was so great, their effo
generally were judged to be both tasteless and faithless
reality. Relative to the painting conventions (and politi
of the time, they undoubtedly seemed so. Paintings tea
us about paintings, but they do so in much the same m
ner as we are taught anything else. If the disparity betwe
what is known and what is to be learned is too great,
learn little or nothing. Even the worldly cosmopolite
modern times must develop a new framework of vis
understanding when confronted with previously unfam
iar styles of depiction. Indeed, the attempt to fit a stra
style into familiar terms invariably distorts both the
and the new.

Arnheim pointed out that pictures are created as so
tions to representational problems within the constrai
of the medium. Recognition of this fact by both obser
and artist means again that pictures are judged as pictu
Even the viewer who says, "That doesn't look like a t
to me," has separate criteria for judgments of trees and
pictures of trees. Trees are not judged as "lifelike" or "
lifelike," but as alive or dead. I do not mean to exami
the issue of whether criteria for judgments of "interesting
"unusual," "beautiful" and such are the same for trees a
for pictures of trees – a matter greatly outside my area
competence. I wish simply to argue that within a cultu
representational pictures comprise a recognizable class
objects, much as do houses. And the rules for the co
struction of the members of the class, be it pictures
houses, are familiar to the consumers in the culture.

Tacit knowledge of construction rules

To say that the rules of construction, or generation,
known to consumers within the culture does not mean t

the ordinary consumer could either build a house or paint a picture. The knowledge is tacit – not necessarily conscious or explicit. It is operative in that the observer can sort cases reliably according to the rules and recognize violations of them. Perhaps more importantly, the observer is bound by tacit knowledge of the construction rules of the culture in judging what pictures look "right." Anecdotes certainly occur in the literature to support the argument that judgments of realistic portrayal are culture bound, such as Gombrich's (1972b) account of the Japanese gentleman who could make no sense of the "distortions" of Western perspective on first encounter, but later found them to be more lifelike than his traditional conventions.

We also have some cross-cultural psychological research that in its own way does not go much beyond anecdote for reliability of information. This one example is presented to give the flavor of the work. Beveridge (1940) presented West African (Gold Coast) students with eighty colored postcards: forty of famous European paintings and forty of Japanese, Indian, and Persian pictures. (The reason for the selection of these specific comparison groups is not clear.) The students were asked to cite their preference when presented with the forty pairs of pictures, matched East with West roughly by subject matter. The students preferred the European paintings 86.5% of the time. To interpret this consistency of preference, one need only consider the words of the author of the study, who wrote: "We must remember, however, that these subjects had been used to seeing European paintings from their earliest school days, whereas Oriental art was new to them." West Africans, like their European counterparts, prefer the familiar. One can't help but wonder how Beveridge would have interpreted the opposite outcome. Good cross-cultural work is difficult to do and difficult to find. The reader is referred to a review of the cross-cultural work on picture perception by Hagen and Jones (1978), for more information on the subject.

We move now from the relation between cultural values and what "looks real" in representational pictures to a reinterpretation of some traditional views of representation in light of the geometrical formulation of natu[ral] perspective.

Two views of representation

The pictures used in this book represent the world in so[me] way. Indeed, I have defined "representational picture" [to] mean one that *looks* like the world, even to the relative[ly] naive. But how is it that representational pictures look li[ke] the world they picture? Two seemingly contradictory a[n]swers have been proposed to this question in a long deb[ate] that I will not be deal with extensively here; I will c[all] them *Conventionalism* and *Resemblance Theory*.

Conventionalism

One group of scholars, led by the philospher Nelson Goo[d]man, has argued that pictures perform their represen[ta]tional function by means of shared but arbitra[ry] conventional codes of depiction. Goodman, in his bo[ok] *Languages of Art*, (1968), assumed no relationship of rese[m]blance between ordinary and pictorial visual informatio[n] and conceived of pictures as vehicles for conventional sy[m]bolism. One learns to read the conventional symbols o[f a] culture's pictures just as one learns to read the conventio[nal] words of a language. As the word *cat* does not resem[ble] the animal, so the picture of a cat need not resemble [its] subject matter in the flesh. Goodman's explanation of t[he] nature of representation is quite possible logically, but n[ot] practically. My restriction that the representational pictur[es] under discussion are accessible even to the relatively nai[ve] precludes use of his formulation. More to the point, t[he] rather consistent findings of the cross-cultural literature [on] picture perception in the pictorially naive do not suppo[rt] Goodman's hypothesis. There is no reliable evidence th[at] pictorially naive people are incapable of either perceivi[ng] or drawing pictures of isolated *objects*. For the perceptio[n] of *spatial layout* in pictures, the findings are less consiste[nt] and subject to some heated debate. It is safe to conclu[de] that it often takes a short period of time for the pictorial[ly] naive to learn to attend to the depicted contents rather th[an] to the medium (paper, canvas, whatever), and the accuracy and flexibility of their pictorial spatial perceptions are often limited in apparently surprising but understandable ways. What is important is that complete failure of spatial perception in pictures by the naive is almost unknown in the literature. Unless one wishes to argue that a completely arbitrary code of depiction can be acquired, learned, and understood in a truly astonishingly short period of time, then the hypothesis that pictures function as representations without a basis in resemblance is untenable.

Resemblance theory

The second answer often proposed to the question of how representational pictures look like the world is that they *are* like the world they picture. Here we have two apparently mutually contradictory positions. The first is what I call the "little pictures" or "perspectivist" theory of representation, which proposes that there is a one-to-one mapping of the visible surfaces of the world onto the picture plane, and from there onto the eye. The simplest version of this resemblance theory argues that natural perspective describes the "little pictures" on the retina – the retinal images that serve (so it is said) as the basis of visual perception. Similarly, linear perspective describes the larger pictures painted out there in the world; and, pictures being pictures, what is true of natural perspective must be true of linear, and vice versa. The second position on Resemblance Theory holds that pictures succeed as representations because they contain the same kind of information as the world they picture. Both points of view are presented here.

Gibson's defense of linear perspective. James Gibson (1971) in a reply to Goodman's conventionalist theory, defended the "naturalness" of linear perspective constructions by pointing out that the critical differences between natural and linear perspective lie not in the constructions themselves, but in the constraints on viewing imposed on the latter. Gibson argued that *any* linear perspective construction, properly viewed from the correct monocular station point, the center of projection as defined in Chapter 3,

would look natural and realistic to the observer. It is lo[
ically and sometimes practically possible to produce a trom
l'oeil display that will fool the observer into thinking [
or she perceives a three-dimensional scene. However, t[
successful creation of such a display requires not only
constrained viewpoint, but usually occlusion of the edg
of the picture and motionless view by the observer as we
Gibson points out that these restrictions are almost nev
observed in the ordinary process of viewing pictures, ar
that it is this failure to observe the necessary restrictior
that makes linear perspective look "unnatural."

Gibson's defense of the naturalness of linear perspecti[
was based on a limited logical analysis of the problem, n[
on systematic empirical investigation, and the position [
arrived at is true and defensible only in a limited sense.
quick review of some of the empirical observations ar
research will make clear what those limits are, and speci[
more precisely the differences, such as they are, betwe[
natural and linear perspective. (Remember that linear pe
spective was originally called *artificial perspective*.)

Maurice Pirenne, painter and physicist, in *Optics, Pair[
ing and Photography* (1970), was at pains to point out t[
numerous differences between the projections occasion[
by natural and linear perspective. Many of the differenc[
specified by Pirenne reduce to consequences of differenc[
in projection surface; the retina is curved, the canvas
question usually flat. Thus in an ordinary frontal phot[
graph of a long wall, the top and bottom of the wall a[
not seen to converge; for the observer staring at the wal
however, the convergence across the retina would be ve[
great. The form of any projection is determined entire[
by the relation between the object being projected and t[
projection surface, relative to the center of projection. Tl
picture surface case and the retinal-surface case illustrat[
in Figure 5.1 demonstrate that it is quite possible to crea
a linear perspective construction on a curved surface th[
differs very little from a natural perspective image on tl
retina. Of course, an argument on the relation betwe[
natural and linear perspective based on retinal images do[
not really make much sense, since retinal images do n[
actually exist. The eyeball is constantly moving and

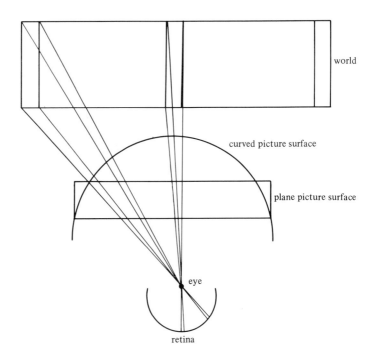

world

curved picture surface

plane picture surface

eye

retina

Figure 5.1. Difference in the forms of the projection of an object onto a flat and curved picture surface and onto a curved retinal surface.

possessed of irregularities in curvature and lens quality (there is no film strip behind the lens.) The eye does not function like a movie camera; that may be the easiest way of conceiving of optical-information structures, but it is not the most accurate. However, for the purposes of this discussion, the important point is that it is possible to subtend, retinally and pictorially, angles of the same size and shape. The differences between a flat projection surface and a curved one are in the retinal (foveal) case trivial.

A more telling criticism of the assumed kinship between natural and linear perspective comes also from Pirene and is reinforced by the informal observations of Nelson Goodman (1968). Both Pirenne and Goodman argue that there are certain cases in which linear perspective cannot be considered to be a subclass of natural perspective. To make this point clear, imagine that you are looking out a window, without moving your head, at a scene in front of you. If you trace on the window the exact outlines of the objects in that scene, then the sizes and shapes of the angles subtended at the retina by the pattern traced on the window should be the same as the sizes and shapes of the angles occasioned by observation of the scene itself. Is a good tracing a good picture? Pirenne demonstrates that the accurate tracing of a sphere seen at the edge of the visible field is a flattened circle, an ellipse; such an ellipse should then be seen in a painting as a sphere, in proper context. But it is not. A flattened circle at the edge of a painting is seen either as a funny-looking squashed spheroid or as a failure in drawing. There are many such mechanically correct perspective constructions that simply do not appear to be correct to the adult Western observer. It is very hard to account for these "failures" of linear perspective with a traditional "little pictures" theory of the relationship between natural and pictorial perspective.

It is indeed true that there exist "failures" of linear perspective not attributable just to neglect of the observation constraints, as Gibson had argued. It is true that linear perspective often must be modified from mechanical correctness in order to look natural and realistic to Western adults. What is equally true, and considerably more important, is that these "modifications" are not modifications at all, but limitations on the range of acceptable perspective. It is not enough that a perspective construction for a picture be projectively correct; it must also be generated within certain cultural conventional constraints in order to look good to members of the culture. Linear perspective is the Western post-Renaissance selection from among the representational options of natural perspective. Like any other selection, linear perspective describes a set of substructures in natural perspective used for depiction purposes by the artists of a specific time, place, and culture. Consumers of art in the culture, artists and public alike, possess tacit knowledge of the construction rules that circumscribe the pictorial subdivision of natural perspective proper to their culture. They know which pictures have been generated according to the rules and which have not. Pictures created according to the rules look natural and realistic; other pictures look distorted. Until recently, such assertions on the role of culture and convention in the evaluation of pictures had to be taken on faith or accepted as working hypotheses. In the past ten years, however, empirical investigation of the perception of pictures has received considerable attention, and the tacit knowledge

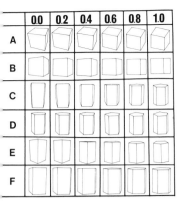

	0.0	0.2	0.4	0.6	0.8	1.0
A						
B						
C						
D						
E						
F						

Figure 5.2. Images of cubes and prisms varying in degree of perspective convergence, where 1.0 is no convergence and 0.0 is extreme convergence. (From M. Hagen and H.B. Elliott, 1976. © 1976 by the American Psychological Association. Reprinted by permission of the author.)

hypothesis has received considerable support. The most pertinent literature will be described briefly as it touches on cultural definition of appropriate perspective.

Recent research on tacit pictorial knowledge. In 1975, Horacio Reggini, an engineer, devised a computer program that would generate images varying in degree of perspective convergence for any object of particularized dimensions viewed from a specified station point. Figure 5.2 gives examples of images of cubes and pentagonal prismatic solids generated by his system. The column of images under the index numnber 0.0 is the ordinary Western perspective that would occur at the specified distance and angle of view. Across the columns, as index numbers increase in size, the perspective convergence across the object from front to back decreases. Amount of perspective convergence across an object can be thought of in terms of the difference between the size of the visual angle subtended by the front surface of the object and the size of the angle subtended at the back. Under index number 1.0, the perspective convergence is nonexistent. This is called axonometric perspective or, more commonly, parallel perspective. (The terms *axonometric* and *isometric* depend on the specific axes of the projection and need not concern us here.) Reggini's program generated a series of images that varied from familiar Western perspective to unfamiliar Oriental perspective, in graded steps.

In 1976, with a student, Harry Elliott, I showed these pictures to Western students under a variety of conditions: one at a time, three at a time, six at a time, monocularly, binocularly, at an arbitrary station point, and at the station point correct for the 0.0 conic projection. Students were instructed to choose the most natural and realistic picture, to choose the best picture, or to choose the most accurate drawing. They held the model objects, the cube and pentagonal solid, in their hands prior to testing so there was no ambiguity about the subjects of the depictions. For all the tested conditions and under all sets of instructions, the results were generally the same. Students chose as preferred pictures those with either no convergence or minimal convergence, 1.0 and 0.8, 75 percent of the time. It is impor-

tant to note that the perspective convergence in *all* of th
pictures was mechanically correct for some station poin
at ever-increasing distances as one moves from left to righ
across columns. Yet these Western subjects limited the
choices of natural, realistic, and accurate to only a sma
subset of those correct images. It is this particular selectio
from among the possible that really distinguishes Wester
linear perspective from the broader ranging natur.
perspective.

Because the pictures in this original study were rath
lifeless, colorless, and limited as a class, Rebecca Jones an
I undertook a replication of this study with what are calle
"more ecologically valid" pictures: color photographs o
ordinary objects like picnic baskets and step stools (Fi
5.3). The objects were photographed at greater and great
distances to produce mechanically the varying convergenc
generated by computer in the earlier study. Essentially th
students' task was the same, and basically so were th
results. The major new finding resulted from the differ
ences in the stimulus dimensions of the objects portraye
In the earlier study, we discovered that for a pictured obje
to appear natural and realistic to a Western adult, it mu
be photographed, painted, or drawn at a distance at lea
ten times as great as its rough front-to-back dimension
We called this the *Zoom Effect*. But the formula applic
only to objects that are roughly cubical. For objects wit
longer orthogonal axes, which extend into the picture plane

*Figure 5.3. Photograph of an
"ecologically valid" common object.
(Photograph supplied by the
author.)*

the preferred convergence is necessarily greater, and can be determined by breaking the object into square segments. For example, consider a box four times as long as it is wide. Were it a cube, the preferred convergence would be about 10 percent from front to back. The rule cannot be the same for a long rectangular box, or its picture could not be distinguished from that of a cube. So the preferred convergence is approximately 10 percent from the front of the box to the point that is roughly as far along the box as the front is wide, that is, it constitutes the first square subsegment of the box top. Convergence, then, is preferentially minimal, but not, for these Western subjects, nonexistent – at least not with elongated objects like rectangular boxes, roads, and railroad tracks.

In a follow-up study to the adult work, Rebecca Jones and I (1978) tested the original Reggini pictures with small children. Children also were asked to choose the best picture. We found that children do *not* perceive pictures as adults do. The youngest children, at the 0.0 station point, chose the extreme convergence (0.0) pictures, or pictures as similar to these as possible, as the best pictures. This choice was almost never made by an adult in any condition. Like the adults, the children had been shown the models before testing and had handled them, but the models had not been placed at any specific or consistent distance. Yet, the children treated the pictures as if they were looking at the three-dimensional model itself, rather than at images of the model. That is they chose exactly those pictures that exhibited the perspective convergence that would be occasioned by the objects themselves when viewed at the picture-viewing distance. This consistency of preference operated only when view was monocular from a close position; under the free-view condition the littlest children exhibited no consistent preference for any of the pictures. Somewhat older children, seven to eight years, appeared to be in transition between the performances of adults and those of the younger (two to four) children.

It is interesting that the very young children functioned not according to a *culturally* determined criterion of correctness, but to an *environmentally* determined one. They responded essentially to ordinary environmental (retinal,

if you will) information, and not to cultural conventio
Given the very close viewing distance, extreme conve
gence across the object would necessarily be present in t
light to the eye if the picture were indeed the object
pictured. The developing awareness of children of the se
arate world of pictures will be dealt with in Chapter 1
For now, what is important to realize is that the Weste
post-Renaissance system, so often hailed as the only tru
visually valid system of depiction, is itself clearly a cultu
acquisition.

Paintings teach us about paintings; pictures educate t
viewer about the *pictorial* possibilities of perception. In th
regard, the insensitivity of young children to the constru
tion conventions of their own cultural style of depictic
is especially interesting. Children respond to the possib
ities of ordinary visual experience, and perceive accordin
to environmentally structured light. They must learn
perceive pictures as pictures, to make judgments abo
pictorial content in terms of pictorial structure. The ta
knowledge of construction rules so evident in the jud
ments of the adults was clearly missing in the judgmer
of the youngest children. The cultural subdivision of na
ural perspective that comprises the depiction system of
particular culture is arbitrary in its delimitation of natu
perspective. The rules can only be learned through fam
iarization with the style of a specific culture.

Thinking of Western linear perspective as a subdivisic
of natural perspective with cultural rules restricting its ran
and application leads quite naturally to consideration of t
second major resemblance theory: invariance. We shall s
that, in a certain sense, "little pictures" theory and inva
iance theory are two formulations of the same thing, an
not contradictory or mutually exclusive at all.

Resemblance theory II

Invariance theorists argue that pictures succeed as repr
sentations of the world because they contain some of t
same kind of invariant information in reflected light as t
objects or scene depicted. James Gibson was the maj
advocate of this theory. Gibson, despite his defense in 19

of the "naturalness" of linear perspective, had nothing invested in the "little pictures" theory of the relationship between natural and linear perspective. Because he explicitly rejected the importance of individual retinal images for perception of the world, his argument on the similarities and differences between the images generated by linear and natural perspective was motivated, seemingly, by a desire simply to clear the air of polemic confusion. In 1971 and 1973, Gibson argued that the true similarity, formal and perceptual, between pictures and the world they depict lies not in the presence of perspective, but in the shared possession of invariant information specifying world properties. He argued that a picture, by definition, is a surface treated so as to contain the same kind of invariant information as the section of the world it depicts. Since invariant information is not specific to particular single view or images, it is not confined to pictures containing photographic, perspectival fidelity. The existence of successful trompe l'oeil displays like that shown in Figure 5.4 shows clearly that approximating a one-to-one map of scene to picture with very fine detail creates a very successful representational picture. On the other hand, detailed, section-by section copies are manifestly absent in innumerable displays such as caricatures, line drawings, and non-Western art. Gibson extended his argument to consider even the cases of caricatures as successful depictions of people by virtue of the invariants they carry for the person's persistent or characteristic properties.

In Gibson's last formulations before his death of the relationship among natural perspective, linear perspective, and invariants, he seemed to assign invariant structure only to natural and not to linear perspective. He wrote in 1979 that the sole function of perspective in a picture is to place the viewer in the scene depicted, not to enhance the reality of the depiction. He said:

The term *perspective* is generally misunderstood. The theory of projection on a transparent picture plane to a station point is a Renaissance discovery that is properly called *artificial perspective*. The theory of the ambient optic array from an environment to a point of observation should be called *natural perspective* and is not at all the same thing. (p.283)

The separation of invariant structure from perspective structure is the heart of the problem. The invariants display a world with nobody in it, and the perspective displays where the observer is in that world. One can depict without a fixed point observation, just as one can visualize without a point of observation, although it is not easy to understand how. But depiction

Figure 5.4. Old Models, by Williams Harnett. (Courtesy of the Museum of Fine Arts, Boston. Reprinted by permission of the Charles Henry Hayden Fund.)

with a point of observation is the more natural sort, and the photographic picture is necessarily of this sort. (p. 284)

Gibson's last treatment of the problem of information in representational pictures seemed to reflect a certain degree of discomfort with his earlier extension of invariant information to pictures. Indeed, in *The Ecological Approach to Visual Perception*, (1979), Gibson treated "awareness" mediated by pictures as a special field of study. However, my thesis in this book is that the concept of "invariant," *mutatis mutandis*, can be of invaluable help in understanding the perceptual basis of representational art, even if not in the form proposed by Gibson. As I explained in Chapter 2, Gibson's conceptualization of the concept of invariant was considerably broader than the geometrical concept offered here. In 1979, Gibson saw the geometric and quasi-geometric invariance concepts as too limited in application to have much heuristic value in perceptual theory. It should be clear that I think we have only just begun to appreciate the possible applications of the concepts of geometrical invariants and groups of transformation to perception, especially in the field of representational art. I believe that at some very basic level, what representational art represents is natural perspective in a pictorial medium. Despite the manifest differences between the concept of invariants and the "little pictures" perspectivist concept of representation, the two ideas are quite intimately related. In order to understand this relationship, within a context of geometrical theory, we must examine pictorial possibilities of capturing the optical structures described in Chapter 3.

Pictures and optical structure

In order to understand how the optical structure of natural perspective relates to the perceptual content of representational art, it is necessary first to consider in some detail the nature of pictures themselves. The terms of this analysis are familiar already from the presentation of the hierarchy of geometrical mappings in Chapter 3, and from the application of these geometrical concepts to visual perception. We will consider now the special character of pictures as mappings of the world they represent.

Pictures as types of mappings

Pictures are particular types of mappings of one plane set of planes) onto another usually known as *projectio* Projections occur in each of the geometries presented Chapter 3. Projections can be described by the constrai on their generation, on the way they are made; that they can be described in terms of the parallelism or cc currence of the lines of the projection, and the paralleli: or intersection of the planes, original and image, of ● projection. Table 5.1 illustrates each of projections that ● occur in each of the four geometries in terms of th● constraints.

Table 5.1. *Mechanical generation*

Mapping	Generation	Character
Metric	Planes are parallel Projection lines are parallel	Distance and area 1 :
	A B C D / *A′ B′ C′ D′* (P, P*)	
Similarity	Planes are parallel Projection is central	Distance and area are changed by constant scale factor
	A B / *A′ B′* (P, P*, CP)	
Affine	Planes are not parallel Projection lines are parallel	Distance is multiplied by different constant ● every line direction

(continued on facing pa●

Table 5.1. (*cont.*)

Mapping	Generation	Character

| Projective | Planes are not parallel
Projection is central | Distance is subject to varying distortion |

The first mapping is Metric: The object and image planes are parallel and the projection lines are also parallel. The second mapping is a Similarity. The planes are parallel and the projection is a central projection to a point on the normal to the image. The third mapping is Affine. In this case, the projection lines from the object to the image are parallel, but the two planes are not. In the last mapping, a Projective projection, the planes are not parallel and the projection lines meet at a center of projection.

Invariants of each projection type

Although these projection types have been geometrically classified, the distinctions are only marginally descriptive.

Since each type of geometry listed subsumes all those b
low it, the Metric and Similarity mappings are, of cours
also Affine and Projective. Likewise, the Affine mappir
itself is also Projective. A general rule to remember is th
if *neither* planes nor projection lines are parallel, then tl
mapping is only Projective. If *either* planes *or* lines a
parallel, then the mapping is Affine or a Similarity; if bo
are parallel, then the mapping is Metric.

Because each type of projection belongs to one of tl
geometries in a proper sense, then the invariants peculi
to that geometry are preserved in that projection. Thu
for example, Metric projections preserve distance and ang
size, even when the projected figures have been mov
laterally, reflected, or rotated. Similarity projections pr
serve all of these properties except that distance is chang
by a constant, and, of course, area as well, Affine proje
tions preserve ratio of division, betweenness, collinearit
and parallelism, but not angle size; distances are chang
according to the coefficient of compression ($A'B' = kA$
for each axis of compression. Thus, k is different for d:
ferent line directions in the plane. Projective projectio
preserve cross-ratio, harmonic properties, and the proper
of being a conic type. Distance is multiplied by a consta
when the planes are parallel (Similarity) and are often great
distorted when the planes of the projection intersect.
central projection with two parallel planes (and appropria
center of projection) is really a Similarity, odd as that m.
seem, and thus actually has all of the properties proper
a Similarity including the multiplication of size and di
tance by a constant. This is why a wall photograph
frontally does not converge to the sides in the resulta
photo.

Constraints

Representational pictures may be profitably described ar
analyzed as belonging to these different families of pr
jections, but the endeavor is subject to certain importa
constraints and considerations.

First, as I explained in Chapter 4, geometry itself do
not deal with armchairs and footstools, automobiles a

people, except in a formal, logical sense that need not concern us here. Geometry deals with points of no dimension, lines of no width, and planes of no thickness and of infinite extent. In analyzing pictures as geometric projections, however, we are not really talking about projecting the ideal points, lines, and planes of geometry, but the units of visible texture, edges, and surfaces of the world.

Second, two concepts closely related in the analysis of optical information, of pictures as projections, may be fundamentally different in geometrical theory. For example, in geometry, Affine parallel projections and Projective central projections may be considered to be fundamentally removed from each other in various formulations of the projective plane. These formulations, or models of the projective plane, are not relevant here; nevertheless, it should be borne in mind that the characteristics of and relationships among the geometries described here exist only in certain formal, mathematical contexts and disappear in others. The contexts in which they do exist are that of the Euclidean plane, and what is sometimes called the "real" projective plane. We concern ourselves only with these.

Characteristics of pictorial projections

Visible versus ideal

In translating the four fundamental types of geometrical projections into categories of representational art, several issues are raised. First, representational art is concerned with the depiction of surfaces in the world, not with ideal planes: The various surfaces in the world comprise the original planes to be projected, and the picture plane, be it glass, film, or canvas (or whatever) is equivalent to the image plane. Consider, for example, the picture in Figure 5.5 of a building, road, and trees. The "world" surfaces to be depicted consist of the ground surface with the road, the front, top, and side of the building, and the front faces of the two trees (if one can speak of the faces of trees). These are the surfaces visible to an observer from a certain point of view or station point.

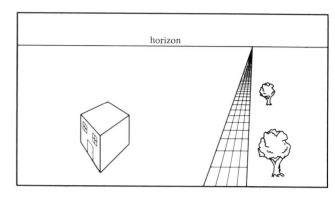

Figure 5.5. *World surfaces depicted in the image plane.*

Mechanical conditions and form

Second, the form of the projection, which the represe[n]
tational picture will take, is dependent on two things: t[he]
spatial relations among the surfaces to be depicted and t[he]
picture plane, and the spatial relations among the lines [of]
the projection. The *planes* may be parallel or intersectin[g,]
the *lines* may be parallel or convergent. In determining t[he]
form of the projection these two variables of image creati[on]
also determine which invariants will be present in ea[ch]
type of depiction. The simple but prototypical exampl[e]
of each projection type in Figures 5.6–5.9 should clari[fy]
this. Table 5.2 summarizes station-point options.

Prototypical examples of pictures in each geometry

We shall take as our examples projections of the front fa[ce]
of a rectangular building. Figure 5.6 shows a projecti[on]
generated when the picture plane is parallel to the fro[nt]
face of the building, using parallel projection lines. Th[en]
the projection is Metric (or Orthogonal), and shape, si[ze,]
angles, and parallelism all are preserved as invariants in t[his]
projection. Figure 5.7 shows a projection also generat[ed]
with parallel planes, but the lines of the projection conver[ge.]

Table 5.2. *Station point options*

Number	Distance	Projection lines	Angle	Planes
Single	Close	Convergent	Frontal	Parallel
Multiple	Medium	Parallel	Oblique	Intersecti[ng]
	Optical infinity			

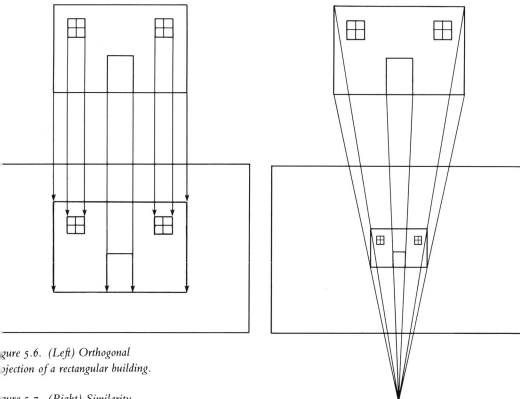

CP

to a point. This creates a Similarity projection in which shape, angle size and parallelism, and perpendicularity all are invariant but the image has undergone a scale change and is smaller in size than the original. The third example, an Affine projection, illustrated in Figure 5.8, leaves scale more or less unchanged because the projection lines are parallel. However, shape and angle size are quite different from the original despite the invariance of parallelism in such projections. (Shape and angle size necessarily change together, but the distinction is useful for clarity.) Finally, Figure 5.9 shows a *Projective* projection (a cumbersome term) generated with projection lines converging to a point with picture plane and building face not parallel to each other. Because this type of image is Projective *only*, shape is distorted, angle size is altered, parallelism is lost, and a scale change occurs as well. Invariants are the rather simple ones, like betweenness and collinearity, and the seemingly exotic ones like cross-ratios of points and lines and the

103   CHARACTERISTICS OF PICTORIAL PROJECTIONS

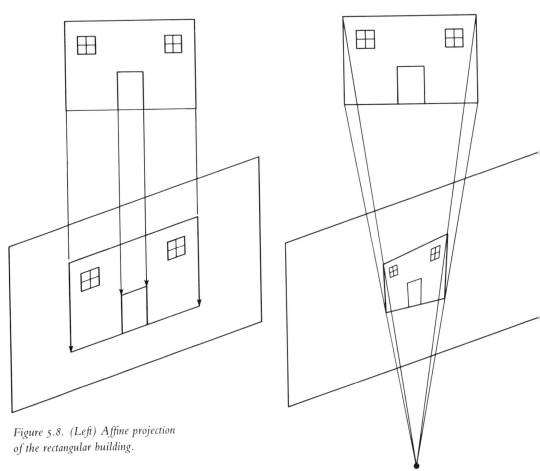

Figure 5.8. (Left) Affine projection
of the rectangular building.

Figure 5.9. (Right) Projective
projection of the building face.
CP = center of projection.

harmonic properties. The invariants for each geometry a
summarized in Table 5.3.

In representational pictures, the type and number of i
variants preserved are a direct function and immediate co
sequence of the means of generating the images. Just
we ascended the geometrical hierarchy, gaining transfo
mations and losing invariants as we went, so also do v
"lose" invariants as we move from Metric to Similarity
Affine to Projective pictures. It is interesting to note th
the pictures most familiar to Western post-Renaissance o
servers are those that contain the fewest invariants. Ho
ever, as I explained in Chapter 3, the invariants captur
in such pictures are exactly those that remain invaria
across *subjective movements of the observer:* the cross-rati
of points and lines and the derivative gradients of si

Table 5.3. *Transformations and invariants*

Geometry	Transformations	Invariants
Metric	Translation Reflection Rotation	Size Shape Distance Angle size Straightness Parallelism Length Ratio of length Cross-ratio Collinearity Area Betweenness Position of center of gravity Perpendicularity
Similarity	Motions Radial homothetic	Angle size Shape Straightness Parallelism Ratio of division Cross-ratio Collinearity Betweenness Position of center of gravity Betweenness
Affine	Similarities Skew reflection Compression Skew compression Hyperbolic rotation Elliptic rotation Shear Parallel projection Metric projection	Parallelism Collinearity Ratio of division Betweenness Cross-ratio Straightness
Projective	Affinities Central projection	Cross-ratio Harmonic division Collinearity Straightness Betweenness (Textural Gradients)

linear, and texture perspective. It may be that what W
erners call "realistic" information is pictorial informa
that is invariant under individualistic movement-gener.
change.

Pictorial projections and the presence of perspective

Most of the pictures in representational art are of m
surfaces, like the building, road, and trees in Figure
(This does not imply, however, that Figure 5.5 itse.
art.) Moreover, the pictures that most frequently occu
Western post-Renaissance art are central, projective ¡
jections in which, characteristically, the ground plane i
right angles to the picture plane. The surfaces of most o¡
objects in the scene rest on the ground plane at vari
angles relative to the picture plane. Thus, for all of th
surfaces, the Projective "distortions" of shape occur. H¡
ever, when a single face (sometimes more) of an objec
fact is oriented parallel to the picture plane, the image
that face is given by a Similarity projection preserv
shape (angles and parallelism). An example of the dif
ence in the appearance of these images is given in Fig
5.10. In the center example of the figure, the image
of the wall from top to bottom, across its extent, is ev¡
where the same, with no convergence, because the s¡
angle intersected by the wall is cut by a picture plane ¡

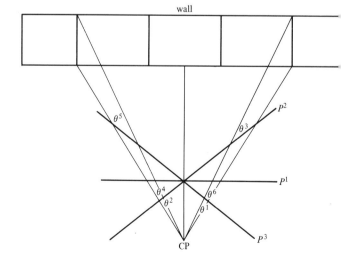

Figure 5.10. Three central
projections of a wall in different
orientations with respect to the
picture plane. θ = angle;
P = picture plane; CP = center of
projection. (Adapted from Pirenne
1970).

allel to the wall. Thus, the triangle formed by the vertical extent of the wall and the projection lines to the eye is similar to the triangle formed by the vertical dimension of the image of the wall on the picture plane and the projection lines to the eye; in similar triangles, the sides are proportional. However, in both the top and bottom examples in the figure, convergence across the wall is very much in evidence. Because the picture plane is not parallel to the wall, the side of the picture plane nearer to the wall will intersect a larger section of the visual cone subtended by the wall than will the farther edge. The two triangles are not similar. Thus the image of the wall on the picture plane will converge to smaller and smaller size in perspective with increasing distance between picture plane and subject. The presence or absence of convergence, of perspective-shape "distortion," is thus entirely a matter of spatial relations between original surface and picture plane in central projections. Similarity projections are often nested in a pictorial composition that is otherwise only Projective. These nested Similarities may somehow serve to anchor the composition as a whole perceptually in ways that are not well understood.

An interesting example of variable perspective effects is familiar through photographs of tall buildings taken with an ordinary fixed-lens camera. By "fixed lens camera" I mean one in which the optical axis of the lens is perpendicular to the film plane and immovable. When the photographer shoots up at the building the film plane is at an angle relative to the front of the building; that is, the film plane "intersects" the building plane (Figure 5.11). Thus the lower part of the building is closer to the film plane than the top, so the visual cone subtended by the bottom of the building will be cut by the film plane at a wider point than at the top. Therefore the image of the building will converge from bottom to top in the resultant picture. (Keep in mind that with such photographs, the images are reversed and inverted on the film plane, and reversed and inverted again in developing, in what is essentially an identity transformation.) Because this bottom-to-top convergence is frequently unacceptable to the photographer or prospective skyscraper dweller (for a variety of reasons)

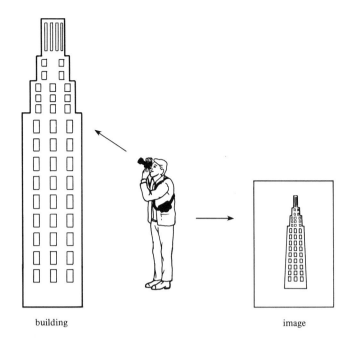

Figure 5.11. Fixed-lens image of a tall building.

building   image

photographs of such buildings are usually taken wi
view camera to "correct" the convergence (Figure 5.
A view camera has a variable relation between lens
film plane so that the lens can be pointed up at the buil

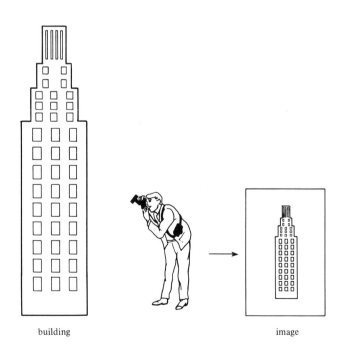

Figure 5.12. View-camera image of a tall building.

building   image

while the film plane remains parallel to the front face of the building. The two images in Figures 5.11 and 5.12 illustrate the difference in the appearances of the building photographed in these two ways: Maintaining parallel surface and image planes produces a Similarity projection with all the Similarity invariants preserved — at least with respect to the front of the building being photographed. Perversely, the principal gain of this maneuver is the loss of perspective convergence.

Perspective convergence can also be lost or "corrected" by assuming a different Similarity station point for each face of an object to be depicted; for example, one center of projection for the front face of a building and one for the side. This technique turns a two-point central projection into a double Similarity image. The multiple-image planes are of course each parallel to their respective object-surface sources. Architects accomplish a similar end in plan drawings, with what are called "orthographic" projections. In these projections, the lines of projections are parallel, and three different image planes are used, one each for the front, side, and base (top) of a building. Each image plane is parallel to the relevant building face. Thus, since both projection planes and projection lines are parallel, the projection is Metric and all metric invariants of shape, angularity, and parallelism are preserved. Of course, the images are subjected to a scale change to avoid awesomely unwieldy plans.

There is still a third method of "getting rid" of the convergence that attends most central projections of multisurface scenes. This technique consists of moving the center of projection so far away from the surfaces to be projected that the converging projection lines approximate the parallel. This distance need not be as far away as infinity, not even as far as the sun that gives us approximately parallel light rays. Optical infinity is very much closer. The visual-angle curve of Figure 2.6 shows angle size plotted with distance as a multiple of object size. To illustrate angle-size change as distance from object to observer increases, we will consider the changes in appearance of a transparent cube of unit size one (1). When the front face of the cube is as far away as it is big, $Distance = 1$ $Size$,

then the front face subtends a visual angle of only 51
and the rear face, at $D = 10S$, 28.7°, a very great chan
in angle size. When the front face of the cube is at a dista
ten times as great as its size, $D = 10\ S$, then the front f
subtends a visual angle of any 5.7°, and the rear face a
$= 11S$, 5.2°, a difference in angular size of less than
percent. If the cube is moved away to a distance forty tin
as great as its size, then the front face occupies a vis
angle of only 1.43°, and the rear face 1.39°. The conv
gence from front to back at this distance is thus minuscu

Lest it seem as if this distance were so great as to ren
its application in the ordinary case trivially rare, consi
the number of not very large objects in a room of
ordinary house. Matchbooks, letters, salt shakers, ci
rettes, pincushions, and toasters all reach a degree of tri
convergence at very short distances. Convergence in n
ural perspective is an ever-present aspect of normal vis
experience only until the observer is too far from the ob
to detect the convergence or attend to it as informati
The existence of no convergence, minimal convergen
and trivial convergence in ordinary visual experienc
what provides the basis for depiction techniques that e
ploy no convergence while retaining a single observer s
tion point. Just as the natural perspective across object
great distances shows no convergence in ordinary visi
so can pictures painted as if the artist were at optical infin
contain little or no convergence. No convergence occ
as "naturally" as the modest convergence usually cal
"perspective" when employed in Western pictures.
shall see that the no-convergence subsection of natural p
spective provided the depiction option for many cultu
across several centuries of time.

Each of the three techniques of "correcting" conv
gence so far discussed – multiple parallel planes, para
projection lines, and very distant centers of projection
transform familiar Western central projection images in
something very different in appearance but very similar
kind. They all follow the same"laws" of image generati
but assume different values for the variables specified
those laws.

Exercise of artistic option

The techniques of image generation discussed above were all concerned with, or at least presented in terms of, "getting rid of convergence." But the goal of artists across time and around the world has hardly been to get rid of convergence. Indeed, many scholars argue that it wasn't until the early fifteenth century that artists could even "find" it. (This is not the place for a review of the dating issue of the discovery of perspective. Edgerton [1975], White [1967], and Ivins [1964] provide extended treatments of the subject.) Suffice it to say that the complete absence of awareness of perspective convergence in pre-Renaissance times and non-Western cultures seems unlikely in the extreme given the multistructures of natural perspective described in the preceding chapters. Unless one wishes to argue for the existence of truly amazing racial or cultural differences in perception or for excessively speedy mutation of vision, it is probably safe to conclude that all peoples see much the same way and, generally speaking, they always have. This does not preclude, of course, dramatic cultural differences in the aspects of vision to which a people attend or attribute value in artistic creation.

Artists are by no means "fixed lens cameras." They are, at least by my definition, skilled adults capable of picking and choosing among the varieties of visual experience for the structure of their compositions. Thus an artist may choose to make single or multiple images of his or her subject; to stand near to or far from the subject, even if that stance is only metaphorical, imaginary, or vicarious; and to conceive of the picture plane as parallel or intersecting the surface plane(s) of the subject, even if such conceptualizations belong only to the realm of tacit knowledge. The selection of any of these options involves the artist in another set of choices: which invariants to depict (and which variants). To a great extent, the selection of the station-point options outlined in the previous section determines the range of invariants that can and will be depicted in a composition. Again, artists are not mindless automata but active creators. Their creative visual activities within the realm of representational art are governed perceptual laws but are not wholly determined by the Nevertheless, selecting a certain station-point option scribes the character of subsequent image generation. T character is describable formally in geometrical terms. I ages generated according to a specific geometry cont certain types of invariant information about the scenes tl represent and not others. Thus, station-point option termines in a necessary, logical progression what an ar can "say" representationally about a subject, and the art of different cultures have quite clearly chosen to say v different things.

A third set of choices, of depictive options, also aris again because the artist is not a passive recorder of inv iants in projections, but is a maker of *objets d'art*, of objo with more facets of being than simply representation. ' objects of art with which this book is concerned are pa: ings or pictures on more or less flat surfaces, so the ar engaged in the creation even of a three-dimensional presentational picture also must be occupied with the *t dimensional* surface demands of the composition. We h so far spent a great deal of time on the three-dimensio demands of representation with no attention to two-mensional compositional demands. However, the t components of composition play off against and with e other in ways unique to art. It is this interplay more t anything else that separates art from ordinary visual perience; its character in different cultural styles will explored in Chapter 8.

The categorization system

Every artist engaged in representational depiction n assume a *station point* relative to the subject, to be depict even if the subject is only in the mind's eye. Physica there are only so many stances an artist can take:

1. The artist can assume a single or multiple station po
2. The picture surface can be frontal or oblique to dominant surfaces of the object.
3. The artist can stand close to, at a moderate distance at optical infinity from the subject.

Compositionally, for the case of multiple subjects to be depicted, again the artist has a limited number of options:

1. Objects can be arrayed in rows, or not.
2. Objects can have uniform orientation relative to the picture plane, or not.
3. Picture plane and subject planes can be parallel or intersecting.
4. Projection lines can be parallel or convergent.

These eight compositional options, sixteen if multiple station point is counted, can be categorized according to the four different geometries, on the basis of generation:

1. If both planes and projection lines are parallel, the picture is a Metric projection.
2. If planes are parallel, but projection lines are convergent, the picture is a Similarity projection.
3. If the planes intersect, but the projection lines are parallel, the picture is an Affine projection.
4. If neither planes nor lines are parallel, the picture is a Projective projection.

These four geometries comprise a categorization network for representational pictures in terms of the *station-point assumption* made by the artists within a tradition, that is, in terms of a geometrical description of image generation and appearance. Also, these four descriptive geometries are subjected to the added constraint that cultural depiction styles differ in their relative emphasis on two- and three-dimensional compositional demands. *Any representational painting, any cohesive style of representational painting, can be categorized in terms of (a) the station point assumed by the artist, (b) the invariant aspects chosen for depiction, and (c) the balance between two-dimensional and three-dimensional demands.* Points of comparison given by this system are on continua, so no dichotomous or categorical classification of works or styles is possible and disagreement about placement of styles is inevitable. What is important is that placement of any representational painting is possible, not that it is debatable.

The categorization system allows for the systematic analysis of perceptual similarities and differences among works of representational art entirely in geometrico-perceptual terms. It reveals surprising degrees of kinship among quite

diverse styles and explains the kinship in terms of ge
metrical subsets of natural perspective. This system re
firms natural perspective as the explanatory structu
umbrella for production and perception of representatio
pictures because all of the geometries are present in natu
perspective. It is the task of an artist or of the artist's cultu
to select from among the available options a set of info
mational substructures for depiction. The reasons directi
choice may vary considerably from culture to culture.
one culture a long-distance stand may be the product o
philosophy about the role of the artist in the creation o
work of art; in another culture the same option may be
function of the purpose the painting is to serve for
possessors. Such speculations belong properly to the rea
of the art historians and are outside the scope of this boo
The analysis presented here is only perceptual; its purpe
is to aid the classification or interpretation of paintin
geometrically through identifying modes of represen
tional depiction. But the goal of representational art
never reducible to representation alone. In fact, it is n
clear that representation per se has ever been the prima
concern of art.

Limited as the categorization system is for the elucic
tion of the aesthetic values of paintings, it has much
offer to further understanding of the varieties of realis
in depiction. The chapters that follow will look at fo
quite distinctive depiction systems in terms of the vist
geometry occasioned by the station-point assumption ma
by the artists in each of the cultures, the invariants availa
for and used in depiction, and the relative emphasis
two- versus three-dimensional composition. Once the fo

Table 5.4 *Four styles: station point options*

Style	Number	Distance	Angle	Lines	Planes	Geometry	2D/
European	S	Middle	Oblique	Convergent	Intersecting (Parallel)	Projective (Similarity)	3I
Egyptian	M	Optical infinity	Frontal	Parallel	Parallel	Orthogonal	2I
Northwest Indian	M	Optical infinity	Oblique	Parallel	Intersecting	Affine	2I
Japanese	S	Optical infinity	Oblique	Parallel	Intersecting	Affine	3I

styles have been presented as clearly as possible, the analysis will be extended to categorize most of the coherent styles of depiction known to the author. Table 5.4 is included for convenient reference.

6

Station point options: analysis of style

Certainly we must not imagine that an internal mechanism runs automatically and produces, in any conditions, the said series of forms of apprehension. For that to happen, life mus be experienced in a certain way. But the human imaginative faculty will always make its organisation and possibilities of development felt in the history of art. It is true, we only see what we look for, but we only look for what we can see. Doubtless certain forms of beholding preexist as possibilities; whether and how they come to development depends on outward circumstances.

Heinrich Wölfflin, *Principles of Art History* (19

Construction rules and realism

The construction rules for generating pictorial images scribed in Chapter 5 demonstrate in at least a formal w that such a representational taxonomy is possible. Exa ination of different art styles will clarify the effects of co struction rules on each style and will permit a forr geometrical analysis of the rules and their consequen for appearance. Because each set of construction rules every coherent depiction style is derived from the availa options determined or provided by the structures of natu perspective, we will see that each style is perceptually va and will produce, necessarily, lifelike images for those w have been educated by familiarity with that option. I in this sense that a controversial remark by Goodman (19 can be seen to be simultaneously true and false. He wro "That a picture looks like nature often means only tha looks the way nature is usually painted."

Every coherent art style is *consistent* in its selection of station-point option. A shift in option determines a shift in style. More striking than the shifts of style, however, is the remarkable consistency of option selection within a culture across great spans of time. This consistency allows for reliable categorization of style, and permits comparisons of one style to another. The four styles to be analyzed in this chapter are post-Renaissance Western art (fifteenth to eighteenth centuries), traditional Japanese art, Northwest Coast Indian art, and ancient Egyptian art. The styles have too many exemplars to be handled in any single volume, so selections have been made by personal preference and prejudice. The analysis of style in this chapter will be primarily in terms of the artist's stance relative to the subject; in Chapter 7, the geometrical consequences of that stance for the depiction of invariant information will be discussed.

European painting

It seems odd to be writing of European post-Renaissance painting as if it were a single entity stretching from the early fifteenth century to the present, but it is really no odder than imposing the same huge categorization on the other art styles with which we are concerned. The Western post-Renaissance method for depicting form and layout remained essentially unchanged from the early Renaissance to the radical revolution of the Cubists. The geometrical basis for the generation of the pictures remained the same across that time span. What changed was the method or technique for manifesting that mode of generation. *Techniques of implementation are independent of the underlying geometrical structure of the composition.* Nearly all the paintings of this era (and there are, of course, exceptions) were generated by a common principle, and share a single selection of station-point option: The paintings are nearly all single-station-point constructions. The distance to the center of the projection is moderate, that is, it is seldom closer than ten times the size of the objects to be depicted, and never at optical infinity for the dominant surface or series of surfaces in the picture. The image plane is nearly always *oblique* to (intersecting) the majority of the surfaces to [depicted.

Single station point assumption

In its simplest terms, the single station point option mea[that the artist chooses the vantage point from which he she wishes to paint the scene and paints only what he she can see from that point without moving. Of cours the procedure is seldom that simple, and many scen painted by the Western post-Renaissance artists are co structed, not actually viewed. The essential point for o purposes is that they are constructed *as if* viewed from single vantage point. The rules for such construction co prise the controversial body of knowledge known as t science of perspective. The quibbling over history, fa and application in this field is astounding, and I will n here enter the lists. The single-station-point character perspective constructions is somewhat less controvers than other matters and is critical here.

Because there is so much misunderstanding about bo concepts and terminology, the presentation below of "si gle station point perspective constructions" will be undu lengthy. The material will be presented in historical co text because the early writers were quite clear about wl they were doing if not why they were doing it, and t principles articulated are valid across the whole period Western perspective art.

Generation of Western perspective constructions. Leon Batti Alberti is considered by many to be the father of mode perspective. In *On Painting* (1436, 1966) he set out clea the construction rules for single-station-point perspecti By "clearly" I do not mean that there is no controver over his exact meaning. Of course there is. Presentatio of Alberti's work are usually accompanied by interpre tions of it. This presentation will be no different, but intent is to clarify confusions about the meanings of t terms *station point*, *vanishing point*, *distance point*, and *cen of projection* in service of the argument that Western p spective whatever else it may be, is essentially a system single vantage point construction. Alberti conceived of the picture plane as an open window (why it must be open I do not know) placed between the artist and the scene to be depicted. The basic component of the scene was the ground plane, which was considered to be covered in a regular grid or checkerboard of squares. The artist's problem, then, was to transfer the grid of squares on the ground onto his picture plane in a geometrically correct (projective) manner. Once the ground plane had been properly projected, it was an easy matter to construct the objects resting on it. Alberti (1436, 1966) explained the procedure in the following manner:

> First of all about where I draw. I inscribe a quadrangle of right angles, as large as I wish, which is considered to be an open window through which I see what I want to paint. Here I determine as it pleases me the size of the man in my picture. I divide the length of this man in three parts. . . . With these braccio [parts] I divide the baseline of the rectangle into as many parts as it will receive. To me this base line of the quadrangle is proportional to the nearest transverse and equidistant quantity seen on the pavement. Then, within this quadrangle, where it seems best to me, I make a point which occupies that place where the central ray strikes. For this is called the centric point. This point is properly placed when it is no higher from the baseline of the quadrangle than the height of the man that I have to paint there. Thus both the beholder and the painted things he sees will appear to be on the same plane. The centric point being located as I said, I draw straight lines from it to each division placed on the base line of the quadrangle. These drawn lines, [extended] as if to infinity, demonstrate to me how each transverse quantity is altered visually. (p. 56; brackets are Spencer's)

Figure 6.1 shows that, up to this point in his procedure, Alberti has accomplished three important things: First, the use of the size of the depicted man as a measure for determining the size on the picture plane of the nearest visible ground squares sets the scale factor for the whole composition; the width of one square is about one-third the height of a man, in the scene and on the picture plane. Second, the fixing of the centric point at about the height of the man fixes the horizon to which the sets of parallel edges will vanish (most of those not parallel to the picture plane); the horizon is a horizontal line drawn through the centric point and is more properly placed at the figure's

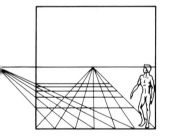

Figure 6.1. Construction showing *race line, central vanishing point, and horizon.*

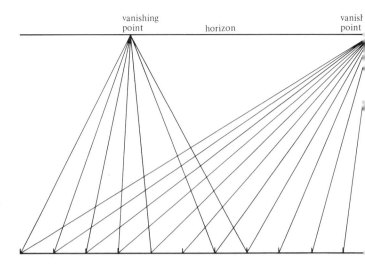

Figure 6.2. Change in lateral shape
of projected squares as vanishing
point is moved laterally on the
horizon.

eye height than at the top of his head. Third, the constru
tion so far has established the lateral edges of the projectє
squares on the picture plane. As the centric or vanishiɪ
point is moved laterally along the horizon line, these shapє
change, as can be seen in Figure 6.2. The simplest way
think about these shape changes is to conceive of the pictu
plane as gigantic, with the centric (vanishing) point in tⅡ
exact center. Then introduce a rectangular frame that iɪ
tercepts only the center, or the left-hand, or the right-haɪ
portion of the construction (Figure 6.3). In this way it cₐ
be seen that moving the centric vanishing point from lє
to right in no way alters the basic character of the coɪ
struction; it simply shows what section of the overall prє
jection was selected for depiction.

At this point, the major missing aspect of the constru
tion is the determination of the degree of perspectiˇ
compression of the *longitudinal* (near–far) edges of tⅡ
squares with increasing distance. We know that the neaɪ
far dimensions of the squares will be projected smaller aɪ
smaller in a regular gradient of compression, but we haˇ
not yet determined that gradient. There are several waˇ
of doing so. Alberti's method is not particularly clear, bₑ
it will work. He writes:

I take a small space in which I draw a straight line and this
divide into parts similar to those in which I divided the baseli:
of the quadrangle. Then, placing a point at a height equal to t.
height of the centric point from the base line, I draw lines fro₪

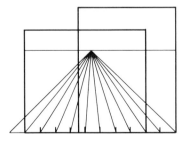

Figure 6.3. The sectioning of a
single-vanishing-point construction
by the picture frame or boundaries.

this point to each division scribed on the first line. Then I establish, as I wish, the distance from the eye to the picture. Here I draw, as the mathematicians say, a perpendicular cutting whatever lines it finds. . . . The intersection of this perpendicular line with the others gives me the succession of the transverse quantities. (1966:57)

"As the mathematicians say," this is quite confusing and requires the use of an auxiliary drawing that must then be transferred to the original construction. As can be seen from Figure 6.4, this is not at all necessary. Since one already has the base line marked off into scaled-down squares, and the horizon line on which to locate "a single point above and perpendicular to" the base line, there is no need to redraw them. Simply connect this single point on the extended horizon to each of the marks on the base line; through this converging family of lines drop a line perpendicular to the base line.

That perpendicular is the picture plane (rotated in space 90°) and the distance between it and the single point on the extended horizon line is the distance between the picture and the station point to be occupied by the viewer. The distance between the center of the scene and this "distance point" determines the range of depictable compression with distance in the picture; the location of the perpendicular picture plane determines the precise gradient of compression (what Alberti calls the coordinates) for the

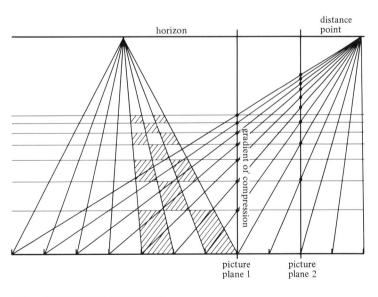

Figure 6.4. Construction showing trace line, horizon, distance point, and two picture planes.

particular construction. The closer the picture plane is t
the distance·point, the steeper the gradient; the farther th
plane, the greater the truncation of the foreground. Hor
izontal lines are drawn across the construction from th
points of intersection on the perpendicular, and the pro
jection of the ground plane grid onto the picture plane i
complete (Figure 6.4).

An alternative method of determining perspectiv
compression with distance is depicted by Jan Vredema
de Vries in Figure 6.5. In this construction, the artist ha
essentially placed equivalent distance points both to th
right and left of the center of the painting, has connecte
the two points to each of the base-line segments, and ha
drawn horizontals across the points of intersection of th
two families of diagonals. (Almost exactly the same con
struction would be created by constructing the perpendic
ular picture plane right in the center of the constructio
through the central vanishing point, and determining i
points of intersection with a single set of the diagonal:
The gradient of compression obtained is almost exactly th
same, although displaced half a square.) The question c
the equivalence of the two methods described (Alberti
and Vredeman's) for determining the degree of perspectiv

Figure 6.5. Alternative construction
method. (From Vredeman 1968.)

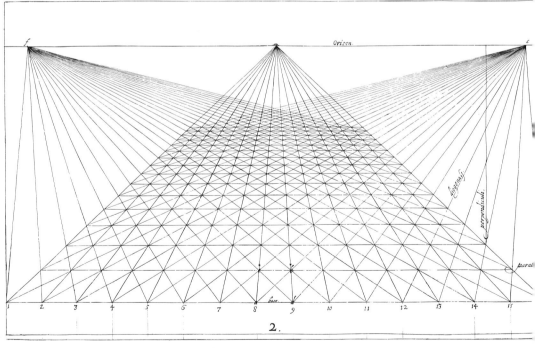

compression in a picture is subject to much heated debate. It is clear, however, that something very close to equivalence can be demonstrated mechanically as can be easily seen by comparing the constructions in Figures 6.4 and 6.5.

Terminology and confusions. I have said that Western perspective is single-station-point construction, but the procedure illustrated in the Vredeman figure shows *two* distinct points. Lest one think that the use of two distance points in the construction really implies two places for the artist and observer to stand, it must be made clear that in a "bifocal" construction such as that of Vredeman, the two points are both on the horizon and equidistant from the central vanishing point. Thus they are essentially *one and the same* point simply repeated for convenience in determining the longitudinal compression. That this "one and the same point" is referred to as "the distance point" is also quite confusing. The distance suggested by the use of the term, is, in fact, the actual distance between viewer and picture specified by the artist, yet the distance point is in the same plane as the picture, which seems to make no sense. Again, the confusion follows from an expediency technique and not from a real contradiction in terms. The actual station point or distance point for the artist or viewer is, of course, in front of the picture, at the height of the horizon line, and at the distance determined by the construction. But one cannot draw easily in three-dimensional space, so a two-dimensional equivalent is used. The station point is simply "rotated" in space through 90° to the right or left until it lies in the horizon line at the distance determined by the artist. The artist then places a picture plane, which has been rotated as described along with the station point, so that it appears not as a plane but as a perpendicular line, between the rotated distance or station point and the center of the construction, as shown in Figure 6.5. Where this plane is placed will determine the amount of perspective compression because that varies with distance. Thus, whether the construction uses one or two distance points, it determines one and only one station point. Technically, this station point is the center of the projection of the depicted scene onto the picture plane as in an ordinar᾿ central projection described in Chapter 3. The easiest wa᾿ to become comfortable with the mechanics of this pro᾿ cedure is to tack strings to the points of intersection of th᾿ checks on a checkerboard, gather the strings to a knot, an᾿ play with the effects of moving the knot, the strings an᾿ a frame rigidly in space.

The term *center of projection* also suffers from multipl᾿ usage and misusage. In the sense just described, the geo᾿ metrical center of projection is not in the construction ex᾿ cept when rotated into the distance point; the geometrica᾿ center of projection is in space in front of the picture pro᾿ jection, as when one holds the knot of strings away fron᾿ the checkerboard. But the term is also used to indicate no᾿ the center of the projection transformation, but the cente᾿ or middle of the projected image. The center of the image᾿ must be, by definition, in the middle of the image, but th᾿ center of the projection transformation may be anywher᾿ in the space in front of the picture. The projection cente᾿ is located in space directly opposite the center of the pictur᾿ image only when the artist has framed the central vanishin᾿ point in a single construction into the center of the picture᾿

Vanishing points: a few words. The artist does not need t᾿ use the one-point construction method we have discusse᾿ here; a two- or three-point system that gives no centra᾿ vanishing point may be used. Moreover, even in a single᾿ point construction, the artist need not center the pictur᾿ around the central vanishing point. As shown in Figur᾿ 6.5, the artist may use any subsection of a larger construc᾿ tion for the actual picture, thus placing the center of th᾿ projection, and the observer's station point, almost any᾿ where in the space in front of the picture. Figure 6.6 show᾿ an elegantly symmetrical one-point construction, but thi᾿ is something of a rarity since the earliest days of the Ren᾿ aissance. More common are the asymmetrical construc᾿ tions such as that shown in Figure 6.7. In this construction᾿ the geometrically correct station point (center of the pro᾿ jection) is directly opposite the vanishing point in the up᾿ per-left-hand section of the picture. The station point i᾿ always directly opposite the central vanishing point in con᾿

Figure 6.6. Construction symmetrical about the central vanishing point. (From Vredeman 1968.)

structions that have such a point, but is far more difficult to locate in pictures that do not, such as three-point constructions. Moreover, although we conventionally group perspective constructions as having one, two, or three vanishing points, it must be kept in mind that every system of parallel lines in a picture has its own vanishing point (Figure 6.8). It can be quite confusing to discuss station point as being directly opposite this or that vanishing point, as can be seen from Figure 6.8; this example is rather a simple one because it is overlaid on a central one-point construction. A picture, be it basically a one-, two-, or three-point construction, can have an indefinitely large number of vanishing points, but has only one true vantage point or station point – the center of the projection tranformation.

Summary of Western single station point assumption. Most of the confusion about the terms *station point, center of projection, vanishing point,* and *distance point* arises because explanatory texts, including this one, usually take the simplest case of the one-point construction to illustrate the basic

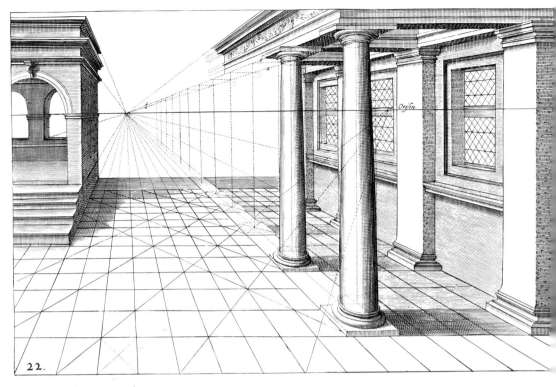

Figure 6.7. *Assymmetrical perspective construciton with station point opposite vanishing point on the left. (From Vredeman 1968.)*

components of Western perspective. In this case, there are special congruencies and correspondences among these points that lead the reader to identify one with the other. Since most of these identities do not survive in the transfer to more complex constructions, misconceptions are inevitable. For our purposes, it is enough to remember that any single central projection of a scene through a picture plane to a center of projection has one and only one station point coincident with the center of that projection. When the observer stands at that point and gazes at the picture, he receives in the light to the eye the same structure as that reflected from the framed scene itself to that vantage point. At that point, at the center of the projection, the scene and the picture are projectively equivalent, at least in terms of the major edges of surfaces and lines in the picture.

The clearest examples of such pictures to hold in mind are ordinary, noncomposite photographs where the center of the projection is at the nodal point of the lens; but even in nonphotographic Western paintings, the single station point, single center of projection assumption is operative. Of course, artists are not photographers, and even pho-

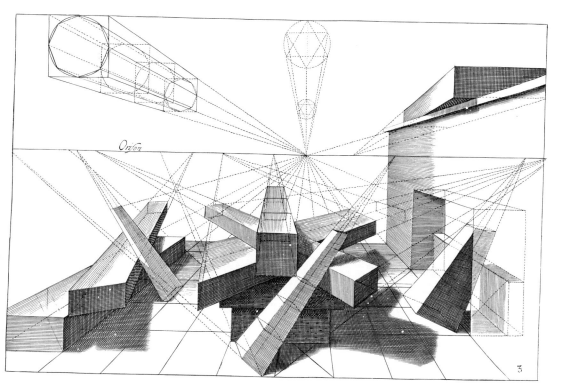

Figure 6.8. Construction showing multiple vanishing points, one for each set of parallel lines. (From Vredeman 1968.)

tographers are not photographers in the automaton sense intended here, so it is well to remember that, although the assumption of the single station point will characterize the general case in Western post-Renaissance art, it will not describe each particular instance without some exceptions and modifications.

Modifications of the single point construction. Western post-Renaissance art typically but not always, uses single station point constructions. Exceptions to the rule abound; many single-point constructions have been modified in some way. However, without photographic evidence from the artist's vantage point at the scene depicted, it is difficult to tell if this assertion is, in fact, correct. The few cases we do have of photographs of painted scenes are generally quite difficult to interpret for reasons following the reduction in the degrees of freedom occasioned by the use of cameras. For example, Sir Ernst Gombrich's (1972b) well-known example of a photograph of Wivenhoe Park from the vantage point presumably occupied by Constable quite misleads the viewer about the extent of the painter's alterations

Figure 6.9. (above) Wivenhoe
Park *by John Constable. (From
National Gallery of Art,
Washington, D.C., Widener
Collection, 1942). (right)
Photograph taken from same vantage
point. (Gombrich 1972b. Reprinted
by permission of Princeton
University Press.)*

of the relative size of the depicted figures, although th
was by no means the art historian's intention (see Figu
6.9). The photographic comparison was intended to illu
trate the complexities of translating light into paint, n
the problems of perspective and size constancy. Yet con
parison of the photograph and painting leads one to believ

128   STATION POINT OPTIONS

that Constable undertook considerable alterations of the relative sizes of the near and far figures, particularly that of the house. He may have done so, but comparison of the Gombrich photograph to the painting does not force one to that conclusion. The photograph can be seen simply as an enlargement of the central portion of the painting with severe cropping or "clipping" of the periphery of the image.

Figure 6.10 shows the same effect with two photographs of the same scene: The picture at the bottom is simply a blowup of that on top, cropped to the same size. The cropping or truncation, in conjunction with the enlargement, mechanically produces the effect of relative size alteration with no need for further manipulations by the artist. This follows, of course, from the nature of the visual-angle curve.

The best photographic work we have in service of explicating Western modifications of the single station point mode of construction is that of Pirenne (1970). Pirenne noted that, in paintings such as Raphael's *School of Athens*, spheres are depicted as circles, not as the ellipses required by projectively correct perspective. Pirenne used a pinhole camera to produce unmodified single station point images of spheres, columns, and balusters, all quite surprising in appearance to the Western eye (Figure 6.11). According to Pirenne, Western artists modify single view perspective in the case of almost all objects with curved surfaces whose shape is familiar to the spectator. Moreover, he observed from his analysis of paintings that human figures also are usually depicted like the spheres, from different subsidiary centers of projection each placed in front of the position in the painting of the figure concerned. Thus, an artist would paint the various figures "rather as if he had done their portraits, each portrait being placed in a separate part of the painting" (p. 123). Pirenne also noted that in *School of Athens*, the architectural background that extends over most of the painting was drawn in perspective as a unit, from a single center of projection, but that should not be taken to mean that curved architectural units like columns were not subject to station point alteration by perspective artists. An example from Jan de Vries Vredeman shows

Figure 6.10. Two photographs of the same scene. In the bottom picture, the picture is blown up and cropped in a telephoto effect. (Photographs supplied by the author.)

just such a selective correction in a perspectivist drawing of columns (Figure 6.12).

The photograph in Figure 6.13 by Pirenne, taken from an angle relative to the columns similar to that of the Vredeman station point, shows that the more distant columns become thicker relative to their height than the nearer ones. But in the Vredeman, taken from a manual on perspective, no such alteration in proportion is depicted. It must not be assumed, however, that the unwillingness of Renaissance artists to depict curved objects and human figures in exact perspective from a single center of projection reflects ignorance. Robert Smith (1974) suggested that

Figure 6.12. Independence of columnar depiction from perspective rules: selective correction. (From Vredeman 1968.)

application of exact perspective to the human figure simp did not occur to the artists. In light of drawings such that by Vredeman in Figure 6.14 this explanation seer unlikely. The Renaissance artist was clearly aware of t correct perspective appearance of figures and curved o jects, but found the appearance unacceptable. Again, a:

Figure 6.13. Angular perspective in a pinhole photograph of the columns of the Basilica at Paestum. (From Pirenne 1970:124.)

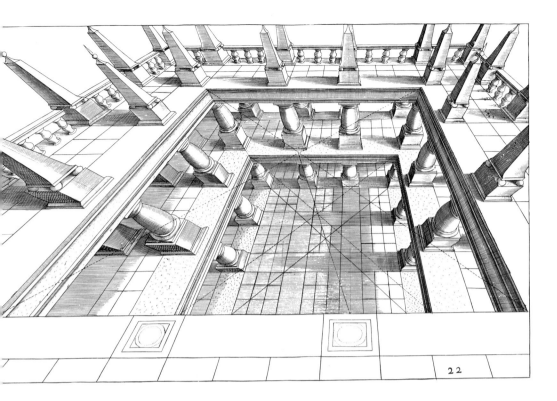

22

have repeated, the formal geometric limits of a picture-generation system will never be identical to the artistic limits. Artistic composition is directed, not dictated, by geometry.

Moderate distance assumption

We have seen that Alberti, in 1436, first presented comprehensively the system of perspective construction. Since the system is really just simple central projection, there are, of course, no constraints on its application in formal terms. Yet constraints on the *range* of construction in the Western perspective mode have a history as long as the perspective system itself. Even Alberti, in this earliest presentation of the system to the art world, wrote that the painter must move away from the subject until he finds the "correct section of the visual pyramid" to capture in the painting. He wrote: "[T]hey (artists) move away from what they are painting and stand further back seeking to find (the point) from which they know everything can be more correctly viewed."

133 EUROPEAN PAINTING

Sixty years later, Leonardo was far more explicit in specification of where the Renaissance artist should st: in order to produce a picture that will look natural several viewers observing at the same time. Acknowle ing that the "correct" place to stand to view the im clearly is at the center of the projection, Leonardo sta in his *Notebooks* (1970):

A diminshed object should be seen from the same distance, he: and direction as the point of sight of your eye or else y knowledge will produce no good effect. And if you will not cannot act on this principle – because as the plane on which : paint is to be seen by several persons you would need sev points of sight which would make it look discordant and wr(– place yourself at a distance of at least ten times the size of objects.

He also suggested a viewing distance of twenty times object height or width (whichever is greater) if the ar wished to produce an image that could be viewed s cessfully from almost any vantage point.

Perhaps because of these artistic predecessors, Alb Einstein, the physicist, suggested a similar formula depicting perspective without distortion in a letter Maurice Pirenne. Einstein wrote: "[T]he spectator will e ily compensate intuitively for this deformation (of viewi from the wrong station point) when the angle which fines the boundary of the object is small, so that all visual rays strike the plane almost perpendicularly" (renne 1970: 99). Neither Alberti nor Leonardo nor Einst(ever explained the basis of his reasoning about perspect: "distortion" and its correction, yet each technique p: duces the same effect. It is very interesting to realize tl what all three prescriptions accomplish is an approxim transformation of a Projective projection into an Affini even in some cases, a near-Similarity, in which shape : proaches invariant status. The two pictures in Figure 6. illustrate the increase in Metric shape properties as the d tance of the projection center is moved farther away. T is, of course, a rather odd way to write of geometry, t artistic construction is not a simple geometric exerci One should not be misled by the fact that invariant featu: increase as distance from subject grows into believing tl

ure 6.15. Two photographs of a
ue: (left) subtending an angle of
and (right) an angle of 20°.
om Pirenne 1970.)

such an increase necessarily guides artistic choice of longer
station points. We do not know what cultural reasons determine the desirable number of invariant features in pictures. To understand Western perspective constraints, it
may be enough to recognize that the Renaissance emerged
from the highly Affine art of the Middle Ages, a tradition
from which to evolve but not to discard totally.

Heinrich Wölfflin also addressed the issue of the distance
of the station point in *Principles of Art History* (1932), pointing out that the painters he calls Baroque (Tintoretto, Rubens,
and others) frequently fancied unusually close or distant station points; the former to emphasize recessional movement
through the plane, the latter to minimize it. Vermeer's *The
Concert* illustrates the use of a fairly close station point (Fig.
6.16).

Figure 6.16. Vermeer, The Concert. *(Reprinted by permission of the Isabella Stewart Gardner Museum, Boston.)*

Limits on allowable distance: very close views. Observation Western paintings clearly documents the wide range distances that can be assumed in moderate distance co structions. A middle range station point assumption cove a lot of ground, so to speak. However, what is critical f our purposes is that such an assumption by no means co ers *all* of the available ground. Baroque station points m frequently be quite near the scene depicted, closer th classical compositions, but they seldom if ever depict co sistently the perspective foreshortening geometrically pr ent and photographically apparent in such close poin Vermeer himself is reputed to have used a *camera obscu* but this was hardly commonplace. Severe diminution c casionally may be tolerated across a scene, but almost never across an object, particularly not across the human figure. The photographic analysis by Robert Smith (1974) of *Dead Christ* by the fifteenth-century artist Mantegna illustrates the persistent use of a perspective correction factor in close-station-point post-Renaissance constructions. Smith shows that although the perspective diminution across the slab on which Christ's body rests is appropriate to a very close station point, approximately one-and-a-half meters, the figure of Christ is not similarly foreshortened. The proportions of the figure are consonant with a much longer station point, as is generally the case in post-Renaissance compositions. If a figure would be strongly foreshortened in the foreground of a close-station-point composition, then a longer station point is assumed for that figure. There are always exceptions, of course, because artists are, almost by definition, experimental, but they are rare and hardly characteristic of the style of that period.

Smith's use of the term *distortion* for strong, but projectively correct, foreshortening, illustrates the strength and persistence of the moderate distance bias even in modern Western thinking. Distortion is present in the *appearance* of a close projection but *not* in its geometry. Leonardo's dictum that the station point should be placed at a distance at least ten times the size of the object is observed by post-Renaissance artists, art critics, and historians, both before and after him, and is apparent even in Baroque compositions that would be rejected by Leonardo as violating the spirit of the law.

With respect to figural foreshortening, even modern artists and photographers rarely produce images of the kind shown in Figure 6.17, a perfectly correct central-projection image, taken with a 50–millimeter lens on a single-lens-reflex camera. There are exceptions, certainly, such as the famous photograph of Joe Louis by Art Kane, but much of their striking quality is due to their exceptional character within the Western tradition. From the Renaissance to the present, the prohibition against close station points with attendant strong foreshortening has been observed within the Western perspective mode of depiction.

Perspective diminution of an extreme degree is also sel-

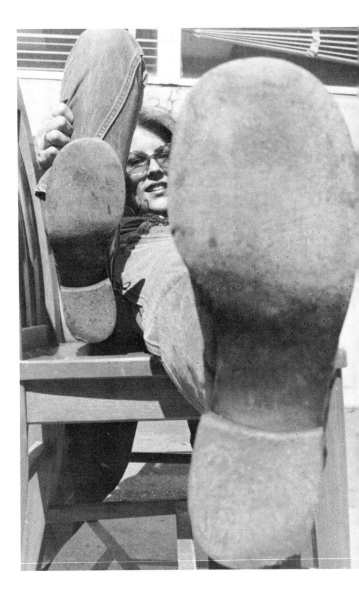

Figure 6.17. Single-lens-reflex photograph shot with a 50-mm lens eighteen inches from the near foot. (Photograph supplied by the author.)

dom seen across post–Renaissance scenes as a whole, though more frequently than across single figures. Everywoman's anecdote often used in psychology class to explain size constancy is illustrative here. Many peop have taken a picture of the Grand Tetons or similarly enc mous mountains with the intention of impressing frien with their immenseness. Yet, somehow, in amateur p tures, the mountains look like molehills. The usual exp nation is that in "real life" our constancy mechanis operates and we perceive the great size of the mounta relative to the small size of the spouse in the foreground. Erwin Panofsky, the art historian (1955), explains that our mind automatically rectifies the visual diminutions and distortions in favor of a more "objective" relation among the various quantities. In pictures, the correction mechanism presumably fails. A variety of unnecessarily elaborate explanations for this phenomenon have been proposed by a number of people, including myself. A more parsimonious explanation than any of them is based on familiarity with pictures within our tradition. We are not used to seeing molehill-sized mountains in pictures because Western artists seldom depict them so. If the mountains in the background appear too small, if the overall perspective diminution in the picture is too great, then the Western artist corrects it according to the Western station-point convention and has done so for 500 years. It is not at all surprising that amateur photographs that violate the convention look odd to the Western viewer. It would be odd indeed if they did not.

Very long views. Similarly, Western post-Renaissance artists do not tolerate in their compositions the *absence* of perspective convergence across a scene. That is, the station point in Western post-Renaissance art is never at optical infinity. Perspective may be appropriate to a station point at a very great distance from the subject, but not to one at optical infinity. An excellent example of a long-distance, but middle-range, Western station point is provided by Ansel Adams's famous night shot of a farm. In this photograph, the "shot" is very long; the perspective diminution is very slight. But once again, perspective diminution with increasing distance is by no means absent. Artistic compositions may have played with the limits of the Western range, but they seldom violated them.

Summary of distance limits. Perspective convergence within a single station point projective construction is the defining characteristic of Western post-Renaissance art up to the twentieth-century moderns, but we have seen that only a limited section of the possible range of convergence has been permitted. It is very important to keep in mind that

the limits of the formal projection system itself are *no.*
same as the culturally determined limits on its artistic
plication. The formal, geometrical limits of the syster
image generation are considerably broader than the ac
application of the system in the creation of real pictu
Nevertheless, the formal characteristics of the system
vide its defining attributes and describe its most cha
teristic members.

Oblique angle assumption

Western post-Renaissance art exemplifies a Projective
jection system, which means that the projection lines fi
subject to station point are convergent, and the angl
picture plane to subject plane is oblique (see Chapter
The existence of convergent projection lines is a neces:
consequence of assuming a station point at a mode
distance from the subject, a custom followed almost w
out exception in this traditional Western art style. B
assumptions, implicit and explicit, of the construction
tem are that the ground plane, that ubiquitous checke
surface, is generally horizontal, and the picture plan
mounted vertically, perpendicular to the ground pla
The picture in Figure 6.18, a classic Dürer engraving
lustrates the spatial relationship between ground sur:
and picture surface, among other things. Surfaces obli
to one another intersect. That is, geometrically, planes
either parallel to one another and *not* intersecting, or t
are *not* parallel and intersecting.

In this translation from geometry to depiction, the
veats outlined up to this point should not be forgotten
geometry (generally speaking) an object of thought is eit
one thing or another, belongs to one category or to
other. In the depiction system presented here, a cer
style of depiction belongs in the main to one category,
may shade at times into another. This is particularly t
at times of transition, either temporal or geographical.
the Projective projection system that characterizes West
post-Renaissance art, most world surfaces depicted
oblique to the projection surfce, to the picture plane. 1
artist, however, has considerable latitude in the arran

ment of "world" surfaces to be depicted; after all, frequently such surfaces exist only in the imagination of the artist. In effecting certain aesthetic compositional goals, the artist may create orderings of objects never evident in random "snapshots" of nature. However bound by cultural rules, the artist is never simply a rule-run machine. The consequences of this artistic latitude in the deployment of depicted surfaces in space, and cultural variation and consistency in that deployment, will be explored in Chapter 9. For now it is important only to keep in mind that the product of convergent projection lines and intersecting surfaces (world and picture) is a Projective projection system and characterizes Western post-Renaissance art. The example that follows, traditional Japanese art, exemplifies an *Affine* projection system.

Japanese painting

Japanese painting covers a time span from about 700 A.D. to the present, but the domain of concern here is not early Chinese and Indian Buddhist iconography but painting in the *yamato-e* style. By this I mean painting in the Japanese rather than the Chinese style, generally depicting ordinary events in the lives of the people (that is, in the lives of the rich people, usually). The end of a coherent yamato-e style may be marked by the influx of Chinese hanging-scroll ink paintings of landscapes, in the fifteenth century, although many examples of the style are found after that time. Japanese paintings of the designated style are single station point constructions with that station point at *of* *infinity*. The picture plane is *oblique* to most of the domi surfaces depicted. The long-distance viewpoint spec parallel projection lines, whereas the oblique angle spec intersecting subject and image planes. Together they scribe an Affine projection.

Single station point assumption

Consideration of paintings like the two shown in Fig 6.19 seem to suggest that Japanese art used multiple p constructions, but that conclusion is a misinterpretatio compositional technique. In "Foundation Ceremonie a Buddhist Temple" from the late fourteenth-century, Nambokucho period, the founding of the temple itself, historical event, is depicted in the top portion of the ture, and the festivities commemorating the event ar lustrated in the bottom section. In "White Path Cros Two Rivers" from the Kamakura Period (1185–13 Amida Buddha is depicted in the Western Paradise in top portion of the scroll, the narrow white path symb of the faith necessary for entering the Western Paradi in the center of the scroll, and earthly life with its ter impermanence, and obstacles to goodness is shown in foreground in the bottom portion of the scroll. Japar artists did not use the pictorial space in the Western m ner, one framed window for one event or scene. Rat they showed different events, different spheres of bei different areas, or different time "zones," all in the sa bounded pictorial space. These units are customarily, though not always, separated by bands, as in these figures, by wavy clouds of gold and silver, or by text. painting shown in Figure 6.20, "Scenes of Kyoto," rather late but illustrative example of the use of the cl technique to separate scenes and demarcate space.

Encapsulation of scenes by clouds and separation of eve by text was particularly common in continuous-narra scroll paintings from the Heian and subsequent peric Figure 6.21 from a sixteenth-century copy of *Genji l nogatari* (Tale of Genji), an illustrated novel, shows sev scenes in sequence. It can be seen that although the ma

*igure 6.19(a). "Foundation
*eremonies of a Buddhist Temple."
*rom The Seattle Art Museum,
*ugene Fuller Memorial
ollection).

foot–long hand scroll has numerous separate scenes or events
depicted, each is a single station point unit, albeit projected
to an infinitely distant artist. The scenes from *Genji Monogatari* also illustrate the unusual height of the station point

143   JAPANESE PAINTING

Figure 6.19(b). "White Path Crossing Two Rivers." (From The Seattle Art Museum, Margaret F. Fuller Purchase Fund.)

in yamato-e. In fact, it is the *height* of the station point in Japanese art, rather than its distance, that seems so strikingly different from the conventional Western station-point assumption. Recall that in Western post-Renaissance art, the ordinary height of the station point is at eye height or above five-and-a-half feet off the ground. In Japanese painting the height is many times as great as that. This "aerial" view permits depiction of great expanses of space, like the scene in Kyoto, and imparts a great feeling of impartial observation to the whole. Aerial observation also engenders a logical consequence in the roofless technique (also "wall-less"). Removing the roofs of buildings permitted the depiction of interior scenes without the artist having to descend to the height of the door, or to enter the room being shown. The Japanese artist is not placed by perspective in the composition of the picture, nor is the observer. The work of art created is a separate entity unto itself, an object of contemplation, not an extension of the self. A Japanese composition does not depict a personal, momentary view through a window, subject to change from the slightest of observer movements.

Optical infinity distance assumption

James Gibson described Japanese parallel perspective works as lacking a fixed point of observation like that determined by a Western construction, but this characterization is not quite correct. Japanese paintings certainly have a fixed station point, but this point is at optical infinity some specific direction from the subject. In Japanese paintings showing long-distance views, the artist–observer is obviously on one side of a building or another; one object is clearly in front of another relative to the viewpoint, even to the extent of partial and particular degrees of occlusion or overlap, and some objects in any composition are clearly "nearer" to the viewpoint than others. The perspective at optical infinity in an Affine construction is proper to a particular station point or angle of view. If it were not, there would be no consistency of depiction of the various angles formed by the several structures depicted in figures 6.20 and 6.21. A station point at optical infinity removes

Figure 6.20. Cloud technique for separating spatial units in "Scenes of Kyoto." (Courtesy of the Museum of Fine Arts, Boston, Bigelow Collection.)

the spectator from the scene depicted, but it does not re move the scene from the spectator.

That the distance of the station point is at optical infinit is evident from the absence of size diminution for figure with increasing distance. In Japanese, as in Western ar distance from the picture plane covaries with height on th plane, so that the farther the figure, the higher its placemer in the picture. In Figure 6.21 figures higher and lower c the plane are virtually interchangeable, despite their di ferent depicted distances. No informative relative-size re lationships would be destroyed by interchanging them Also, the absence of vanishing points, explicit or implici

for parallel edges of objects in the scenes testifies to the very great distance of the station point. At optical infinity, there is no apparent convergence of parallel edges with distance.

If Japanese Affine constructions were machine produced, there would be no exceptions to these rules. Because Japanese artists were clearly not machines, there is considerable variation in the spatial aspects of their depictions, particularly in background layout. A particularly striking exception to the parallel-edges rule is shown in Figure 7.7 from *Hasadera Engi*. Not only are the edges of the building depicted as not parallel; they are *divergent*. Divergent per-

Figure 6.21. Three scenes from the
Tale of Genji. *(From Shikibu*
1979.)

spective like this also crops up occasionally in early Chinese art and, more frequently, in Western religious art before the Renaissance. It was never adopted anywhere with enough consistency to be called a style of spatial depiction. The failure of artists to adopt divergent perspective as a technique for spatial layout is due, I believe, to the complete absence of divergent perspective occasioned by observation of the ordinary environment. There is no place for an observer to stand and view a rectangular building such as that depicted in Figure 7.7 where the light reflected from the building would be structured in such a way. There is nowhere to place a fixed-lens camera so that a single shot of the building would show divergent edges in the image. However, it is possible, photographically, either to use a view camera or to take multiple-fixed-lens shots of a building from different angles and piece them together to form divergent-perspective images. There is no evidence that equivalents to these compositional routes were ever followed; that they were not is clear from the consistency of depiction of the angles or corners of other objects and figures in scenes where divergent perspective occurs across a particular object. I believe that the occasional use of divergent perspective in art, like the occasional creation of anamorphic displays, reflects simple experimentation with layout techniques on the part of isolated artists. John Ward, an art historian of the northern Renaissance, argues that its presence in Gothic art springs from reverence for the holiness of the depicted subjects; converging edges would have compressed the holy bodies in an unsaintly manner (personal communication). Ward's explanation does not account for the failure of the reverent artists to use parallel perspective, also a technique of noncompression employed by both contemporaries and forebears. Whatever the reasons for the occasional appearances of divergent perspective, it is never *characteristic* of any coherent art style, and is certainly not characteristic of the Affine constructions of traditional Japanese art.

The first signs of the breakdown of a consistent Affine style occur in the landscape-painting techniques adapted from the Chinese. The art historian Ienaga (1978) marks

the end of the era with Sesshu (1420–1506), who, accord
to Ienaga, first "treated depth realistically." By this Ien
means that Sesshu was one of the first Japanese artists
employ atmospheric effects and size diminution to spec
increasing distance. The artist Shūbun (1420–1450) u
similar techniques, reinforcing the break with traditi
The paintings in Figure 6.22 by Sesshu and by Shūl
illustrate these effects.

The detail from the Shūbun (Fig. 6.23) shows disti
size diminution from the big trees in the foreground to
tiny trees on the mountain in the background. The mid
ground in this kind of landscape painting is often sim
filled with hazy atmospheric effects, giving the impress
of very great distance. Great as the space depicted wa:
traditional works, it was never as great as in these landsc
paintings. In the catalogue notes on the Shūbun landscap
the Seattle Art Museum specialists note: "The graded s
tial recession of coast and mountain gives a sense of infir
spatial depth." The distance depicted was great indeed,
it was by no means infinite. In such landscape paintin
the station point is not at optical infinity and size di
nution is evident. It may be that the depiction of si
enormous expanses of space encourages the use of n
Affine techniques.

In any case, the introduction of size perspective ma
the end of the Affine era and the beginning of a comp
period of development and experimentation fueled by c
tural influx from increased trade and travel, and expos
to Christianity and European art. These influences
volved a change in perspective through adoption of a clo:
but still very distant, station point, and thus to a Project
projection system.

The later-occurring moderate-distance constructic
often generated rather startling stylistic juxtapositions, l
that shown in Figure 6.24. Japanese "baroque" expe
ments with close station points also appeared in the s
teenth century and later in compositions like that depic
in Figure 6.25. However, these belong, not to traditio
Japanese painting, but to the dawn of a new style, a n
cultural option, much as Giotto's pictures belong more
the Renaissance than to the Gothic past.

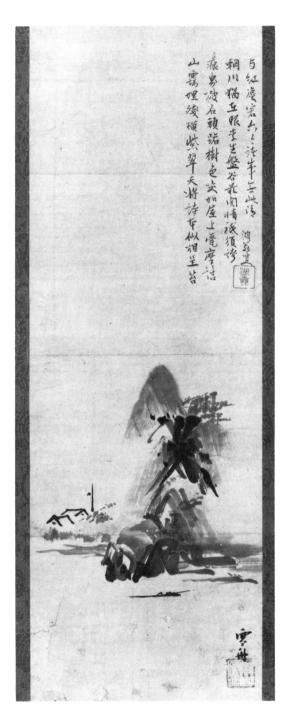

与紅塵隔又若半空此湾
輞川猶五眼生生盤谷蒙閔情祗須誇
痕思波在頭踞樹色尖加屋上瓷磨之話
山靄埋幾橫紫翠天將詩古似祖堂苔

Figure 6.22. Nonaffine Japanese compositions: (left) "Landscape" by Shūbun; (right) "Landscape" by Sesshu. (From The Seattle Art Museum, Eugene Fuller Memorial Collection.)

151 JAPANESE PAINTING

Figure 6.23. Detail from landscape by Shūbun in new style. (From the Seattle Art Museum, Eugene Fuller Memorial Collection.)

Figure 6.24. "Western" perspective
in a Japanese picture. Interior of a
Kabuki Theatre. (Courtesy of the
Museum of Fine Arts, Boston.)

153   JAPANESE PAINTING

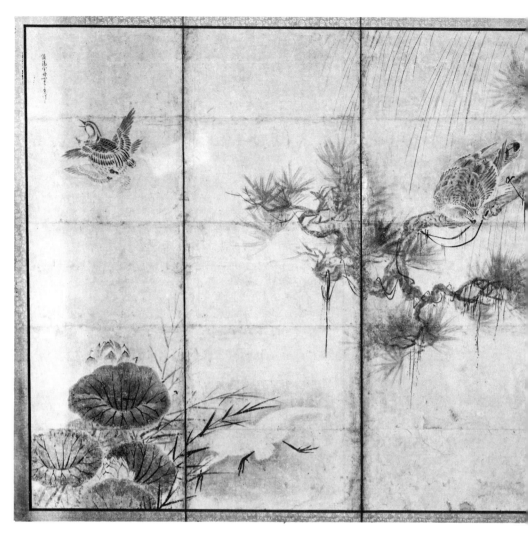

Figure 6.25. "Baroque," close station point: "Falcons, Herons and Trees." Attributed to Sesshu. (Courtesy of the Museum of Fine Arts, Boston, Fenollosa-Weld Collection.)

Oblique angle assumption

It should be clear by now from observation of Figures 6.19 6.25 and from the painting shown in Figure 6.26 that t picture plane in traditional Japanese painting was obliqu not only to the ground plane, but also to the domina surfaces of nearly all depicted objects. The aerial view the corners of buildings, what would be three-point pe spective in the West, was commonplace. Also, human fi ures and animals were seldom if ever depicted en face. A in Western art, the picture plane was mounted verticall intersecting the horizontal ground. However, because t

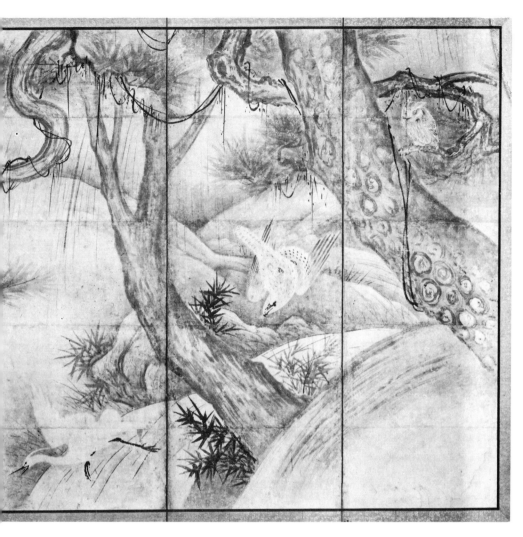

height of the station point was so great, the section of the
picture plane bounded by the picture itself is considerably
different from the Western equivalent. The difference in
the two image-generation techniques is illustrated in Figure
6.27. Again, the complexity of the image construction is
much increased by the depiction of multiple objects rather
than of a single one. The Japanese artist in the multiple
object case, like his Western counterpart, is faced with a
greater number of choices. Yamato-e selections for single
object depiction or the painting of whole scenes all involved parallel projecting lines and intersecting planes, giving always an Affine projection.

Figure 6.26. A complex scene illustrative of the intersection of ground plane and picture plane. (Courtesy of Museum of Fine Arts, Boston, Fenollosa-Weld Collection.)

Traditional Japanese art is Affine because it employs parallel projection lines with intersecting planes, and a single station point. But it is not necessary to assume a single station point to create Affine images. A very different form of Affine image generation was undertaken in the art of the Northwest Coast Indians.

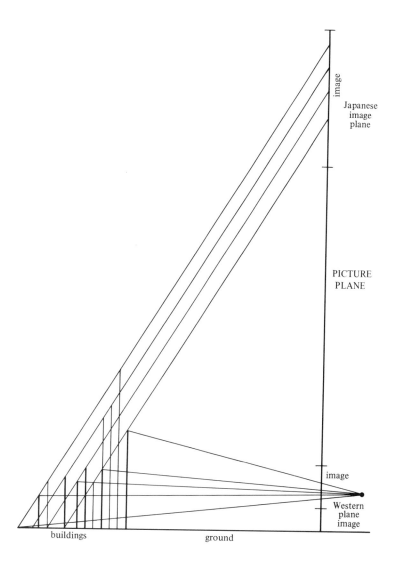

Figure 6.27. Difference between Japanese and Western art in height of the station point.

Northwest Coast Indian art

Unlike European or Japanese art, the art of the Indians of the Northwest Coast is a multiple station-point style, with the station points at optical infinity and the picture plane intersecting the dominant faces of the depicted objects, usually animals. This art style has received a great deal of attention from the anthropologists, perhaps because it is the most highly developed system of two-dimensional representation found in a so-called primitive culture. Although the anthropologists have made the style familiar

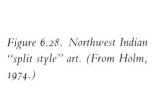

Figure 6.28. Northwest Indian "split style" art. (From Holm, 1974.)

and accessible to the rest of us, generally in the form il
lustrated in Figure 6.28, a brief review might prove useful
This style of depiction is usually called split–style art, a
least by non-Indians, because it appears that the anim
depicted has been split down the back and then spread ou
in the available space. Other techniques include dislocatin
the split details, representing one creature by two profiles
using symmetry, reducing, stylizing, and accentuating cer
tain features in schematic characterizations. However, Bi
Holm, the art historian and anthropologist, in his boo
(1974) on the analysis of form in Northwest Coast India
art, points out that those principles, basic to the art styl
though they are, deal only with the representation of th
depicted contexts and not with the "composition, desig
organization, or form."

Holm writes:

The different degrees of realism in this art seem to result nc
from a variety of concepts of representation but from the artist
preference (more or less strictly bound by tradition) in handlin
the given space. In each case individual parts of the creatur
represented assume their conventional form and the degree c
realism (that is, resemblance to the visual form of the creatur
in nature) achieved is due to the arangement of these conver
tionalized body-part symbols. (1974:11)

Holm then offers what he calls three rather loose categorie
of design, descriptive of the actual handling of design ele
ments. The three categories are:

1. *Configurative design*: when the animal represented retain
   a basically animal-like silhouette, perhaps occupying
   large part of the field to be decorated, but not distorte
   so as to fill the field entirely, yet the design still exhibi

*igure 6.29. (left figure)
Configurative wolf design. (From
Iolm 1974.)*

*igure 6.30. (right figure) Beaver
a an expansive design. (From
Iolm 1974).*

the characteristics of the art style. The wolf design on the woven spruce hat in Figure 6.29 is configurative.

2. *Expansive design*: when the animal is distorted, split, or rearranged to fit into a given space, but the identity of the essential body parts is still apparent; the anatomical relationship of one part to another is also maintained to some extent. The beaver design on the woven spruce hat shown in Figure 6.30 illustrates expansive design. Expansive design is what is generally meant by split-style art.

3. *Distributive design*: when the parts of the represented animal are so arranged as to fill completely the given space, consequently destroying any recognizable silhouette and ignoring natural anatomical relationships. Space-filling demands compete with representational demands, making recognition of any specific animal impossible although individual animal parts may be recognized (Holm 1974: 11–13). An example of distributive design is given in Figure 6.31.

The analysis of Northwest Coast Indian art as an Affine projection system applies only to configurative and expansive designs, and primarily to the latter, to the split-style designs. Whether a design is configurative or expansive can be seen as a consequence of the determination of the dominant face of the animal for the purposes of the particular depiction. Where the dominant face is the face

159 NORTHWEST COAST INDIAN ART

Figure 6.31. Distributive design showing unrecognizable animal. (From Holm 1974.)

itself, the design is generally *expansive* and the geome[try] *Affine*; where the dominant "face" is the side profile vie[w] the design is generally *configurative* and the geometry M[et]ric. Since both design types are multiple station point [it] will be clearest to begin with that assumption and t[hen] work through the operation of the oblique angle assum[p]tion for each type.

Multiple station point assumption

In his introductory remarks to *Primitive Art* (1955), Fr[anz] Boas broke representational alternatives into two ca[te]gories. He pointed out that in graphic representation [of] objects, the artist may assume one of two points of vie[w.] It may be considered essential that all the characteri[stic] features of the object be shown, or the object may be dra[wn] as it appears at any given moment. Boas argued that, [in] the former case, our attention is directed primarily tow[ard] those permanent object traits that are most striking a[nd] critical for object recognition, while less characteristic f[ea]tures are considered by the artist to be irrelevant. If [the] artist is interested solely in the visual impression recei[ved] at any given moment, then the salient features of that p[ic]ture direct attention. Boas claimed: "This [latter] meth[od] is more realistic than the other only if we claim that [the] essence of realism is the reproduction of a single mom[en]tary visual image and if the selection of what appear[s]

Figure 6.32. Wooden hat design representing sculpin. (From Boas 1955:225, Fig. 224.)

salient feature to us is given a paramount value" (pp. 71–2). He wrote that as soon as the artist is confronted with the problem of representing a three-dimensional object on a two-dimensional surface and showing in a single, permanent position an object that changes its visual appearance from time to time, he must make a choice between the two representational techniques.

It is easily intelligible that a profile view of an animal in which only one eye is seen and in which one whole side disappears may not satisfy as a realistic representation. The animal *has two* eyes and *two* sides. When it turns I see the other side; it exists and should be part of a satisfying picture. In a front view the animal appears foreshortened. The tail is invisible and so are the flanks; but the animal has tail and flanks and they ought to be there. (p. 72)

Boas found both the perspective and the symbolic techniques in primitive art. He called the technique of depicting characteristic object features in combination "symbolic" because "the essential parts are symbols of the object." Boas pointed out that it is possible to find examples of this technique of depicting multiple views in European art, even in Michelangelo, but his analysis of Northwest Indian art is all that is relevant here. Boas developed his analysis of the symbolic technique in Indian art by first explaining designs on curved discontinuous surfaces like hats and bracelets and then moving to designs on flat continuous surfaces. Although this suggests that the evolution of the art style itself followed such a course, there is no evidence that it did. Such a suggestion leads to unnecessary conclusions and obscures the multiple station point character of Northwest Indian art. Figure 6.32 shows a wooden-hat design representing a sculpin. Boas wrote that this shows a top view of the animal lying with its lower side on the surface of the hat. The artist opened the back of the animal for the crown of the hat, splitting and distending the middle as it was distributed around the field. Figure 6.33 shows the design representing a bear, for a bracelet. Boas (1955) wrote:

Figure 6.33. Design for a bracelet showing a bear. (From Boas 1955:223, Fig. 221.)

The animal is imagined cut in two from head to tail, so that the two halves cohere only at the tip of the nose and at the tip of the tail. The hand is put through this hold, and the animal now

surrounds the wrist. In this position it is represented on t[he]
bracelet. The method adopted is therefore identical with the o[ne]
applied in the hat, except that the central opening is much large[r]
and that the animal has been represented on the cylindrical su[r]
face, not on a conical one. (p. 223)

These methods are not really identical at all. The ho[le]
in the middle of the back of the fish is not the same as t[he]
split down the back of the bear. It is perhaps the intr[o]
duction of the term *split-style* that leads to this conclusio[n]
If the bear design is considered to be composed of the le[ft]
and the right profile views of the animal joined togeth[er]
at the nose and mouth, with anatomically adjacent par[ts]
generally arranged together but distributed across the avai[l]
able field, then it can be seen quite simply as a multip[le]
station point construction. The picture of the sculpin – t[he]
bullhead fish – is a single point construction. The bullhe[ad]
has no characteristic features on its belly; all is apparent [in]
a single top view. This is a limiting case in an imag[e]
generation system that uses multiple-station points to ca[p]

Figure 6.34. A classic split-style design for a bear. (From the cover of Holm 1974.)

ture all the critical features. That "split style" is an over-simplification of what is really multiple viewpoint construction should be evident from the example in Figure 6.34. This design shows a bear, with the head in the lower middle section, the forepaws on either side, the body in the middle of the painting (decorated with another face), and with the two hind paws placed out on the left and the right hand sides of the painting. Clearly this is no simple splitting of the animal from nose to tail. It is the presentation of half-a-dozen views of the animal's body, highly stylized but retaining anatomical integrity in the distribution pattern across the surface. Such prototypical split-style designs can readily be seen as multiple station point views, as is obvious from consideration of the two designs from Boas in Figure 6.35. These are both double-profile views of bears, joined at the face to give a full-face impression to the design. Boas warns that in most of these views, the face is not shown from the front, but in double profile, as indicated by deep depressions at the axis of juncture. Generally, the joining takes place below eye level, usually at the nose, indicating that the upper parts of eyes and forehead are not one structure. The resulting angularity is evident.

Optical infinity distance assumption

An optical infinity distance assumption generally means that the artist observer is not placed in the composition

Figure 6.35. Double-profile views of bears. (From Boas 1955:224–5, Figs. 222 and 223.)

itself, that the object or scene depicted is not constructed as an extension of the visual space of a single person. There is no attempt to create a picture so that "both the viewer and the objects in the painting will seem to be (standing on the same plane," as Alberti (1956) put it. The animals and occasional humans depicted in Northwest Coast Indian art are not captured in a single frozen slice of time; they are not part of anybody's momentary glance. Boas writes that the Indian depiction system represents the animal's most characteristic parts; his analysis provides a list of conventionalized symbols for many of the creatures. For example, a beaver is represented by large incisors, a large round nose, a scaly tail, and a stick held in the forepaws (The tail and teeth alone are sufficient.) The sculpin (bullhead fish) is represented by two spines rising over the mouth and a continuous dorsal fin; the bear is shown with large paws, large mouth set with teeth, protruding tongue, large round nose, and sudden turn from snout to forehead.

Pictures of bears contain the bear's distinctive features and pictures of beavers contain the beaver's features, but something equally important is true. The distinctive or characteristic body parts of the animals depicted are by no means arranged at random across the available field. In the designs that retain true representational character – in the sense that the depicted contents are accessible to the relatively naive – organic integrity is maintained despite (or because of) splitting, spreading, reducing, and "symmetrizing". A look back at Figures 6.30 and 6.31 will reveal that anatomical arrangements of body parts are generally maintained in both configurative and expansive designs. The two sides of the split wolf in the configurative design (Fig. 6.29) are shown adjacent to one another and joined at the hip. Moreover, the head is joined to the body at its usual and accustomed place as the body is joined to front and hind limbs. Even the expansive split-style beaver design retains anatomical logic in the arrangement of parts. The head is depicted at the front, with the head and teeth in organically correct spatial relation to each other and to the ears at the top of the head. Forelegs are adjacent to the head, just as the hind legs are adjacent to the turned-up tail at the back. Distinctive body parts are certainly present but so are all the basic body parts visible from the front, side, and rear. It is far more descriptive of the actual appearance of these works to say they represent multiple views of a single object rather than multiple individual body parts. A single body part, such as the beaver's hatched tail, may be critical for identification of the specific animal depicted, but it fails to characterize the composition as a whole.

The emphasis by historians and analysts on characteristic features has generally diminished analysis of multiple-view representation in a single picture. Northwest Coast Indian art is a mode of depicting the visual concept that combines views of the object while retaining fidelity to the structural skeleton of the object itself. The joining of front, side, and rear views of animals in a single painting, and the joining of two profile views of a single animal in a painting preserves the three-dimensionality and the constant shape of the animal as no single view could do. The particular views selected generate either Affine or Metric compositions, depending on the image plane. In either case, the projection lines are always parallel. There is never any foreshortening of bodies, no depiction of the hind legs as apparently smaller than the nearer forelegs. The animal is depicted wholistically, in timeless form, not bound to a single station point or a close foreshortened view. Perspective variation, on the other hand, is an accident of the moment, fundamentally personal in its here-and-now quality. Generally speaking, cultural styles in which the station-point option is multiple also assume a distance point at optical infinity, giving a parallel projection.

It may be that combining views of several body parts, each with a different perspective proper to the various viewpoints, all into a single painting would make the painting uninterpretable. Perspective implies appearance in a momentary glance; multiple disparate perspectives would imply a hydraheaded observer. Perhaps whatever drives a culture to faithful rendition of the multiplicity of object views also urges that the distance assumed will be at optical infinity. The lack of interest in, or the explicit rejection of, depiction capturing one of the highly variable perspectives available on close viewing of an object seems to involve

Figure 6.36. Metric example of Northwest Indian art: a slate carving of a sea monster. (From Boas 1955:233, Fig. 238.)

distancing of subject from artist in both a metaphorical and literal sense. Such distancing, however, still leaves two options available to the artist for the positioning of the image plane relative to the subject, each having different consequences for the generation of the image and its geometry.

Oblique angle assumption

Where the dominant face of the depicted subject is the face itself, the design is usually expansive and the geometry Affine; where the dominant face is the side-profile view, the design is usually configurative and the geometry Metric. An example of the Metric style is shown in Figure 6.36, a slate carving of a seamonster. The dominant face shown is the overall side view of the monster, giving a basic configurative design. The image plane is parallel to the side creating, in conjunction with the parallel projection lines, a Metric projection. Such configurative compositions are often single viewpoint as in the seamonster design, or minimally split multiple point constructions, as in the drawing of the wolf in Figure 6.29.

Side-view Metric compositions are relatively common but another type of Metric composition, the full-face construction, is not. Boas (1955) pointed out: "There are very few designs which can possibly be interpreted as full-face views of animals. . . . [T]he face of the shark is always shown in this manner, because its symbols appear best in this position. The only other animal which is painted or carved on flat surfaces in full front view is the hawk or thunderbird, whose symbol is the long beak which descends to the chin" (p. 235). Figure 6.37 shows a clear example of a full-face Metric composition depicting a shark with the body itself shown in at least four different aspects while the head is shown in only one. *Single* station point, full-face Metric compositions seem to be very difficult to find except for occasional examples like the thunderbird shown in Figure 6.38. Indeed, a single station point construction unimproved by the addition of even a single other aspect is a *rara avis* indeed in Northwest Coast Indian art.

Neither the side-view nor the full-face construction

Figure 6.37. Full-face composition depicting a shark. (From Boas, 1955:229, Fig. 233.)

Figure 6.38. Single-station-point view of a thunderbird. (From Boas 1955:236, Fig. 244.)

constitute what most of us consider to be the most characteristic images of Indian art, the so-called "split-style" compositions, like that shown in Figure 6.36, in which the face is the dominant, but by no means the only surface of the animal to be depicted. Many of these classic-style pictures seem to be Metric, but on closer examination it can be seen that they are not. Boas argued that pictures such as the bears (Figs. 6.33–35) are properly seen as two profile views of the animal's head, joined usually at the nose and below. The vertical depression, the absence of joining above the nose, argues that Boas is correct. I agree, except that I conceive of the two profiles as two views available at two station points, rather than as two isolated features of the animal juxtaposed. It seems a trivial difference in interpretation until the geometrical consequences of either assumption are considered. A view of an object from a specific station point is constrained physically and logically to so many options like near–far, parallel or oblique, with certain geometrical consequences for each assumption. The depiction of a body part, or object part, in isolation, as a thing not viewed but merely existent, always must be Metric. If I ask you to draw the top of a coffee cup, you will draw a circle. So will everyone else. If I ask you to draw multiple views of the coffee cup showing its most characteristic features, you might again draw a circle for the top. But you might not. Thus one interpretation allows for the appearance of non-Metric images in addition to the Metric ones. This is the view that both are available in natural perspective of an object. The argument that an art style consists of depiction of body parts without reference to natural perspective, without reference to possible varieties of appearance, cannot account for the appearance of any non-Metric images in the style.

I think non-Metric images abound in what Boas called split-style depictions, like those of the bears. The images of the bears shown in Figure 6.35 can be interpreted so: The image plane is oblique to both the left and right side view, what Boas calls the profiles, of the object; intersecting planes run parallel to the side surfaces of the face and body itself. These intersecting surfaces and parallel projection lines give an Affine projection, as is evident from the nasal depression line, the absence of joining, vertical space above the noses. What is remarkable ab that space to me is not that it is empty, but that i bounded by an angle. The left side of the face is at an ar to the right; the right side of the composition rises diagonally as a whole to the right of the field, and the side of the composition rises up to the left. This is a cla hallmark of an Affine composition. This diagonal lay is similar to the ubiquitous oblique angles in the buildir houses, temples, and palaces of the Affine Japanese wor Boas remarked on this angularity frequently in his disc sion of the patterning on carved and painted boxes, that shown in Figure 6.39.

Generally speaking, wherever the viewpoint is cle ly multiple, wherever the animal is "split" and spre around the available space in an expansive design, so of the views, at least, are oblique and the compositio Affine. It is very important to remember that Metric g metry is nested in Affine geometry, that Metric images v be found in Affine construction schemes. In the treatm of Egyptian art that will follow, we shall look at a depict system that is *only* Metric: the cultural style of anci Egypt.

Egyptian art

Ancient Egyptian art gives the impression of being a more formalized system of depiction than either Japan or Renaissance art, and a far more static one in terms artistic variation within the prevailing convention than of the three systems discussed so far in this chapter. have no evidence that it was anywhere written in anci Egypt that the artist must assume a certain stance relat to the subjects and arrange them just so in space, yet close to 3,000 years, with the slightest of variations, spec prescriptions for the generation of images held. Anci Egyptian art was generated from *multiple* station point *optical infinity*. Since the image plane was always *para* to the most characteristic aspects of the objects represent the system was one of Metric projection.

Figure 6.39. Affine angularity of construction in painted boxes. (From Boas 1955:263, Fig. 274.)

Multiple station point assumption

My statement that the station point in Egyptian art was multiple and at optical infinity oversimplifies the case. The station point is usually single across simple objects and multiple across more complex objects like humans and birds, but it really depends on the particular object illustrated. If the parts of an object, or the arrangement of parts, can undergo radical changes such as those that take place in the human form when the figure sits and then stands, or in birds as they fly, and then perch or walk along on the ground, then these changes were deemed important enough to require a multiple station point treatment for the figure. When birds were drawn flying, the wings were shown on the top and the body from the side; these views were combined so that for the whole bird the composition was multiple station point. The birds shown in Figure 6.40 should be contrasted with the belly-up, spread-wing treatment of the thunderbird in Figure 6.38. In Egyptian art, the bodies of birds were depicted from the side or the top. When birds were perching or walking, they were drawn sideways from a single station point.

Human beings were nearly always multiple station point figures whether they were standing or sitting, because each

Figure 6.40. Egyptian birds. (From Capart 1923).

part of the body seemed to demand specific characterization for adequate depiction of its shape. Whether the figure was sitting or standing, hips were in profile along with face and feet, and the shoulders and eyes were frontal. A classic such "profile" is shown in Figure 6.41 (top) along with the minimal changes in depiction style over time (bottom). The depictions of birds and humans are, as far as I can tell, the only items that force the categorization of Egyptian art as multiple station point within a single object. Nearly every other object and animal was depicted from a single station point in some characteristic aspect. Animals were nearly always depicted from the sides (later sections) as were inanimate objects like boats, boxes, vases, furniture, and weapons. Inanimate objects were usually shown in a simple architectural elevation with no ground plan visible whatsoever.

Boas (1955) pointed out the frequency with which Metric "architectural" drawings occur in "primitive" art, using Egyptian art (as well as Northwest Coast Indian art) as an example. He wrote of Egyptian paintings: "They are not by any means proof of an inability to see and draw perspectively; they merely show that the interest of the people centered in the full representation of the symbols" (p. 73). Boas did not distinguish between Affine and Metric constructions; nevertheless, his point is well taken. However,

the difference between Egyptians' pictures of single objects
and architects' drawings of those objects is that the Egyptian drawings include only elevation or plan whereas the
architect's drawings include both. In Egyptian drawings
each object depicted generally has a single station point.
The single views selected by Egyptian artists should be

compared to the common sections of depicted objects lustrated in Figure 9.5.

In Egyptian art, scenes, unlike single objects, are alwa and clearly multiple station point products with para image and subject planes. Each subject – person, obje or animal – is painted as if it or each of its most char teristic parts were right in front of the artist. Never i single station point assumed for the entire scene even complex New Kingdom compositions. For example, layout method for the pond in Figure 6.42 is clearly multiple station point technique combining characteri aerial and frontal views of persons and objects; the hunti scene depicts not successive planes in space, but rat simple sections of a complex scene, with each section a each object within a section having its own station poi This kind of construction is similar to that of Raphao *School of Athens*, in which the artist painted each hum figure as if he were standing for his portrait directly front of the easel.

This multiplicity of station point across scenes creat at least for the Western eye, certain difficulties of int pretation of the spatial relations among components. C jects seem to be placed in the two-dimensional pictu space primarily with regard to their two-dimensional pearance; as it is with single objects, so it is with subco ponents of "scenes." Left–right spatial relations are cle but the only reliable information for near–far relative the station points is given by the overlapping of one figt by another. As can be seen in the example of the hunti scene in Figure 6.42b, overlapping gives the *thinnest* po sible distance between two objects especially in the high stylized version prevalent in Egyptian art. Additional the appearance of a series of figures overlapped in dep often seems to be determined by formal similarities, as the depictions of the elands and oxen in Figure 6.42b, a not by any concern for the clarity of the three-dimensio layout. The emphasis in ancient Egyptian art is certain on clarity of depiction of subject matter, but the mul plicity of station point makes this a bit hard to understa at first. The explanation probably lies in the criterion clarity itself. If each object is to be depicted so it appe

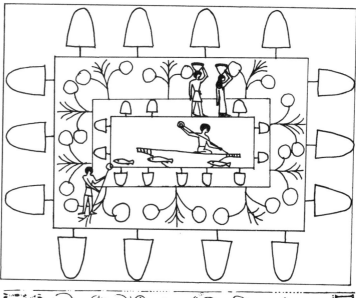

Figure 6.42. Two techniques of depiction of spatial layout in Egyptian art. (top, Drawing by author – after Capart 1923; bottom, from Groenewegen-Frankfort 1951.)

to be what it is, as clearly and timelessly as possible, then, surely, depicting it in its various, temporary positions in space certainly must be irrelevant.

Generally, the relations of one object to another in Egyptian art are formal and not spatial. If a king is depicted in a boat, the depiction conveys the information that he had

a boat or was a hunter–fisher, or will be in the after
not that at one point in his life he went duck hunting
sat just so. This same indifference to the moment is evic
in the Egyptian assumption of a station point at the dist:
of optical infinity. Both Japanese and Northwest C
Indian art make the same assumption; the formal g
metrical consequences for all three styles is the same,
the specific appearance of images is very different fi
style to style, partly owing to the differences in num
and angle assumptions and partly to other conventic
factors.

Optical infinity distance assumption

The supposition of a station point at optical infinity g
hand in hand with a multiple station point assumpt
where the intent is the depiction of objects in their clea
most recognizable forms. It cannot be said too often
any artist engaged in transforming three-dimensional
ids into two-dimensions forms is forced to order prior
for depiction. One can't do everything. Observatio
hundreds of Egyptian paintings supports the belief
recognizability was a primary concern of the Egyptian ar
When we remember that Egyptian art was the art of t
paintings, and that tombs were filled with objects pres
ably intended for the comfort of the deceased in the af
life, we have a clue to the importance of recognizabilit
a primary artistic goal. It might well have been the
that objects painted in tombs possessed the same deg
of "solidity" as objects truly present, at least as far as
interests of the dead were concerned. However, it is
really necessary to understand the intention to apprec
the quality of the product. Most painted objects in Eg
tian art are Metric projections of their three-dimensic
counterparts, insofar as such a thing is possible. For n
objects, it is rather as if a bright light were shone on
object from a great distance, creating a shadow form
be filled in by the artist in color. These Metric projecti
preserve the most invariants and are thus the most "
ognizable" images.

  Of course, a station point at optical infinity has o

consequences as well. There is no foreshortening across objects, and no size diminution covarying with increased distance. All objects are at the same distance relative to the artist–observer. Size relations in these pictures give no reliable information for relative worldly size. Figure 6.41 is an excellent example of size presented without regard to spatial placement.

Since the station points are at optical infinity, the relative size relationships mean nothing for relative distance. It sometimes seems that certain techniques of horizontal stratification across the field imply the display of successive areas in space, as in the hunting scene in Figure 6.42b, but more probably this inference is made only by the modern beholder and was not by the ancient artist. One is tempted to draw the same conclusions about the relation between height on the field and relative depth for Egyptian art as for Japanese painting, but the conclusions are probably not valid. The problems involved in the depiction of complex spatial layout in a system as Metric as the Egyptian will be discussed in the section, "Scenes with many surfaces," in Chapter 9. We will consider briefly the remaining component of the Egyptian system, the frontal–parallel *angle* assumption.

Frontal–parallel angle assumption

Most of the implications of the frontal–parallel angle assumption have already been drawn in the discussion of station point and distance. A Metric projection system requires that the image plane be parallel to the dominant plane of the subject. In Egyptian art, the dominant plane is determined with great consistency. The selection occasionally depends on the varieties of possible characteristic activities of the subject, as with birds, but not in most cases. The overwhelming impression gained from Egyptian art is of the clarity of the forms displayed. The Egyptian artist appears to have had no interest in depicting the vagaries of appearance arising from an image plane oblique to the dominant plane of the subject. Each object has its own station point; each object is viewed from a distance so great as to obviate projective alteration of its charac-

teristic features, and those features are copied faithful
onto a parallel image plane. This means of effecting sim
plicity of rendition has other ramifications in pictorial com
position that will become apparent when we look mo
closely at the Egyptian's particular geometry.

Indeed, the formation of the four art styles that I hav
subjected to geometrical description can be seen in an er
tirely different light from the traditional one when th
implications of such a "hierarchical" geometrical analys
become clear. That each style is a valid visual geometi
sectioning the domain of natural perspectives has eno
mous implications for theories of "how pictures work
the outline of those implications is the subject of the ne
chapters.

7 Invariant information: analysis of style

The sound of a bell is not the bell and the odor of cheese is not cheese. Similarly the perspective projection of the faces of an object (by the reverberating flux of reflected light in a medium) is not the object itself. Nevertheless, in all these cases a property of the stimulus is univocally related to a property of the object by virtue of physical laws. This is what I mean by the conveying of environmental information.

James Gibson, *The Senses Considered As Perceptual*
Systems (1966: 187)

Utility of the analysis

In the preceding chapter, I have tried to show in at least a preliminary way that it is possible to categorize depiction styles in terms of station-point options and consequent geometries. But what is the point of doing so beyond the pleasure and parsimony gained from the simple establishment of a system? There are two main utilitarian justifications for employing the analysis of style presented here.

The most immediate consequence of using the system is the revelation of degrees of kinship among quite diverse styles of depiction that are obscured by conventional categorizations of Western versus non-Western art, or of "sophisticated" versus "primitive" art, and other similar unilluminating dichotomies. It is easy to see that such simplistic classifications of art completely fail to describe or indeed even begin to explain the obvious differences in appearance from style to style; the problem of explaining similarities from one style to another is hardly touched upon. Geometrical analysis of style, on the other hand,

reveals varying degrees of fundamental similarity that a
not apparent upon casual inspection of different stylis
exemplars, obscured as they are by the many variables n
contingent upon geometric aspects of image generatio
No "style" of painting could ever be analyzed fully by
exposition of its geometrical structure, but such an e
position is critical to understanding the basic princip
upon which a more extensive elaboration of the ma
issues of style can rest. The geometrical structures giv
framework of degrees of similarity that permits the e
ploration of the nature of the many differences that disti
guish one style from another. Much of art history
description and exposition of these differences in appe
ance. How much more illuminating it is to look at t
differences in light of the similarities. Kinship networks
similarity give us the foundation required for this task
terms of the formal characteristics of image generation
the station point options.

The second boon of such a system is that it categori
the various depiction styles as Metric, Similarity, Affi
and Projective *projections*, that is, transformations belor
ing to particular *Groups*, thus permitting their expositi
in terms of geometrical *invariants*. Examination of style
terms of the geometric invariants depicted is analysis
art in terms of the kind of information an artist can transr
about objects and scenes within the conventions of sty
The very brief presentation of empirical work on vis
perception of the ordinary environment in Chapter
showed the promise of analyzing information for perce
tion in terms of geometrical invariants, but only a promi
not a program, was presented.

From the work that does exist, however, several thir
are clear: We know that examination of Metric invaria
in terms of equivalence classes will further our understar
ing of the general problem of perceptual identity and si
ilarity; that Similarity invariants can serve as dir
information for approach and recession, specifying yet ag
another set of equivalencies; that Affine invariants spec
growth and aging in ordinary vision, revealing that c
servers are capable of responding to such high-level
variants; and, finally, that the Projective invariants, wh

seem so inaccessible to ordinary perception, provide the basis not only for the gradients that have proved useful in the analysis of visual perception but for informative families of perspectivities as well. Research on geometrical information for vision is in its infancy. It has taken us centuries to begin to solve the problems of appearance created by Euclid's geometrical approach to vision. But the accomplishments are great and the promise is even greater.

Perhaps it will seem paradoxical to argue that the promise of the geometrical approach to the analysis of visual information is more fully realized in the field of representational art than in the domain of ordinary vision, but it is true. It is paradoxical to argue that the artist has more freedom of vision than the observer of the ordinary environment, but it is true. The artist need see only that wonderful terrain viewed through the "mind's eye." The artist is not constrained by the temporary positioning of objects in space or by the place where he is momentarily standing. In a single depiction the artist can "move" many times, showing as many aspects of the object or scene as are required by the composition. Objects can be arranged "in space" at will, ordered and rendered symmetrical, stacked and distributed according to artistic demand. This freedom to be close or far from the subject, to depict it once or many times, to face it head on or study it obliquely, makes it simple for the artist to select from the enormous variety in the optic array just those invariants that serve the purposes of artistic expression.

In representational pictures, the type and number of invariants preserved are a direct function and immediate consequence of the artist's stance relative to the subject, of the formal means of generating the images. That is, the artist's stance or selected station point option determines the geometrical mapping of the picture, a mapping that necessarily preserves some figural invariants, but not others. As we ascend the hierarchy from Metric mappings to Projective, fewer and fewer invariants are preserved. Thus, the selection of a mapping option determines what and how much an artist can demonstrate about the persistent properties of objects and scenes. It is possible to examine specifically

what each depiction system allows the artist to comn
nicate about form and spatial layout. To illustrate the rai
and limitations of each communication system, we v
look again at Metric maps in ancient Egyptian art, Aff
mappings as they occur in pre-Western influence – Japan
and Northwest Coast Indian art – and Projective mappir
(and some Similarities) in Western post-Renaissance ar

Metric invariants and Egyptian art

In any Metric mapping, the following invariants are f
mally preserved in the figure mapped: size, shape, distan
angle size, straightness, parallelism, length, ratio of leng
cross-ratio, collinearity, area, betweenness, position of t
center of gravity, and perpendicularity, ratio of divisic
and harmonic division. If ancient Egyptian paintings
properly characterized as multiple Metric mappings, th
such figural invariants should be evident in them. Of cour
art is *never* the mechanical application of geometry; nev
theless, Metric invariants should be manifest in Egypti
art if its characterization as Metric is generally correct, a
to a greater extent than in contrasting styles. To test t
assertion, we will examine objects like tables and chai
figures both animal and human, and scenes and events frc
Egyptian art.

Scale reduction and similarity

Metric geometry is often called Distance geometry becau
the preservation of actual metric distance is considered fu
damental. Yet in Egyptian art, as in our own Weste
architectural orthographic blueprints, the image is su
jected to a scale change. Egyptian images are occasional
"life size," but this is by no means characteristic of t
style. So although Metric mappings allow for the pres
vation of exact size information, no art style, including t
Egyptian, avails itself of the opportunity afforded, pi
sumably because of logistical considerations. Even wh
painting murals, one has only so much wall space. Y
Egyptian pictures do not therefore fall into the Similari
mapping group, although the invariants preserved are i

deed those proper to the Similarities. Egyptian pictures were conceived of and generated as minimally transformed, one-to-one presentations of the most characteristic or informative properties of objects and events and their *Metric* characteristics. A distance point at optical infinity is not quite the same as no station point, a dubious construct at best. A station point at optical infinity assumes some spatial orientation relative to the subject, however minimal. Likewise, a distance point (or series of them) at optical infinity with parallel subject and image planes does not produce pictures equivalent to sets of Similarity images because nowhere in such pictures is there any evidence of the near–far convergence of line or diminution of size that would ordinarily appear in a series of Similarity images. Euclid's Proposition 5 (Figure D.1.)describes the appearance of such Similarity images, clearly absent in the art of ancient Egypt. In fact, no art style is really consistently generated in terms of Similarities; Similarity projections always occur as special cases in the context of Projective mappings. Presumably, the adoption of a distance assumption, with the consequent degree of convergence or nonconvergence, is primary, and its special applications, like the Similarities when the planes are parallel, are secondary. Thus we properly see the operation of Similarity projection in the analysis of Western post-Renaissance art and not in Egyptian art. This is a very roundabout way of saying that one should not be misled by the scale reduction in Egyptian art; Egyptian pictures are not Similarities and were never intended to be (Figure 7.1).

The "Shape" invariants

The preservation, indeed the fundamental character, of Metric relations in Egyptian art is seen most clearly in the depictions of shape: angle size, parallelism, perpendicularity, and relative lengths and areas. (Invariants like collinearity, cross-ratio, and betweenness are necessarily present if these others are.) Consider, for example, the segment of the Deir El Bersheh coffin, shown in Figure 7.2, which depicts, among other things, a throne and several tables. Such "carpentered" objects give us the clearest opportunity

of evaluating the preservation of shape – angularity, p
allelism, and perpendicularity. Right angles are preserv
especially in the throne and low table, and parallelism
maintained in the spatial relationship between top and b
tom edges of the seat and table tops, and in the relationsl
between top surface and supporting substructure of
throne and low table. It follows, of course, that perp
dicularity is necessarily preserved, but the "rigidity" of
preservation is quite striking visually. It is clear even fr
the "framing" of scenes that preservation of the right an
and its attendant spatial configurations was a matter
aesthetic (or religious) preference as well as a means
providing shape information about objects and scenes.

Shape information is also given in the rigid presentati
of spatial relationships in the animal chair. The naturalis
treatment in the painting in no way mitigates the striki
severity of line and angle. Smaller objects such as the r
merous vases and braziers are also rigidly presented in
views most informative about shape. Because they are c
jects with clear, upright orientations, and because th
parts are not independently articulated in the manner
the human body, these simple objects are depicted in o

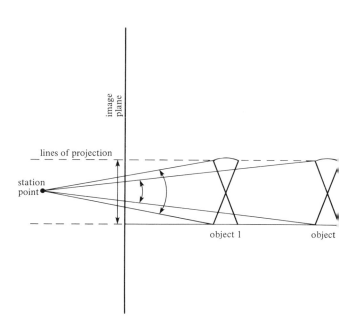

Figure 7.1. Comparison of size
relations in Metric and Similarity
images.

Figure 7.2. Deir El Bersheh coffin, Dynasty XII. (Courtesy, Museum of Fine Art, Boston. Harvard Expedition.)

line by a frontal section through the middle of the object. The result is rather as if each object, such as the vase, were cracked in half, inked along the cracked edge and used as a printing block to determine outline. (It is noteworthy, although not in terms of the geometry of the compositions, that these outline forms were modeled in paint and stone so as to give a nearly tactile impression of volume; curvilinear objects in Egyptian art often look quite solidly rounded, unlike the more carpentered objects, which often look like cutouts.) That these frontal sections (hypothetical though they be) were considered to be parallel to the image plane is obvious when one attends to the rigid preservation of symmetry, a figural aspect quickly destroyed by nonparallel planes.

Shape and the number of station points

The tables and chairs, vases and braziers we have considered were all depicted from single, infinitely distant station points – one for each object. Indeed, because all of these objects are brought forward to a single plane in space, one could argue that there is a single station point for the entire scene. However, this assumes a completely unnecessary and unsubstantiated, imaginary prearrangement in space of the objects to be subsequently depicted from the single point, and there is no evidence of any such interest in spatial layout in Egyptian art. The assertion is especially untenable in light of the fact that vertical arrangement on the picture plane bears no relation to longitudinal (near–far) layout in space. It seems clear that each of these relatively simple objects was depicted from its own infinitely distant but informative station point. Because of their limited and intrinsically rigid articulation and arrangement of parts, these objects are adequately represented by *single* frontal sections containing the critical parts. But objects like bodies, animal and human, do not possess rigid layout of parts, and therefore do not lend themselves to adequate illustration by single frontal slices. Spatial relations among parts vary as a function of position and action and cannot be represented by single sections. Moreover, a single section that is clearly informative about one body part – for example, human shoulders or bird wings – will obscure information about the shape and layout of another part or relation among parts, like torso and hips of a human, and body and feet of a bird. So, in Egyptian art, complex objects with multiple layouts of parts are portrayed from multiple station points. The classic example of this technique occurs with the human figure.

To the Western eye, of course, combining multiple views of a single "object" creates a rather schizoid image. However that may be, it is clear that once again the choices are directed by a fundamental concern for *shape* depiction, even though the shape selected as critical or most characteristic may seem arbitrary. Presumably within the context of iconographic traditions, the specific choices are not arbitrary. Indeed, mute testimony to this point is provided by

Figure 7.3. Old Kingdom human figures. (From Groenewegen-Frankfort 1951.)

the relatively unchanging conventions of depiction across many centuries. For example, the time span covered by the pictures in this book is nearly twelve centuries. It is notable that the nonarbitrary assemblage of the human body parts likewise shows the dominance of shape depiction in Egyptian art, especially in Old and Middle Kingdom art in which the body is generally depicted in sitting and standing semiprofiles (Fig. 7.3). In New Empire art, a much greater variety of positions is depicted, as can be seen in Figure 7.4, but the dominance of the semiprofile for clear shape depiction is still evident. The desire to portray complex objects while providing adequate information about the shape of their distinctive parts is also evident in the many representations of birds from hunting scenes in tomb paintings. A selection of birds from many centuries of Egyptian painting shows attention to the shape of the wings, the body, and the feet, and the relation of wings to body (Fig. 7.5). Sagittal sections are most common for birds at rest, and lateral sections for birds on the wing. I think it important to note that the occasional pres-

ence of a foreshortened human shoulder or bird wing
along with the frequently used technique of overlappin
or occlusion, argues that the Egyptian artist was not un
aware of the frozen aspects of momentary appearance, bu
actively rejected them. Whether their rejection in favor o

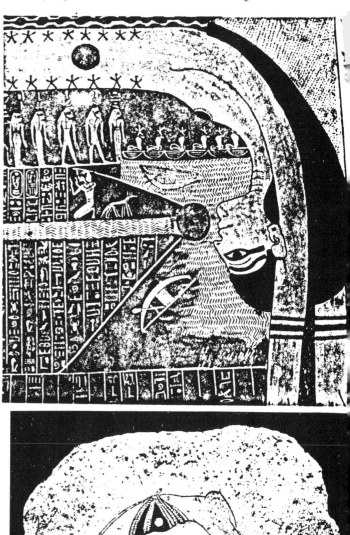

Figure 7.4. Unusual presentations
of human figures in New Empire
art. (Top, from Abbate 1972;
bottom, from Capart 1923.)

Figure 7.5. Various illustrations of birds from Egyptian art. (Top, from Abbate 1972; bottom, from Capart 1923.)

clear metric dimensionality was dictated by religious or aesthetic concerns, or by other factors, does not concern us here, however intriguing the speculation. Whatever the reason for the importance of revealing shape to the Egyptians, their consistent application of metric principles of invariant angularity, perpendicularity, and parallelism in its service allows us to characterize their paintings as Metric mappings with a fair degree of accuracy.

187 METRIC INVARIANTS AND EGYPTIAN ART

Egyptian art is also quite clear about metric and angular relations and proportions *across* bodies. This is quite obvious from observation of the Middle and New Kingdom paintings. Yet observation of Figure 7.2 also suggests the opposite, as metric relations are not preserved across the human figures, although they are across the other, non-human, subjects. But Egyptian art is a style that is subject, as are all styles, to nongeometric, or extrageometric, conventions and constraints in addition to its geometrical ones. In Egyptian art, relative size relations are not invariant in the depiction of human figures. Wives, children, servants, and slaves are usually presented as quite tiny figures relative to the major male figure – a convention that has found expression in more than one art style throughout history.

Occasional artistic variations aside, then, it is clear that the characterization of Egyptian art as a Metric projection system is strongly supported by the evident emphasis in the style placed on the unequivocal depiction of the Metric invariants of size and distance. There is no depiction style, outside of the drawings of modern architects, that is so unambiguous in its Metric portrayal of subjects. Through these paintings we know a great deal about the sizes and shapes of objects that have long become dust and in many cases perceptual judgments of pictured objects are borne out by objects found still intact in tombs. Metric mappings capture more invariants than any other kind of mapping; they provide the greatest degree of resemblance to the object pictured in terms of number of invariant features preserved in the map. In this sense, such mappings as the pictures of the ancient Egyptians, are the most realistic of the world's art styles. We shall see, however, that it is only in the sense of shared invariants that Egyptian art is most realistic. Each loss in invariants also reflects certain informational gains. The Affine projection system of Japanese art is by no means uninformative about its subject matter.

Affine invariants and Japanese art

An Affine mapping will preserve fewer invariants than a Metric mapping. The major loss is the angularity invariant, including, of course, perpendicularity. However, since the projection lines of an Affine projection are parallel, although the original and image planes are not, parallelism is preserved. Indeed, it is the loss of the angle-size invariant in conjunction with the invariant of parallelism that distinguishes an Affine projection from all others. Additional Affine invariants are ratio of division, collinearity, betweenness, and cross-ratio.

In examining Japanese yamato-e art for Affine invariants, then, we shall look primarily for the transformation of angle size joined with a fairly strict preservation of distance between parallel edges of surfaces. It should also be kept in mind that since parallel lines do not meet in an Affine mapping, figures likewise should fail to undergo size compression with increasing distance since figural size perspective is simply a special case of linear perspective. We shall look then at both figural and architectural units to test the assertion that yamato-e art is an Affine mapping system in which original and image planes are not parallel but projection lines are. Again, it is simplest to examine pictures with clear, architectural, "carpentered" units to determine the treatment of angles and parallel lines. Figure 7.6 shows segments of three handscrolls: a scene from *Kibi Daijin Nitto E-kotoba* (Kibi's Adventures in China) from the Heian period, late twelfth century; a scene from *Genji Monogatari* (Tale of Genji), early twelfth century; and a segment of the handscroll *Bakemono no Soshi* from the sixteenth century.

Many Japanese scrolls depict temples, houses, palaces, and terraces like those shown in Figure 7.6 in which it is clear that right angles are not preserved. All the presumably parallel edges of such architectural units, like the top and bottom of a single wall or the two side edges of a terrace floor, can be measured and checked for parallelism. This seems absurdly obsessive as edges like those depicted here seem clearly to be parallel. But it is occasionally asserted that Oriental perspective is commonly divergent rather than parallel; to the Western eye, parallel edges receding into the space of a picture often look divergent because we are accustomed to convergent parallel edges, so to speak, in our pictures. Careful measuring of dozens of more or less randomly selected edge pairs, however, clearly sup-

(a)

Figure 7.6. Japanese buildings and
people: (a) Kibi's Adventures in
China. (Courtesy, Museum of Fine
Arts, Boston, William Sturgis
Bigelow Collection by Exchange.)
(b) Tale of Genji by Shikibu.
(Courtesy, Museum of Fine Arts,
Boston, Bigelow Collection); (c)
Bakemono no Soshi (courtesy,
Museum of Fine Arts, Boston.
Marshall H. Gould Fund.)

ports the assertion that Japanese "perspective" depiction is
Affine, that parallel surface edges remain parallel in the
image. There are occasional exceptions, as in the fragment
of Hasadera Enji (Fig. 7.7), but they are indeed the exception. Although I have no pretensions of being a Japanese
art historian, I have noticed that such exceptions seem to
occur in compositions where the hand of the artist is less
sure.

Where the artist does not use a ruler, or other mechanical
compositional aid, some deviation from parallelism in both
directions is only to be expected. But the presence of occasional variation by no means suggests that parallelism is
not preserved in principle. The invariance of parallelism is
also maintained in figural depiction, providing additional
support for the argument that the geometry of Japanese
art is Affine, and consistently so. A consistent Affine composition will not permit of any regular size diminution of
figures with distance any more than convergence of parallel

191   AFFINE INVARIANTS AND JAPANESE ART

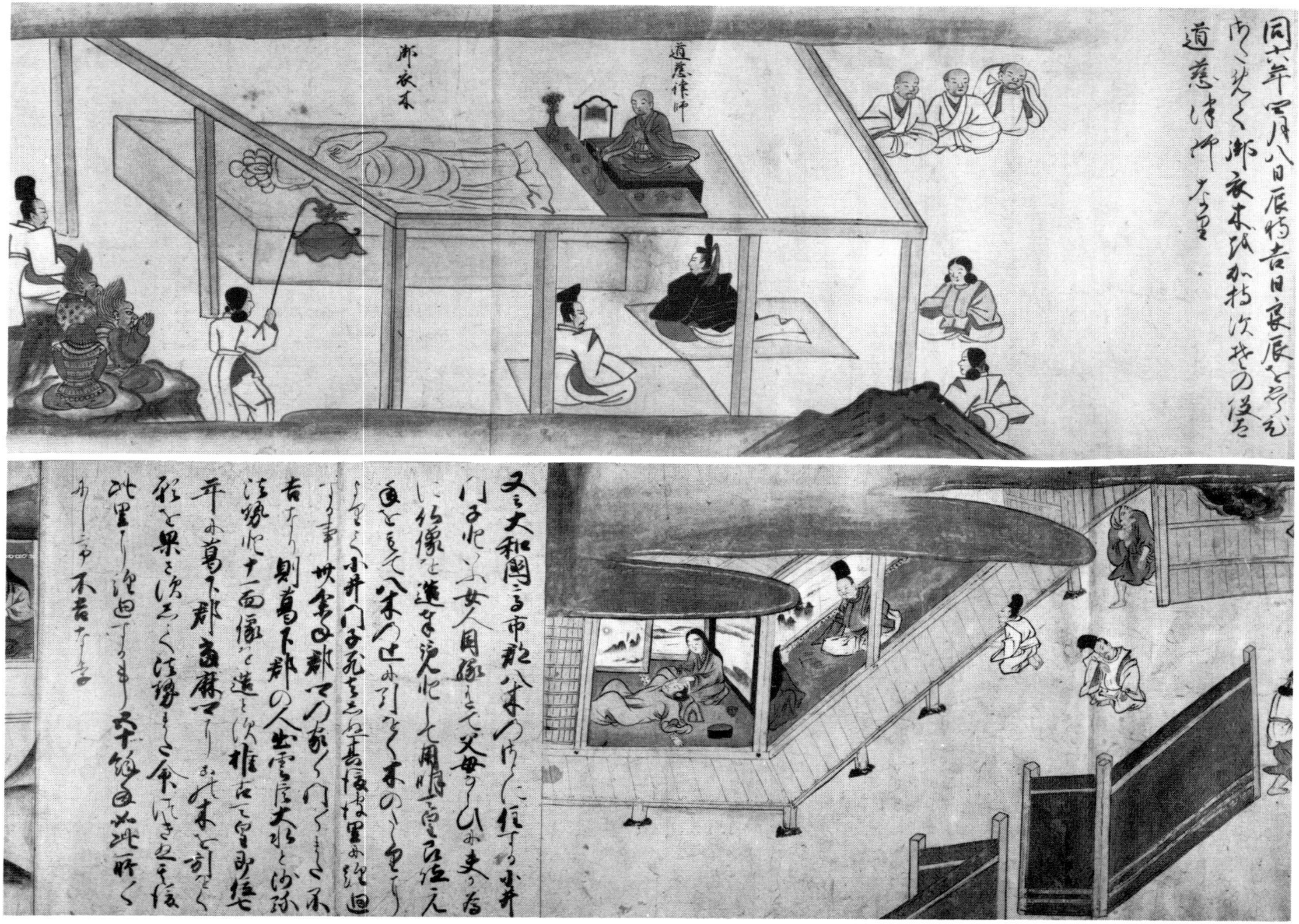

(The Seattle Art Museum, Margaret E. Fuller Purchase Fund.)

Figure 7.8. (top) Sanjō-den Youchi no-emaki ("Scroll with depictions of the night attack on the Sanjo Palace"), from the Heiji Monogatari-emaki ("Illustrated scrolls of the events of the Heiji Period."). This shows Affine treatment of wheels. (Courtesy, Museum of Fine Arts, Boston, Fenollosa-Weld Collection.)

Figure 7.9. (bottom) Hasadera Enji, showing Affine treatment of wheels. (Courtesy of The Seattle Art Museum, Margaret E. Fuller Purchase Fund.)

edges. This seems intuitively obvious when one conside
the case of a depiction of a terrace peopled with figure
If the terrace does not "shrink" into the distance, how ca
figures seated on it do so? Well, easily, if one is not con
strained by geometrical consistency. After all, Egyptian
excepted the human figure from consistent relative si:
relations for religious or status reasons. However, th
Egyptians' otherwise metrically correct images do not j
the observer with contradictory information because fig
ures are not placed in three-dimensional space; everythin
is pulled into a single frontal plane. That Japanese artis
did not combine visually inconsistent geometries in a sing
composition, or indeed in the style as a whole, is simpl
a specific case of a general principle for all art styles. Eac
coherent style is generated in accord with the principles c
one or the other of the geometries, and there exists no sty.
that is a hodgepodge of several geometries. That this is s
is clear; why it is so is not.

The consistent application of the principles of a particul
geometry is beautifully exemplified in Figure 7.8, a frag
ment from the *Burning of Sanjo Palace*, an illustrated hanc
scroll from the Kamakura period (second half of th
thirteenth century.) Because this piece has no carpentere
units, it does not lend itself to angular analysis, but th
lack of size compression in the figures here is clearly Affine
as is the depiction of the wheel. Look at Appendix A i
which a circle is shown undergoing an Affine transfor
mation, in this case *shear*. The same effect is achieve
through Affine projection – parallel projection with inter
secting planes, as explained in Chapter 3. Such elliptica
wheels are a commonplace in yamato-e art. Another ex
ample is given in Figure 7.9 from *Hasadera Enji*.

So what kind of information does Japanese art carry
The major types are information for consistent size rela
tions, parallel edges, and identity of angles. These artist
evince less concern for metric shape, but retain some in
terest in demonstrating viewpoint. The consistency of sin
gle viewpoint is obvious in constructions like the Sanj
Palace fragment, where the wheels and carriage body ar
in a consistent projection. The hallmarks of Affine com
position are probably nowhere clearer than in these ya

moto-e constructions, which contrast strongly with the character of Northwest Coast Indian constructions where, as we have seen, there are neither houses nor terraces, carriages nor wheels.

Affine invariants and Northwest Coast Indian art

Although I have said that the invariant of parallelism is the artistic hallmark of Affine composition, it will be difficult to demonstrate this in Northwest Indian art, also an Affine system. Indian art deals only with animals and, occasionally, human figures. There are no carpentered units, no three-dimensional extended ground space to anchor the composition. The only angles in this art are "accidental," which is to say that they occur in some Indian woven blankets, but only as a function of the weaving technique rather than as a function of the technique of image generation. Figure 7.10 shows a Chilkat (Tlingat) blanket that seems to display a very angular composition; next to it is the same design painted. The painting is a hypothetical copy of the pattern board that served as a model for the weaving, abstracted from the woven design by Bill Holm.

Figure 7.10. (a) Chilkat blanket and (b) "painting" style copy of lateral panel. (From Holm 1974.)

It seems clear that the angularity introduced into the wea
ing is incidental to the scheme of depiction.

Besides parallelism, the remaining Affine invariants a
betweenness, collinearity, cross-ratio, ratio of division, a
straightness. Except for betweenness and collinearity, the
are not easily examined in animal depictions. Their "a
finity" is evidenced best, I think, by the absence of a
projective compression across the body parts of the anim
in the face of evident oblique (intersecting plane) dep
tions. In the discussion of the oblique-angle assumption
Indian art (Chapter 6), we saw that the two sides of t
face of an animal are generally depicted at an angle to o
another and that the whole depicted left side of an anim
generally rises upward in the left field of the compositi
and the right side rises up in the right. Generally, the t
and hind feet of the animal are depicted higher in the fi
than the forepaws. In such a design, if the object wer
box rather than an animal, the edges of the box recedi
in space would remain parallel to one another, albeit at
acute angle to the central edge, as shown in Figure 7.1
which shows a similar animal taken from a box. The si
ilarity is obvious.

I cannot say that Northwest Indian art preserved pa
allelism of object edges, because the style did not dep
objects with parallel edges. However, one can argue bac
wards that the absence of compression of depicted bo
parts with increasing distance rests on an implicit par
lelism invariant, the hallmark of an Affine projection.

This same lack of interest in or active rejection of t
depiction of perspective foreshortening is inextricab
wedded to a distance assumption of optical infinity. T
end result for the Northwest Indian artist is preservati
of information about relative distances in different dire
tions. The other invariants available to the Indian artist a
critical for representation, for nonarbitrary object reco
nition, and include certain fundamental relationships
adjacency or betweenness – again subject to marked st
lization in presentation. By adjacency I mean a notion al
to collinearity except that, again, with animal depictio
we lack the straight lines necessary to exemplify coll
earity in any strict sense. Yet it is evident that the Ind

Figure 7.11. Preservation of "parallel" edges in Indian art. Box made by craftsman at Thomas Burke Memorial Washington State Museum, Seattle, Washington. Photo supplied by the author from er collection.)

artist preserves information about relations within and across body parts, that is, about the situation of one part of the eye relative to another, or the placement of the eye relative to the nose. We see this most clearly in the preservation of the organic integrity of the body of the animal. Franz Boas determined that each animal was represented by certain characteristic features, but it is certainly *not* the case that these features were arranged in two-dimensional space by a roll of the dice. The foot bone is not invariably connected to the ankle bone, because nothing in art is invariable, but it usually is. Adjacency and betweenness are not, of course, uniquely Affine; they are also Projective (with a couple of exceptions) and Topological. But they are among the Affine invariants, they were available to Indian artists, and were illustrated quite faithfully by them.

Probably the invariants most fundamental to the *possibility* of representation – never mind its *fidelity* – are those that are invariant across the most, not the fewest, transformations. Thus the seemingly fundamental shape invariants of Metric geometry may be seen as quite elaborate aspects of depiction. This is the view espoused by Jean Piaget in his exposition of the development of the conceptualization of space in the ordinary environment in children. Rather than deal with the issue here, I will return to it in the treatment of the development in children of spatial depiction techniques in Chapter 10. Whatever the disposition of the hierarchy in acquisition, it is clear that as we move toward Projective projection systems, the artist is left with fewer and fewer invariants to depict, with what seems on the face of it to be fewer and fewer sources of information about the subject matter available for communication. What is left for the Projective artist, and how can we understand the conveying of optical information in Projective pictures?

Projective invariants and Western post-Renaissance art

Westerners are accustomed to thinking of their own post-Renaissance art as the most realistic, highest fidelity, system of depiction. Yet Western art contains the fewest invariants of all the styles so far discussed. Geometric invariants for size, shape, distance, parallelism, and perpendicularity are all lost in Western Projective projection. Under the uniquely Projective transformation, the central projection of a plane onto an intersecting plane, the only invariant figural properties necessarily preserved are collinearity and betweenness, the property of being a degenerate or a nondegenerate conic, the cross-ratios of points and lines, and the harmonic properties. If these conventional invariants of geometry were the only information available for the objects and scenes shown in Western pictures, it is not clear that we could understand them at all, at least not without a great deal of training. How can we explain the seemingly easy accessibility of Western pictures without recourse to learned conventionality as a crutch?

It is my position that Western pictures are informative about their contents primarily because they contain the derived invariants of size, line, and texture spacing and compression, traditionally called perspective in Western art. We saw in Chapter 3 that the gradient invariants are derived from the cross–ratio invariant. Cross–ratio is invariant across change in the center of the projection or the station point of the observer, as the case may be. The gradients are derived from the cross–ratio under the assumptions that the center of projection is a point of observation and the relevant points are on the straight edge of an object or surface. Gradients of spacing and compression are essentially changes in projected size with increasing distance and so are projectively available in the light only at middle and short distance viewing. (However, most ordinary viewing in the ordinary environment is *not* at optical infinity.) Likewise, such gradients in pictures, what we call "perspective," is present only in middle- and short-distance station-point constructions. The rate of change in projected size is, of course, change in the slope of the visual angle curve, as shown in Figure 2.6. The rate of change in visual angle is very rapid near the point of observation, while with increasing distance the rate, the slope of the function, approaches zero change. Long-distance station-point constructions thus become Affine and lose the gradients of compression, while they pick up the invariant of parallelism – a much more intuitively obvious shape component than cross-ratio.

Is it the case that the gradients in Western pictures compensate for the loss of the Affine invariants? Is it true that the system with the fewest invariants generates the most realistic, most faithful pictures of the scenes in the ordinary environment? We have seen that a Metric picture gives quite precise information about the relative sizes and shapes of its objects and, at least in its manifestation in architects' plans, about relative distance in spatial layout. We have seen that Affine projections preserve the shape invariant of parallelism and relative distance in single directions. Can Projective pictures, using just the gradients derived from the cross-ratios, the cross-ratios themselves, and the fundamental invariants of betweenness and collinearity, supply reliable information about the shapes, sizes, and distances of objects pictured?

We saw in Chapter 3 that they can. The existing literature provides convincing evidence that the optical gradients provide at least potential information for specification of the relative sizes and distances of obje and for the specification of shape through slant, given presence of sufficiently textured surfaces. (The informa is potential, it is available to perception; whether it is u is another matter.)

The presence of this additional "perspective" struct in Western painting is said to account for its special cl acter, for what is often called the "objective" mode depiction, and for the illusionistic success of trompe-l'c like pictures (Fig. 7.12). Is that true? Is there really anyth about the Projective specification of information in pict that somehow renders those pictures more "lifelike" t pictures carrying only other kinds of information?

In his discussion of Northwest Coast Indian art, anthropologist Boas (1955) observed that the Western p Renaissance method is more realistic only if it is belie that the essence of realism is the reproduction of mom tary appearance. I think that is both true and not true is true in that most Western people probably feel that c one slice of time should be contained in a "good" pict because Westerners are generally conditioned by the p tographic model. At the same time, the quality of the si image portrayed is at least as important as its "singlene As Gibson argued for twenty years, the invariants dis a world with nobody in it, but Western perspective im

Figure 7.12. Trompe-l'oeil-style painting from Hawaii. (Photograph by H.L. Coffman.)

show where the observer is in that world. The function of perspective is not to enhance the "reality" of the picture, but to place the viewer in the scene pictured. Gibson apparently thought that depiction with a single, fixed station point was more natural than depiction without one.

I do not think Western pictures are either more "lifelike" or more natural; I do think it is true that the *presence* of the scenes depicted is more compelling. Western perspective pictures are constructed as an extension of the viewer's space. They contain exactly those invariants – the gradients – that specify change in point of view, variations in the angle of observation. In a correctly constructed perspective picture, à la Alberti, the scale is even set to human dimensions, the picture window is anchored to the human viewer. The sense of an immediately present space in these pictures is indeed unequalled. This information is unique to Projective pictures. Yet even in these images actually designed to extend the space of the viewer individualistically, the station point is never so close as to exclude the possibility of other viewers. The picture always exists as an object apart, as an object of art. It is more subjective than pictures in other styles, but never entirely so.

Western perspective pictures extend the world of the self. Non-Western pictures portray the world of the self without painting the observer's nose into the picture. Every style captures different invariants. Each invariant of structure specifies something in the world, serves some communicative function within a representation. Presumably, every loss in depictive communication is compensated for by a gain. It would seem so given the number of adherents to each projection style.

8

Compositional demands in two and three dimensions

The control of planes is the essence of Cézanne's achieveme...
I am not so much impressed with the tiny planes that are ke...
distinct and unblended in the familiar chromatic passages or
color modulations. It is the organization of the important
underlying planes – their rotation from static to dynamic
positions, the tensions, the space intervals between them, the
movement into depth and their inevitable return to the pictur...
plane – that is primarily important.

Erle Loran, *Cézanne's Composition* (19...

The role of representation in art

It is probably true that representation itself has never b...
the primary goal of art, even of representational art, p...
verse though that may seem in light of the preceding ch...
ters. It is certainly true that representational art is ne...
reducible to representation alone, even for the port...
painters or trompe-l'oeil artists. This point may well h...
been lost in my overall intent to establish an informat...
based categorization system for representational art in ter...
of station point options and consequent invariant de...
tion. This book is about alternatives for the representat...
of natural perspective; thus it is no doubt understanda...
that the role of representation in art has become somew...
exaggerated. Yet in some very important sense, repres...
tational art in both its cross-sectional and longitudinal ...
tories is the search for successful solutions to the probl...
of depicting three dimensions in two. This book dw...
on only one aspect of those solutions, the geometrical...

projective aspect, and does not touch on others equally susceptible to perceptual analysis. An obvious example is the range of techniques for the creation of a boundary in the light to the eye reflected from the picture: a black line, a colored line, or no line, the juxtaposition of two colors, the blending of two colors on the canvas or off, the addition of lighter pigment or darker, the thickening or thinning of pigment; the creation of shadows and highlights through penumbral blur of edge in light or color, the adjacency of different painted textures within a same colored area, the differential directionality of brushstrokes – to name only a few of the most obvious examples from painting. Another clearly perceptual aspect of painting, in the most limited sense of perceptual, is the use of color: the blending of color, the effects of complementary and contrasting colors, the engendering of "atmospheric effects" through color values, the breakdown of color masses into component colors blended, graded, or juxtaposed, the use of color for emphasis and to direct the attention – again, to name only a few of the more obvious aspects of color vital to art. The deployment of color, the creation of boundaries in the light through various means, the alternatives for depicting spatial layout of surfaces make up much of what is properly called "perceptual" in the world of representational art. A comprehensive book on the perception of art would cover them all. Yet it is likely that even in such a broad-ranging book, a vital component of representational art would still be omitted. The "art" component of representational art is not touched on by formal analyses of spatial layout, or by analyses of techniques for depiction of contour and the deployment of color.

Representational art necessarily entails a geometrical component as well as technique. It is nonsense to exclude these factors from the analysis of representational art, but neither one alone nor both together provides a sufficient matrix for the exposition of the *artistic* component of art. If statements like "That's not art; it's only a picture," and "That's not art; it's an empty exercise in technique" have any meaning, then that meaning does not lie obviously in the range of variables so far discussed.

What is and is not *Art*

For me to essay a determination of what is and is [not]
"Art" would be foolhardy, but it is perhaps not unr[ea]
sonable to espouse the criterion of another. Rudolph [Ar]
nheim recently remarked that the artistic componen[t is]
present in all things that evoke an aesthetic respons[e in]
the viewer. To paraphrase this statement in Gibson[ian]
terms, an "objet d'art" is an object that affords arti[stic]
experience or aesthetic appreciation. By this criterion[, of]
course, many things, manmade and in nature, are "ar[t"]
to varying degrees, but in art, the affordance of aesth[etic]
experience is an end deliberately and devoutly sought [by]
the skilled creator. It is the evidence of such deliberat[ion]
in the resulting works (and the response itself) that p[er]
mits the assignment of a created piece to the category [we]
call "art."

In Chapter 1 I wrote that two-dimensional represe[nta]
tional art, as treated in this volume, is always skilled lab[or,]
the end product of developed technique. Yet this is a b[ook]
about representation in art and not about the varieties [of]
technique. Still there is an aspect of depiction, separ[ate]
from both representation and technique, that must be [ex]
plored in order to develop an adequate categorization [net]
work even for the analysis of spatial layout in art. T[his]
aspect of depiction arises from the fact that representatio[nal]
art is never simply representational or it is not art in [the]
sense intended here. All pictorial representational ar[t is]
two-dimensional as well as three-dimensional in that [the]
artist depicts an object, scene, or event on or withi[n a]
bounded space of some shape. A representational pict[ure]
not only depicts surfaces in space but is itself a surfa[ce,]
relatively flat usually, bounded by a frame or other s[ur]
faces. This is true even for murals and tomb paintin[gs.]
Thus the artist is subject to two-dimensional compositio[nal]
demands as well as to three-dimensional concerns. I h[ave]
dealt extensively with options available to the artist for
depiction of three-dimensional spatial layout in two [di]
mensions, but have not yet touched on the compositio[nal]
component of two-dimensional spatial layout.

Two-dimensional spatial layout

By two-dimensional compositional concerns I mean the artist's consideration of the flat pattern or appearance of a single object or figure, of several figures together, and/or of all figures in the composition relative to the surround. I believe that in all representational art worthy of the name, at least the first of these problems of appearance is a matter for concern. It is certainly not true that all three are present in all styles. Nor is it true that all styles of representational art give equal attention to the problems of two-dimensional appearance of pattern on the picture surface. Some styles seem to be predominantly representational, to be concerned mainly with the representation of the subject matter of the picture; other styles are heavily shaped by a dominant artistic interest in the creation of surface pattern. I believe that it is possible to use the relative degree of emphasis on two- and three-dimensional composition to further elaborate the categorization network for artistic style. Of course, categorization of art styles as primarily two- or three-dimensional is by no means an undertaking in formal analysis in the sense that categorization by geometry is. Nevertheless, taking the two together provides a much fuller examination of the problems and solutions in the area of spatial layout in representational art.

Before attempting a categorization of styles into those primarily two- and three-dimensional, it will be useful to consider briefly some of the components of two-dimensional pattern organization of concern to artists, art critics, and art historians. No attempt at comprehensiveness will be made, and no pretense of general acceptance of terminology is intended. Schools of writing on art differ greatly one from another; so too does the terminology employed and the "concepts" valued. For my purposes some principles of pattern organization from Gestalt perceptual psychology will be of use as well as some concepts borrowed from the art historians. In Gestalt psychology, a pattern is said to be organized, to have "good form," according to the principles or laws of simplicity, proximity, area, symmetry, good continuation, closedness, and common fate.

Thus, according to these principles, a set of elements sho
be grouped perceptually to make the simplest form, so
adjacent elements are seen to belong to the same fig
to maximize symmetry, and so on. Not too long ag
wrote the following in a criticism of Rudolf Arnhei
Gestalt theory of the perception of art:

But even as a theory of representation, Gestalt theory fai
soon as one goes beyond the individual exemplar. Any si
painting can be described in terms of the principles of org
zation employed therein; but a catalogue of paintings so anal
gives us nothing but endless checklists of laws present and abs
Of course, these could provide a sort of . . . articulation m
of painting which might . . . considerably advance our un
standing of similarities and differences among individual p.
ings. But it will not give us Egyptian art compared to
contrasted with that of the Japanese. It will not provide us
an organizational framework for discussing the incredibl
versity of existing art styles around the world. At least, I c
think it will. (Hagen 1980b: 24–5)

Or so I thought at the time. I did not see then that
Gestalt principles of organization could be instrument
describing the two-dimensional appearances of pictures
even in evaluating the weight of pattern organizatior
lative to that of representation in a particular renditio
style of pictorial rendering. But now I believe they c

The Gestalt laws of organization are well known to m
so a very brief reminder of their operation here sho
suffice. The law of simplicity refers to the fact tha
several possible arrangements of elements into a patt
the simplest will be the one ordinarily perceived (Fig. 8
The law of proximity dictates that elements close toge
spatially will be seen as belonging to one figure; the
of symmetry that elements symmetrically arranged wi
perceived as figure. By the law of good continuation,
ments arranged in a simple form or in part of a sir
form will be seen as continuing that form and belon;
to it; and, by the law of common fate, elements in unif
orientation to the axes of the available space will be
as belonging to a unitary form (Fig. 8.2). It must nc
forgotten that these laws combine in ordinary form
ception and they do so as well in the perception of t

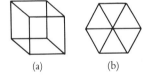

(a)   (b)

*Figure 8.1. The operation of the
Gestalt Law of Simplicity. (After
Julian E. Hochberg,* Perception, *2d
ed. © 1978:137–8. Reprinted by
permission of Prentice-Hall,
Englewood Cliffs, N.J.)*

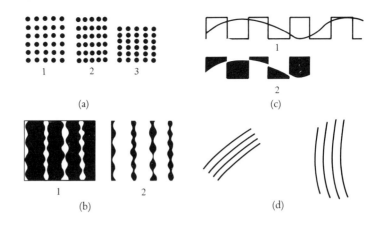

Figure 8.2. Gestalt Laws: (a)
proximity, (b) symmetry, (c) good
continuation, (d) common fate.
(After Julian E. Hochberg,
Perception, 2d ed. © 1978:
pp. 137–8. Reprinted by permission
of Prentice-Hall, Englewood Cliffs,
N.J.)

dimensional form in pictures. The perceptual laws will be
better understood in light of certain terms and concepts
from art history.

Some two-dimensional concepts from the field of art

The first and most critical of these concepts is taken from
Erle Loran's analysis, *Cézanne's Composition* (1963); this is
the "picture format." He writes that the picture format is
a term used with reference to the shape or proportions of
the picture plane, and that a picture format may be rectangular, square, circular, triangular, and so on. "A well-
organized picture must be a self-sufficient and closed unit
within a specific frame or format" (p. 17). Loran's implication of the universality of this principles ignores the existence of objets d'art like Egyptian tomb art and the cave
art of the African Bushmen and the Ice Age artists of what
is now France and Spain. Nevertheless, where there is a
frame or even some physical boundary for the painting
surface, then the format concept is relevant to the problem
of two-dimensional form; where there is not, then there
remains the problem of the determination of the appearance of a single figure and of the flat-pattern appearance
of several figures together without reference to the frame
of the space. Where format is relevant, the concept of
negative space assumes importance. Negative space is the
space between the positive volumes, or more properly,

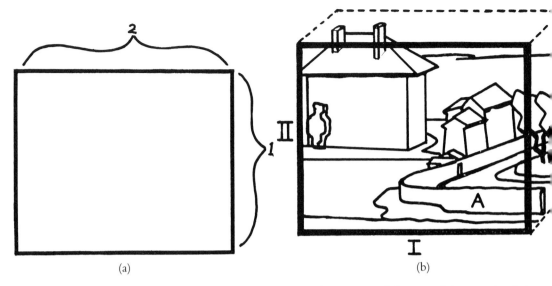

(a)   (b)

Figure 8.3. Negative space between the forms of the solids and the format. (a) The picture plane and the picture format. (b) Negative space and the "picture box." (From Loran 1963:18.)

between the two-dimensional forms of depicted solids, a●
between the forms of the solids and the format. Both
these instances of negative space are illustrated in Figu
8.3.

Aspects of appearance that rely on the interaction
multiple forms together are, again from Loran, two-d
mensional movement, rising and falling movements, line
rhythm, and tensions between planes and axes. Concep
that may be applied to the analysis of single forms a
linear rhythms and tensions within the object. (See Figu
8.4 for examples.)

Gestalt principles and concepts from art criticism

Any art work on a two-dimensional surface is subject
Gestalt analysis insofar as the problem of *form* is releva
to the analysis. Gestalt laws specifically address the pro
lem of form perception. If they have any weakness of utili
in this regard, it is that they deal specifically with t
problem of which elements in a display will be seen
belonging together, and do not deal directly with the iss
of the perception of elements *not* grouped together by t
laws. One must reason on the basis of the artistic conce
of "tension" resulting from failures to apply the rules a
from laws placed in opposition to each other.

Essentially, the Gestalt principles address the questi

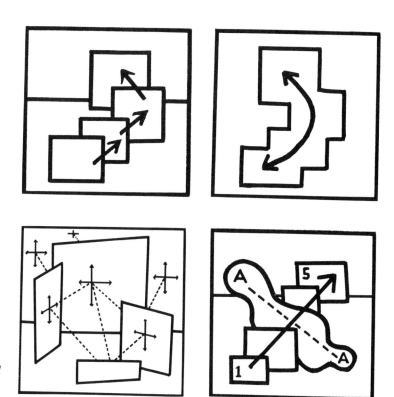

Figure 8.4. Types of interaction of forms together on a two-dimensional surface. (From Loran 1963:21–3.)

of what elements will be seen grouped together as a single form and why, while the more traditionally artistic concepts deal with the facts of appearance after perceptual organization. For example, Figure 8.4a taken from Loran illustrates the operation of the law of closure in the creation of the four individual units, the laws of proximity and common fate in the grouping of the elements into left and right pairs, the law of common fate again in the separation of the "horizon" line from any of the four elements, and the law of symmetry in a reversal of the ordinary application of the law. The picture is not symmetrical: the left-hand pair of elements bear a spatial relation of the one to the other different from that of the right-hand pair, and each is different from the other with respect to the format. It is this lack of symmetry, this creation of balance through proportional alteration of the elements relative to the horizon and to the format, that creates what Loran refers to as tension between the axes. Whatever their weaknesses, the Gestalt Laws of Organization still provide the best tool in perceptual psychology for understanding the variety two-dimensional compositional techniques, just as g ometry provides the best tool for the analysis of thre dimensional representation.

Some art styles emphasize the two-dimensional aspec of composition, space filling, while others primarily er phasize presentation of three-dimensional solids in spac It bears repeating that all art worthy of the name necessari involves attention to both two- and three-dimensior composition, and two-dimensional compositional analy enlightens, to some degree, the "art" component of re resentational art. I have said that two- and three-dime sional compositional concerns may be differentia weighted in a particular exemplar or style of depictic and that the relative degree of dominance of the two pr vides a useful elaboration of the geometrical matri analysis of the representational component. To illustr this, several styles exhibiting a relatively heavy empha on either two- or three-dimensional composition will presented with various examples of each.

Styles emphasizing two-dimensional composition

Four styles will be presented to illustrate depiction mo that show an emphasis on the two-dimensional com nents of artistic construction. Two of these, Egyptian and Northwest Coast Indian art, are familiar from previous three-dimensional analysis; two of them are r Romanesque manuscript illuminations and Cubism.

Egyptian art

In Chapter 6, I argued that Egyptian art depicted obje of different types in certain conventional ways: inanim objects nearly always from the side, animals from the s or top depending on which "view" reveals the most formation about the creature, and humans, birds, and c tain animals from a mixture of viewpoints. I argued that the picture plane in Egyptian art is always conceiv of as parallel to the planes of the objects depicted. T parallelism gave a very slender slice of the world ind

for portrayal, and necessitated certain depiction techniques
to cope with it. One of the logical outcomes is shown in
Figure 8.5, a very late limestone relief: The contents of the
tray on the pedestal, the bread, the two ducks, the shrub-
bery are all tilted forward into the picture plane itself
through the use of an additional station point – in this case,
a bird's eye view. But what is of interest here is not the
devices by which various aspects of objects in depth were
portrayed, but rather the way in which those aspects were
placed on the surface itself. It is clear that symmetry – in

the sense of reflective symmetry across the tray top, iterative symmetry in the case of the hands of the figur dominates this segment of the relief. The areas across wh the principles of symmetry are applied, across which ments are balanced, are often relatively small segment the whole (wall, tomb face). Elements are created w great attention to the appearance of several figures gether, occasional attention to the appearance of a sin element or figure, and little attention to the form of elements relative to a format, to the boundary of the pain surface. One example of design with attention to the r of the format was shown in Figure 7.3, but such examp occur very infrequently.

An excellent example of a painting, rather than re work, that shows the dominance of two-dimensional co position in Egyptian art is the Deir El Bersheh coffir the Museum of Fine arts in Boston (Fig. 7.2.). Althou there is no such thing as format in the Western sense c frame or cut canvas, the Egyptian artist certainly structu the two-dimensional appearance of the elements with gr attention to forms, especially those relatively close toget in the composition. Moreover, certain design elemer like the hieroglyphic border above the heads of the figu in the left-hand detail of the coffin design, as well as gray strip beneath their feet and running perpendicula between the large figure and the vase, do serve as forr for small segments of the composition. Certain structu tensions are played out against this mock format. The agonal thrust of the staff is brought into sharp relief this framing, while the strong vertical and horizontal a of the vases, jars, and table are further reinforced by perpendicularity of the mock format lines.

That the Egyptian artist was quite concerned with form of one element relative to another is evident in treatment of the two jars and their immediate surrou (Fig. 7.2). The striking symmetry of the tall vase on left is highlighted and iterated in the symmetry of negative space between the vase form and the format; symmetry of the brazier on the right is deliberately set by negative shapes that do *not* repeat the simple symme of the positive form. Attention to symmetry and to balar between positive and negative shape are hallmarks of classic Egyptian art, and the lack of a traditional Western format should not obscure this fact.

The dominance of two-dimensional design elements in Egyptian art, particularly of those that deal with the appearance of adjacent or nearby elements, is overwhelming. But two-dimensional dominance is also obvious in the treatment of single figures, as well as of several figures considered as a unit. I believe, however, that use of two-dimensional principles, such as axial symmetry in the depiction of a single vase, owed more to the Egyptian concern for clarity, in terms of information about invariant shape, than to aesthetic concerns for the appearance of the painting surface itself. That is, the form of single elements is determined by the representational intent of the artist, whereas the relations among forms, in this art style, are determined by the two-dimensional aesthetic intent. While both three- and two-dimensional concerns are always operative in any art style, it is clear that in Egyptian art, the latter are generally dominant.

Northwest Coast Indian art

The art of the Northwest Coast Indians is predominantly two dimensional and is divided by Holm (1974) into three categories of design: configurative, distributive, and expansive (Figs. 6.30-32). Configurative designs are determined mainly by interest in the appearance of the single figure, while expansive and distributive designs reflect the artist's interest in the figure relative to the format – what Holm has called "space-filling" concerns. Since Indian art almost never treats more than one figure at a time, the appearance of one figure relative to another is almost never of interest. (The exceptions to this occur in certain visual puns, where more than one animal is represented in the same space.)

Configurative designs, like that shown in Figure 6.29, are generally self-contained units constructed without regard for any other figure or for the space to be covered. This straightforward spread-eagle design is hardly characteristic of Indian art as it is determined by a principle of

Figure 8.6. Argillite platter representing a dragonfly. (Photograph by R.B. Inverarity.)

bilateral symmetry much simpler than the Indians usually employed. A far more characteristic example is shown in Figure 8.6. This composition, portraying a dragonfly, spreads the animal parts throughout the available field in a tightly controlled interplay between subject matter and format. Holm calls this type of design expansive; Boas calls it split-style. Organic regularities of the portrayed animal are preserved in a lawful manner, while the animal is split and its parts distributed across the available space. The extremely stylized elements of the portrayal, as well as the great balance and strong symmetry of the compositions, clearly support the argument that the highly characteristic split-style Indian art is a style dominated by concern both for the appearance of the individual figure in two dimensions and for the generation of that figure within the constraints of the format. Indian art is used to decorate plates, bowls, spoons, cups, doors, bracelets, boxes, and many other items, each with a different space to be covered and decorated. Indeed, one might almost say that the decorative component of this style considerably outweighs the representational component. This is particularly true in the distributive designs like that in Figure 6.31. Representational concerns are obvious in the regular invocation of the animal "symbols" (in Boas's terminology), and in the maintenance of the organic integrity of the creatures depicted, but it is clear that they do not dominate the style. In a very different mode this same argument can be made for manuscript painting of twelfth-century Europe.

Romanesque manuscript painting: twelfth century

Miriam Bunim (1970), in her excellent book on the depiction of spatial layout in medieval painting, argued quite convincingly that Romanesque illumination of the type presented in Figure 8.7 was dominated by two-dimensional or decorative concerns of the artist. She wrote:

In this type (of background painting), which may be designated as Romanesque, the picture plane is partitioned as in the stratified background, but the divisions have no implication, in form or color, of a naturalistic environment. Thus, the background has, like that of one color, a nonrepresentative character. The effect, however, is different, for, although the form of the background itself is, in a sense, abstract and ideal, it does not give the impression of unbounded space, because the divisions in the picture plane create a distinctly delimited, substantial, and vertical pictorial field. (1970: 86)

She argued that since illumination in the Middle Ages was primarily religious in content and was produced in monasteries, there was a strong tendency to preserve traditional forms and to concentrate on content rather than pictorial effect. The sanctity and remoteness of the depicted scenes rendered local and environmental details relatively unimportant, just as the unworldliness of the lives of the monk/artists diminished their interest in imitating the fe[a]tures of the everyday world in painting. Thus, Bunim sa[w] the development of nonrepresentational backgrounds consistent with the monastic view of life. Romanesq[ue] picture planes are partitioned into rectangles, bands, pane[ls] and combinations of vertical and horizontal bands. Figu[re] 8.7 shows two variations on the essential Romanesque for[m] – a picture plane with a rectangular subdivision, or pan[e] interrupting the enclosed area of the nonrepresentative u[ni]form surface. In *Allegory of Sowing and Reaping*, the pan[el] is set apart from the rest of the background by a chan[ge] in color; in *The Adoration of the Magi*, the effect of the pan[el] is highlighted by the addition of pattern into it.

There is no complex tridimensional spatial interrelationship, f[or] the figures remain on a plane in front of the paneled wall whi[ch] curtails any movement in depth. The freedom of moveme[nt] laterally, which the frequent overlapping of the frame (righ[t]) and the segmentation of the figures by the frame attest, indicat[es] the mutually independent although not discordant compositi[on] of the background and the action, an independence that is al[so] indicated by the fact that the background is neither the natu[ral] environment nor an ambient medium in which the action tak[es] place. (1940, p. 89)

Figure 8.7. Romanesque illuminations: (left) Allegory of Sowing and Reaping; *(right)* Adoration of the Magi.

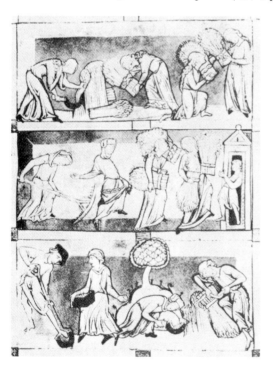

It is certainly true, and can be seen easily in Figure 8.7, that the action in these Romanesque paintings is not confined to the borders of the format in the sense that seems so necessary in more recent European painting. However, it does not follow necessarily that the background and the action are independent, as Bunim asserts. They are only independent relative to the more modern concept of format as impenetrable envelope. I believe it does greater justice to the medieval artist's sense of composition to say rather that these paintings explore the limits of figure and ground in a manner playful and unique to the time. Bunim is right that the colored panels provide controlled contrast to both the color and form of the backlighted figures, but she does not carry far enough her concept of background as focus and foil for figures. Colored panels and bands also highlight negative shape in a visually striking manner not possible with more complex backgrounds, and this interest in negative shape is further manifested in the placement and violation of offsetting borders, colored and patterned. Violations of borders are like violations of symmetry – they rivet the attention on the discordant element. In Figure 8.7b, the king's offering bowl becomes the focus of the entire picture. This focusing is obviously the product of the operation and violation of two-dimensional organizational principles. Because the border, by the laws of good continuation and common fate, is seen to be continuous behind the arm and bowl of the King, the arm and bowl in turn are thrown into relief in front of it.

It is clear that this technique of allowing movements of figures across the framing elements of the composition also has certain three-dimensional consequences. Where the hand and the arm of the king are thrown into relief, they are thrown out into the space in front of the picture plane. The frame defines the locus of the plane, so any object depicted in front of the frame is necessarily in front of the projection plane as well. This thrusting of the figure out in front of the picture plane involves the viewer of the picture in the action of the piece itself. It invokes a special kind of intimacy, a special kind of observer experience not found in the tightly bounded, strictly objet d'art, kind of painting. This was presumably a monastic intention insofar

as these paintings were intended to inspire in their putativ
viewers a sense of reverence for a sacred presence.

The spatial consequences of the technique should no
blind the observer to the primarily decorative componen
of this art style. Decorativeness is evidenced by the repe
itive use of certain stylized and highly two-dimension;
silhouette forms as well as by the almost obsessive intere;
in the use and abuse of symmetries, all against the defi
itively nonrepresentational background pointed out s
clearly by Bunim. I will return to the subject of Christia
manuscript painting in the next chapter since it provide
so clear an example of progressive experimentation wit
geometry in the arts.

Cubism

Cubism was a short-lived style in modern Western pain
ing that generated more commentaries than pictures b
far. There is little agreement on when the style begai
when it ended, and who qualifies as a bona fide cubi;
painter, but there is a great deal of rhetoric about the makeu
of the cubist style and the marks of a cubist painting. Son
of this rhetoric makes sense; some of it is completely ir
comprehensible even when the paintings described are i
front of one's nose. I shall take the analyses that are rel;
tively clear, subject them to one additional constraint, an
circumscribe a domain of style to be called cubist that i
I hope, accessible to the average museum goer. The cor
straint to be added to more conventional descriptions
cubism is that of realism; that is, in this analysis, the pain
ings of interest are those that are representational in th
sense presented in the first chapter. The representation;
character must be apparent to naive observers after a nc
unduly long exposure. If the painting does not seem, with
out a great deal of written text accompanying it, to be
picture of anything, then that painting is not subject to th
analysis presented here. Those familiar with the develop
ment of cubism will see immediately that this criterio
cuts the size of the available body of work to be discusse
substantially. Nevertheless, it is the case that, particularl
between the years 1907 and 1914, painters like Picasso an

Figure 8.8. Les Demoiselles
d'Avignon *by Pablo Picasso, 1907.*
(Collection: The Museum of
Modern Art, New York. Acquired
through the Lillie P. Bliss Bequest.)

Braque, who developed cubism in the footsteps of Cézanne, very frequently created works of art both representational and cubist in form (Fig. 8.8).

Les Demoiselles d'Avignon, painted by Picasso in 1907, is
considered by many to be the first of the paintings in the
new cubist style. Its revolutionary quality, according to
Edward Fry, the art historian (1966), is that it broke away
from classical norms for the human figure and from the
illusionism of perspective. Normal anatomical proportions
were disregarded, anatomical components were reduced
to geometrical forms, and the human image was reordered
at will. Multiple viewpoints were combined into single
forms, multiple images into a single painting.

It is important to realize that whatever the intention of
the cubist artists in the early years, the effect of multiple
viewpoints was not one of objects seen in the round. This
is surprising in light of the explicit acknowledgement that
multiple-station-point images alone were capable of capturing the experience of a sequence of perceptions and
placing them on canvas. Indeed, the opposite was the case,

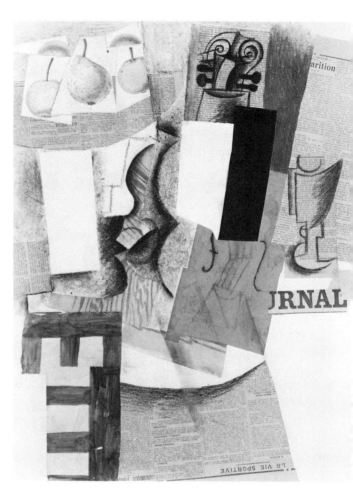

Figure 8.9. "Still Life with Violin and Fruit" by Pablo Picasso, 1913. (Philadelphia Museum of Art: The A.E. Gallatin Collection: catalogue number, 52-61-106.)

and this effect of flattening the space onto the picture surface itself became a hallmark of later cubist painting, as realism disappeared. Picasso's "Still Life with Violin and Fruit" (Fig. 8.9) bears witness to this fact. The multiple images of the violin do not combine to produce the sense of a wholistic object; they remain unintegrated representationally. Their function, unlike the multiple views of the Northwest Coast Indian artists, is essentially two dimensional. There is no notion of preserving organic integrity, the completeness of the three-dimensional form. There is not even any sense of experimentation with the limits of the violations of continuity of line or sequentiality of views. Cubist paintings "progressed" very quickly from the very loose organic integrity of pictures like Figure 8.9 to the visually incomprehensible works like that of Figure 8.10.

Figure 8.10. "Still Life with Violin and Guitar" by Pablo Picasso, 1913. (Philadelphia Museum of Art: The Louise and Walter Arensberg Collection: 50-134-170.)

Picasso's "Still life with Violin and Guitar," also painted in 1913. This kind of painting reminds one forcibly of the distributive designs of the Northwest Coast Indian painters. The subcomponents of the piece are placed on the surface with regard only to two-dimensional layout, and the representational quality is lost. Organic integrity in the broadest sense of the term has not been respected by the painter.

I think that the lack of the development of a cubist technique that preserved representational character while exploring the limits of geometrical analysis of form and multiple images arose from a fundamental ambivalence in

Figure 8.11. (above) photograph of Daniel Henry Kahnweiler *(From Fry 1966.) (right)*Portrait of Daniel Henry Kahnweiler *by Pablo Picasso, 1910. (Courtesy of the Art Institute of Chicago.)*

the intentions of the artists themselves. Did they wish t depict spatial layout or did they not? In early works, th technique called "passage," introduced by Cézanne, is use successfully to depict space in a nontraditional way. Pas sage is a series of more or less intersecting planes that ru together and seem to be simultaneously in front of an behind each other. In perceptual terms, the technique cap italizes on ambiguities of information. In the painting i Fig. 8.11, passage is primarily in service of the two-d mensional composition. The small planes flip back an forth in space creating a surface both flat and dynamic. A the same time, additional representational character is lo through blurring the organic integrity of the figure. Th

Figure 8.12. (above) photograph of Ambroise Vollard (From Fry 1966.) (right) Portrait of Ambroise Vollard by Pablo Picasso, 1909– 1910. (Hermitage, Leningrad.)

picture truly pushes the limits of the representational function of passage. Another, similar, portrait by Picasso, on
the other hand, shows the astonishing effectiveness of the
technique for depicting spatial layout (Fig. 8.12). This portrait of Ambroise Vollard, also by Picasso, is quite incred-
ibly lifelike. The planar composition technique formalizes
the construction two-dimensionally in a manner unprec-
edented in Western European art; at the same time it heralds
a new technique for the realistic pictorial description of
objects extended in space. The similarity between the cub-

ist portrait and the photograph results from one of th
most important – and best realized – insights in the histor
of painting: the depiction of volume does not depend o
surface, and that of surface does not depend on line. Despi
the effectiveness of such a painting, exploring the limi
of this technique for the depiction of three-dimension
space did not much take the fancy of the cubists. The
played with it sporadically, but the bulk of their work an
the clear trend of the times was in the direction of tw
dimensional exploration.

This strong dominance of two-dimensional concerns ov
the obvious potentialities of three-dimensional cubism aris
as much from the cubists' interest in geometry as fro
their ambivalence of intention. As Leon Werth wrote i
an eloquent 1910 essay on Picasso:

I too could invent a few definitive phrases on the art that mu
give the structure of things and must not confine itself to catchir
in a vague tremor the appearance and emotion of the momen
the eye's whim. I could say, too, that true decorative nobili
is a necessary consequence of the search for structures ma
manifest on the canvas by the essential planes discovered by t
painter's mind. I could add that, instead of reproducing in the
photographic or tactile appearances the movement of the mass
in a landscape or the play of the muscles in a body, what matte
is to perceive their laws, and that only the figures of geometr
can yield this without lying (Fry 1966: 57)

I do not think that any cubist ever succeeded in discoverin
the laws of "movement of the masses in a landscape" c
even of the play of the muscles of the body, but I do believ
that volumes can be and were analyzed into essential simp
structures and various geometrical forms like rectangle
triangles, trapezoids, and so on. I think this was an astor
ishing rediscovery of an old concept of form, of forn
recovered from the formlessness of the impressionists an
pointillists, and that this discovery was fueled by the u
precedented interest of mathematicians, philosophers, an
scientists in geometry around the turn of the century.
seems almost inevitable that these forces would have con
bined to strip cubism of its representational character, a
though it does not seem inevitable to me that the successf

development of that aspect of cubism will never take place. I believe that it will. Subject to a developed understanding of the constraints on the selection and combination of images in a multiple image composition, Rudolf Arnheim's promissory remark of twenty-five years ago will become true. Arnheim vowed that with familiarity, the multiple station point images of the cubists would come to seem realistic to us. They will. That they have not is an accident of history.

It could also be the case that the cubists fell victim to the rhetoric to which their stylistic innovations were subjected. More vacuous commentary was never written. Perhaps, after reading passages like the one below, first published in 1912, the cubists simply lost heart for the representational endeavor, or perhaps they believed their own press.

Let the picture imitate nothing; let it nakedly present its raison d'être. We should indeed be ungrateful were we to deplore the absence of all those things – flowers, or landscape, or faces – whose mere reflection it might have been. Nevertheless, let us admit that the reminiscence of natural forms cannot be absolutely banished; not yet, at all events. An art cannot be raised to the level of a pure effusion at the first step. (Gleizes and Metzinger 1966).

On that note, let us look at several styles that did not even attempt to reach the level of pure effusion.

Styles emphasizing three-dimensional composition

Four rather different styles have been selected again to illustrate what I mean by the dominance of three-dimensional artistic concerns over two-dimensional composition. All art worthy of the name shares this duality of concerns. Representational art is never only representational, but many styles are largely representational. This distinction is by no means a dichotomy; it is only a question of emphasis. Of the four styles illustrated here, two of them, Japanese and Renaissance art, are familiar from previous chapters, and two of them, Ice Age cave art and the art of the Bushmen, are not.

Renaissance art

To illustrate that vast domain known as Western po:
Renaissance, premodern, art I have chosen several pair
ings dated fairly close to the dawn of the Renaissanc
Observation of paintings done quite early in the Rena
sance and those done a bit later reveals in dramatic fashio
the transition from a style dominated by two-dimension
concerns to one primarily three dimensional. Figure 8.
shows two human figure paintings, one of the Madon
and Child and one of St. Lucy, by artists born at the ve
beginning of the Renaissance, Cosimo Tura and Frances
del Cossa. The similarity in composition, although not,
course, in the treatment of the figure, between these pair
ings and the Romanesque illuminations discussed above
striking. The same use of background as a decorative fo
and the dramatic exploitation of color to set off one for
against another is apparent in both styles. The strong sym
metries and balanced violations of those symmetries a
also reminiscent of the earlier style. The artistic facto

Figure 8.13. (left) "Madonna and Child" by Cosimo Tura (1430–1495). (right) "St. Lucy" by Francesco del Cossa (c.1435–1477) (National Gallery of Art, Washington, D.C.)

rather than the chronology, that pushes them into a transition stage is the treatment of the human figures, particularly those of the Child and St. Lucy. These figures have a solidity, a roundedness, a feeling of plastic volume generally missing from the earlier style. It is this quality that introduces the dominance of three-dimensionality, even in portrait works, that characterizes Western post-Renaissance art. The illustration in Fig. 8.14 should make this convincingly clear. Leonardo's background for "Portrait of a Woman" is certainly three-dimensional in the impression it gives of indefinitely extended space but it is his treatment of the lady that makes this a three-dimensional painting. This painting also serves as a forcible reminder that backgrounds, however three-dimensional they might be, also, necessarily, create the two-dimensional patterning or framing for the central figure – although perhaps seldom as effectively as in this picture of Leomardo's.

In paintings that are not portraits, it is even easier to appreciate the strongly three-dimensional quality of tra-

Figure 8.14. "Portrait of a Woman" by Leonardo da Vinci (1452–1519). (National Gallery of Art, Washington, D.C., Ailsa Mellon Bruce Fund, 1967.)

227 THREE-DIMENSIONAL COMPOSITION STYLES

ditional Western art. Figure 8.15 is a detail from *The Adoration of the Shepherds* by Giorgione, c. 1498. Giorgione has laid out an entire landscape stretching back into space. He gives the impression of recreating for the observer what would be seen if one were to "stand" where the artist stood, despite the metaphorical quality of that stance. Actually, the Renaissance observer would have required very tall scaffolding and good binoculars to see this scene but such conventions of composition rarely bother the initiated. It is well to remember that even strongly three-dimensional styles are representational within a context of cultural convention. It is as great a mistake to think of such paintings as these as photographic as it is to think of photographs as nonconventional. The Bruegel shown in Figure 8.16 exhibits this same quality of apparent creation of authentic events. Again the artist has pictured a scene to be

Figure 8.15. The Adoration of the Shepherds *by Giorgione (c. 1477–1510). (National Gallery of Art, Washington, D.C. Samuel H. Kress Collection.)*

experienced, not just a pattern to be admired. The painting is certainly an object to be appreciated for its form, color, and balance, but more, it is a landscape to be explored, a place to be as well as a thing to look at. It is this component of pictorial art that changes the emphasis from two- to three-dimensional composition – the shift of focus from the picture itself to the contents of that picture.

Japanese art

This same component, the artist's and viewer's interest in the depicted contents, makes yamato-e art also a predominantly three-dimensional style, particularly the narrative scrolls: illustrations intended to illuminate a story. Figure 8.17 is a segment from the thirteenth century scroll *Heiji monogatari emaki*, the Heiji War scroll. This segment shows a scene partly inside the Sanjo Palace and partly outside,

Figure 8.16. The Harvest *by Pieter Bruegel the Elder, 1565. (All Rights Reserved, The Metropolitan Museum of Art. Rogers Fund, 1919.)*

Figure 8.17. (top) Heiji monogatari emaki (*Tale of the Heiji War scroll*). *Middle thirteenth century, artist unknown.* (*Courtesy, Museum of Fine Arts, Boston, Fenollosa-Weld Collection.*)

Figure 8.18. (bottom) Heiji War scroll: *the carriage is away from the palace. This is a time further along in the scroll than Fig. 8.17.* (*Courtesy*

in which the rebel Minamoto general orders the ex-Emperor into the waiting carriage. The technique is incredible: finely drawn, yet impressionistic in its feel of an activity level and passion so great that one figure almost runs right into the others. It is a wonderful scene two-dimensionally with its severe blocked masses of plain color setting off the wonderfully complex yet surprisingly repetitive central area. But its truly engrossing character is in the story being told, in the events unfolding on this scroll. There is so much happening, so much to look at and experience. This picture is a painting, but it is incontrovertibly a painting of an event that spectators can share centuries after the historical incident. Figure 8.18, a scene from further on in the scroll when the carriage is well away from the palace and surrounded by abductors all ready to continue to do battle, should convince those not familiar with the story of the power of the painting to command and direct the viewer's attention to the represented event rather than to the painting as object in itself. A point that must be made here is subtle but extremely important: Representational paintings that are primarily three-dimensional inform about their subjects in a commanding, but very special way. It is not merely a question of transmitting knowledge about an object, person, or event; these paintings transmit knowledge of a certain type – the tacit knowledge of perceptual experience. All representational paintings succeed as representations because they carry perceptual information about the subjects they picture, but not all paintings carry the same feeling for the spectator of "being there." Orthogonal pictures almost never carry this feeling. They lend themselves to a degree of formalism seldom found in Affine or Projective styles. Orthogonal styles approach what seems to be almost an abstraction rather than an extraction of information about their contents.

The explanation for this perceptual difference among the styles is simple and does not require that Affine and Projective styles be invested with special visual validity. It is simply the case that in the normal experience of the ordinary cluttered environment, objects are many surfaced and those many surfaces are at many different angles relative to the observer. This is true outside the laboratory, true for the binocular observer sitting comfortably in chair looking around or strolling through the environmer Most Affine and Projective styles retain and indeed er phasize this multiangular aspect of ordinary perceptual e perience, but it is not, as is often suggested, a necessa consequence of either style. It is important to rememb that the descriptive geometry has no necessary implicatio for the relative degrees of emphasis on representation on pattern.

Another common belief with little empirical support that strongly representational styles reflect great cultur advancement and, therefore, must have appeared rath late in the history of art or in the history of a people. T issue of cultural advancement is too complicated for a s perficial treatment here but it will be illuminating to e amine briefly the painting styles of two groups of so-call "primitive" people. The first group of people, in sever senses of the word first, are the Ice Age cave dwellers what is now France and Spain, and the second are t Bushmen who lived until fairly recently in what is nc South Africa. Both styles are strongly three-dimensior with some surprising two-dimensional aspects.

Ice Age cave art

Some of the best known of the Ice Age cave art com from Altamira, Spain. The Altamira paintings were do on the ceiling of a chamber approximately twenty yar long and ten yards wide; the ceiling is about five feet hi on the average. On fifteen yards of the ceiling a group about twenty-five animals was painted. Seven of these a imals are shown in Figure 8.19. The paintings are assum to date from 10,000 to 12,000 years ago (although sor scholars say 30,000 years) and have been assigned to t Magdalenian (final) division of the Upper Paleolithic ag (No one really knows how old they are except that th are very old indeed.) Nearly all of the existing copies the paintings are copies of the original copies made by Ab Breuil in the early 1900s; these copies were painted in viv reds, browns, blacks, and blues. It is assumed that t copies are relatively faithful, but it should not be forgott

Figure 8.19. Ice Age cave paintings from Altamira, Spain. (After Fairservis 1955.)

that there are inevitable differences between paintings ma
with watercolor or chalk on paper and those made w
ancient pigments on rough stone. The best evidence of
fidelity of the copies is that the cave paintings themsel
were called fakes upon discovery eighty years ago becau
of their aesthetic effect and technical proficiency, both
ident in Abbé Breuil's copies.

Emphasis on two-dimensional composition requires
tention to the form created by a single figure, to the fl
pattern appearance of several figures together, or to
appearance of the figure or figures in the composition r
ative to the format. Cave art has no format: The edges
the ceiling of the chamber were not used to set off or fra
the figures. There is also no evidence that the artist(s) e
considered the visual relationship of one figure relative
another; there appears to be no evident grouping of
figures. The animals are placed in a roughly equilate
triangle spreading across the ceiling with no evidence
deliberation in the placement. The only evidence of artis
concern for two-dimensional patterning comes from c
tain aspects of stylization, for example, in the treatme
of the horns, tails, and hooves, and from the elegance a
economy of line used in the figures. The strength of t
latter point, however, rests heavily on the fidelity of
copies. Regardless, it clearly seems safe to categorize th
paintings as primarily representational in effect. This
evident from the range and types of postures selected
depiction: Bison are depicted standing, turning, bellowir
and dead or lying down. It is evident in the capturing
what I have called elsewhere the fleeting or momenta
appearance of the subject, in the bellowing bull with
arched neck, in the leaping boar with the legs spread. I
also the case that the artists frequently used what mig
be called a semi-relief technique, either carving into
rock itself or using natural stone protrusions and hollo
to emphasize anatomical variations like the curve of
shoulder or flank. Even in the few examples that I can f
of cave art that does show attention to two-dimensio
composition, like the examples shown in Figure 8.20 fro
the Cueva del Civil, the representational plasticity of
figures is evident in the fluidity of the depicted motic

Cueva del Civil
Province Castellon

Detail from various
Spanish Levant sources

Figure 8.20. Cave art from the Spanish Levant, Cueva del Civil. (After Fairservis 1955.)

Nevertheless, the Cueva del Civil paintings clearly reveal a distinguished sensitivity to the relations among depicted figures, and the playful variations on the stylized figures show an unusual degree of interest in single as well as relative figural patterning. It is this interplay between a high degree of stylization and the kinetic plasticity of the subject, particularly of the human figure, that also characterizes the cave art of the Bushmen.

The art of the Bushmen

Figure 8.21, an early nineteenth-century rock painting, shows the same kind, if not the same degree, of interaction between stylization of the figure and variation in stylization as the ancient Cueva del Civil painting. This painting shows several variations on the figure, as well as foreshortening, profiles, rear views, and squatting, bending, leaping, sitting, and standing. The figures are highly stylized without appearing stiff or stilted. With little interior detail and no

Figure 8.21. Early nineteenth-century rock painting attributed to the Bushmen. (From Bleek 1930.)

use of shadows they nevertheless appear in the round. T technical proficiency is amazing.

In South Africa there are well over a thousand sites which rock art has been found, most of it attributable the Bushmen who used to live near them. These are the products of currently living Bushmen nor of the Bar past or present. According to Willcox (1963), it is vᴇ unlikely that any of the paintings could be more than 2,0 years old because of exposure to the elements, and soᴍ of them are certainly more recent because they depict E ropeans. Most of the paintings show people and anim hunting, dancing, eating, cooking, and fighting. There some inanimate objects, and there are scenes as well single figures. A complication in this kind of art not oft found in others is that present-day analysts have consᵀ erable difficulty distinguishing what is a true "scene" frᴏ what is simply a random placement of objects, and determing the number of artists involved in a "compo tion." There are sometimes many layers of paint put doᴡ over many years. Of course, later artists may have bᴇ

236 COMPOSITIONAL DEMANDS

"finishing" or adding to earlier compositions in a deliberate manner, but we have no evidence one way or another. Bushmen interviewed about some of the paintings in the nineteenth century often told stories about paintings that incorporated most and sometimes all of the elements of the apparent composition, but it could easily be the case that the stories were determined by the paintings and not vice versa. We can really only guess with the aid of internal evidence. It seems from the coherence of the composition and the similarity of treatment of the figures that Figure 8.22 is a single effort, or perhaps two. Figure 8.23, on the other hand, shows a painting that appears to be a mélange

237 THREE-DIMENSIONAL COMPOSITION STYLES

of efforts all occupying the same surface more or l•
haphazardly.

Whatever the degree of integrity of the various co•
positions, what is so striking about these paintings is th•
strongly representational quality. The interest of the a
ist(s) does not lie primarily in the elements of pattern
the symmetries of form, but rather in the clear depicti
of plastic solids. The relations among figures of prima
interest to these artists are three-dimensional, like th•
involved in hunting, fighting and dancing, not two •
mensional. However, this art style is not oblivious to tw
dimensional attitudes. Indeed, the very prevalent iterati•
with variation so common to this style is an unmistaka•
expression of awareness of the possibilities of flat for.
The three bending figures at the top of Figure 8.21 spe•
to this point eloquently. Bushmen art is primarily rep•
sentational, it may even be primarily illustrative of my•
as was often avowed in early commentaries on this a•
but it is not solely representational. Many of the paintin•
are the work of artists in the sense of the word that imp•
skill and training –they are not random scribblings of a•
ateurs, although many of those exist as well. But the effo•
of children and amateurs are not art and will be left •
analysis in the last chapter of this book. The works of t•
Bushmen artists, like the works of all accomplished artis•
reflect the interplay between representation and patte•
between depiction and decoration.

A categorization scheme

This brief illustration of the possibility of categorizing re•
resentational art styles in terms of the relative degree
dominance of two- and three-dimensional compositio•
demands concludes the presentation of the elements n•
essary to the categorization scheme that is the heart of t•
book. We have seen above that art styles can be categoriz•
in terms of the geometry descriptive of their image ge•
eration system, in terms of the station point option select•
by the artists within the style, and in terms of the invaria•
information available to the artist for depiction. With t•
addition of the depiction-versus-pattern component, t•

scheme is stretched a bit to accommodate the artistic as well as the geometrical, the aesthetic as well as the representational. In Chapter 9 an effort will be made to categorize as many of the world's art styles as are accessible to the nonprofessional in the world of art. I hope that the distinctions I do and do not observe will not do great violence to those made in the field of art proper. I will end this chapter as I began it by saying again that this is a perceptual categorization scheme, not an artistic or an historical one. The contrasts among these three ways of categorizing art should be illuminating, not irritating.

9

The categorization system

Writers on art have two ways of approaching a picture: the work can be described or it can be interpreted. But no one would pretend that a description of a picture, accurate and clear as it may be, can bring out all of its functional, symbolic, sociological, historical, and spiritual content, especially when it is a religious work, ritual monument, mythical scene, or a symbol, as is so often the case in the earliest artistic creations. On the other hand, the interpretation of the function or spiritual content of a picture can go astray, leading to irresponsible speculation.

P. P. Kahane, *Ancient and Classical Art*, 1964

Scenes with many surfaces

Despite the excursions in Chapter 8 into what I hope was rather responsible interpretative speculation on the nature of composition, the categorization system presented here is primarily concerned with what might be called the mechanics of representation. As I argued in Chapter 5, the artist engaged in representational depiction has only a very limited number of physical station point options, and the appearance of the picture is largely a result of the selection among those options. The options involve the spatial relations between the original surface and the picture plane in terms of both angle and distance; that is, the dominant plane of each object depicted may be parallel to the picture plane or not, and the projection lines may be parallel or convergent. Figure 9.1 provides a simple reminder of the appearance of those options that will be useful in the categorization that follows. Figure 9.1b shows a Similar

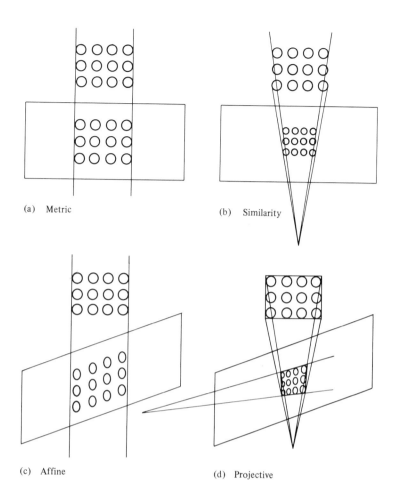

(a) Metric

(b) Similarity

(c) Affine

(d) Projective

Figure 9.1. (a) Metric, (b) Similarity, (c) Affine, and (d) Projective projections of twelve objects in space.

projection of a scene with parallel planes and a fairly close distance. If the distance between the object planes and the image plane is greatly increased, then, as in the first example, the projection lines become parallel and the projection will become Metric. If the object and image planes are *not* parallel, then the projection is either Affine, when the projective distance is at optical infinity, or Projective, when the distance is shorter, as shown in the third and fourth example.

These are useful models but they are very simple. They do not really address the fact that most representational pictures depict not one surface but many. We must consider the arrangement of *all* of these surfaces both relative to each other and relative to the picture plane. The scene itself may be organized so that the multiple surfaces are all arranged in rows in space or placed arbitrarily, and the

241   SCENES WITH MANY SURFACES

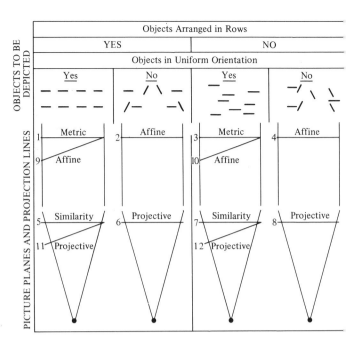

Figure 9.2. Twelve compositional options with objects ordered and not ordered, projection lines parallel or convergent, and planes parallel or intersecting.

dominant planes of each of those depicted surfaces can in various orientations relative to the picture plane. Consider, for example, possible depictions of eight peop There are twelve different compositional options to co sider, shown graphically in Figure 9.2. These options clude all of the depiction combinations of assuming obje to be arranged in rows or not, of assuming the objects to have the same identical orientation relative to the pictu plane, or not, and of assuming their projections to be w either parallel or convergent lines. When all the domina planes of the objects depicted have the same orientatio then they may all be parallel to the image plane, or n Before we consider the actual appearance of the worl art in terms of these options, a word about the concept "dominant object planes" is in order.

Dominant planes and characteristic aspects

Real world objects are not two dimensional cutouts, b voluminous solids. So, whenever I speak of an image pla parallel to or intersecting the object plane, I mean by "o ject plane" something that must be defined intuitively the most informative plane of the solid; that is, the tw dimensional form must "inform" the viewer about the shape of the three-dimensinal solid. But the determination of what is informative for shape is hardly a simple matter.

Consider, for example, the depiction of the human body, what is usually called the "figure" in art. The body can be arranged in space in an indefinitely large number of ways, and an indefinitely large number of hypothetical planes can be passed through each of these arrangements. Then, as we have seen, the image plane can be either frontal (parallel) or oblique (intersecting) to each of these subject planes. Figure 9.3 gives several examples of possible arrangements of the human body in space. The same variety of form depiction, in this case for birds, is given in Figure 9.4 a pair of six-fold screens from seventeenth-century Japan (Edo period). The multiplicity of aspect in this picture is almost photographic in its variety, although the composition certainly is not. It is clear from these two examples that the artist can generate a very large number of two-dimensional images of solid shapes.

The question the artist must answer, compositionally if

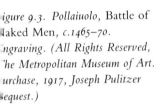

Figure 9.3. Pollaiuolo, Battle of Naked Men, c.1465–70. Engraving. (All Rights Reserved, The Metropolitan Museum of Art. Purchase, 1917, Joseph Pulitzer Bequest.)

Figure 9.4. Seventeenth-century Japanese screen: "Crows", Ido Period. (The Seattle Art Museum, Eugene Fuller Memorial Collection. Pair of sixfold screens in ink and lacquer on gold paper.)

not explicitly, is *which* of the possible subject planes is mo informative for the purposes of the composition, and do it remain so whether the image plane parallels or interse it. It is clear from the discussion in Chapter 7 on info mation in pictures that a purpose of the composition m or may not be the clear depiction of three-dimension shape, through either single or multiple views. Where *single* view for each object is selected (unlike Egyptian d pictions of humans), the views that give the most info mation about the spatial relationships among parts of objec are (a) a frontal section (separating front from back) throu the human body and through upright objects like trees and vases; (b) sagittal slice (separating left from right) through birds and most animals; (c) and a lateral (separating top from bottom) section through relatively flat creatures like lizards. Figure 9.5 illustrates the passing of these planes through each of these types of being. I argued in Chapter 6 in the analysis of Egyptian painting that "recognizability" as a major goal of depiction results in the attempt to rep-

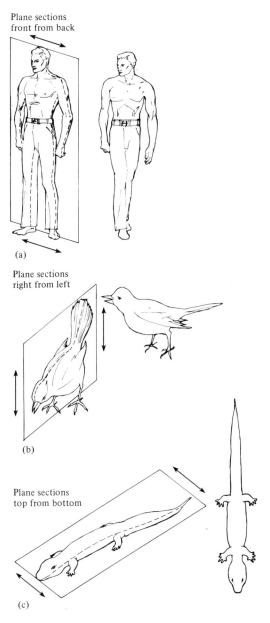

Plane sections
front from back

(a)

Plane sections
right from left

(b)

Plane sections
top from bottom

(c)

Figure 9.5. Frontal, saggital and lateral sections through beings of different types.

245   DOMINANT PLANES

resent these object types (or parts of objects like the huma figure in Egyptian art) in their "most characteristic a pects." Egyptian "semiprofiles" are fascinating example of a modified frontal slice for the depiction of human Northwest Coast Indian art provides a notable illustratic of the customary "rules" for depicting animals in sagitt split-style. The concept of "most characteristic aspect" clearly cultural, at least in the specifics of the renditior although the consistency across cultures with which sp cific aspects are selected is striking.

Despite the consistency, it is far easier to describe wh constitutes the most characteristic aspect of an object *aft* the fact than before. Several scholars have tried to defir the criterion of most characteristic aspect formally, wit varying degrees of success. Julian Hochberg (1977), th noted perceptual psychologist, discussed the concept i terms of a visual *canonical form* that must be present fc successful depiction. Canonical form, he presumed, is som sort of prototype or reference form for the object, cor taining all the feature relations distinctive to it and lackin those that are shared, irrelevant for identification, or ur informative for shape. In theory, each object has a singl discoverable canonical form critical to imaging. I argue in Chapter 4 that canonical form defined in this way prob ably doesn't exist.

This conceptualization of the canonical form notion pr supposes a rather large reference library in the minds c artists and viewers filled with air-brushed snapshots of a familiar objects and object types. That such a library c filing system exists is assumed by a great many worker in the field of pattern recognition. A static film library c prototypes is not, however, the only theoretical alternativ available to describe the perceptual structures necessary t object recognition through two-dimensional representa tion. I argued in Chapter 4 that Ernst Cassirer's *generativ* concept of perceptual form, the concept that perceptu identity is attributed to apparently altogether heteroge neous figures by virtue of their being transformable int one another by means of group operations, provides much more dynamic and general approach to the problem of canonical, or easily recognizable form. A related, bu much less geometrical, concept comes to us from Rudolf Arnheim. In 1969, following Gurwitz, Arnhiem offered the concept of *renvois*. He explained that for any object there is an indefinitely large number of projective views of that object available to the perceiver, artist, or consumer. A certain subset of these views contains *renvois*; these are referencing aspects or views that point beyond the given view to adjacent, subsequent ones. Aspects with *renvois* make reference to the simplest three-dimensional solid that could have generated them; thus, according to Arnheim, the structural skeletons of projections or images with *renvois* are directly related to the structure of the object depicted.

Exciting as this notion is, the primary difficulty with it lies in the absence of independent, a priori, criteria for distinguishing aspects with *renvois* from those without it. We have no means of describing clearly what is meant by a *direct* relationship between the structural skeleton of a projection with *renvois* and the structural skeleton of the solid object. We know that all projective views of an object, be they Metric, Similarity, Affine, or Projective proper, have a direct relationship to the parent object determined by the appropriate, reversible projective transformations. If we wish to say that a particular depiction of an object is related to that object in a uniquely informative way, then we need criteria more specific than that of "direct" relationship. We need specification of *degrees* of relationship, of degrees of similarity between object and image. We saw in Chapter 4 that such information is much better described in terms of geometrical consequences of the station point assumption, of the artistic options for creating a picture.

Options and styles

Generally, it can be seen from Figure 9.2 that Options 1,2,3,4,9, and 10 involve a distance assumption at optical infinity, giving either an Affine or a Metric projection; Options 5,6,7,8,11, and 12 assume a near to moderate station point distance, giving Similarity or Projective images. That is, Options 1 and 5, 9 and 11, 2 and 6, 3 and

7, 10 and 12, and 4 and 8 are identical each to the other except for the distance assumption. The assumption of variable oblique angles between the original surfaces and image plane is taken in Options 2, 4, 6, and 8 (because the slants of the objects vary), and a constant oblique angle in 9, 10, 11, and 12 (because all the objects pictured have the same slant). The parallel picture–object assumption is made in Options 1, 3, 5, and 7.

It is easy to classify each of the styles with which we have been concerned in terms of one or more of these options. Option 8 corresponds to much of Western post-Renaissance art in which the object surfaces are at various angles of inclination relative to the image plane, objects in space are arranged freely, not in rows, and the projection lines are convergent because the station point distance is moderate – giving a Projective projection. In Western post-Renaissance art, the central spatial relationship is one of perpendicularity between the picture plane and the ground plane. Each of the other sets of parallel edges in the depiction is drawn at its own angle of inclination, each so with its own vanishing point. In Western construction, very little is depicted parallel to the picture plane, other than the occasional building face or wall, so Options like 5 and 7, though possible, seldom occur. The normal Western case was shown in Figure 6.8, in which the only surface parallel to the picture plane is the square prism face in the center of the picture. Options 5 and 7, projections of surfaces parallel to the picture plane, are, of course, Similarities, and therefore show perspective change only in size, not angles. Option 6 also corresponds to Western-style art, but in this case the spatial arrangement of original objects is contrived into rows.

Option 4 corresponds to the conventional Japanese (pre-seventeenth century) compositional choice, in which, like the Western counterpart, objects are arranged freely in space, on the ground at various angles of inclination relative to the picture plane, while the projection lines are parallel because the distance assumed for the station point is at optical infinity. If the picture is of a single object, or of objects with no apparent or specified loci in space, then one need consider only the relationship between the image plane and the single dominant object surface. This is the general case in Northwest Coast Indian art where objects are depicted without reference to a ground plane or architectural units. Nevertheless, Northwest Coast Indian art also reflects the choice of Option 4 where object and image planes are oblique and intersecting. In this case, however, only one object from two angles is commonly depicted without reference to context. The use of Option 1 is exemplified in Egyptian art: Objects are generally arranged in rows in space, each object is usually arranged frontal to the image plane, and the projection distance is at optical infinity so the projection lines are parallel.

Options 4 and 8, traditional Japanese and European, generally deal with the "world as it is"; that is, objects are *not* usually arranged in rows in space, nor are they usually in uniform orientation to the picture plane. Egyptians, in their selection of Option 1, arranged objects and planes in space (not physically, of course) to accomplish a certain appearance in composition of orderliness, symmetry, and repetition. In a manner rather similar to the Egyptians, Classic European art tended toward frontal compositions with objects clearly arranged in rows along successive planes in depth. Of course, this tendency reflected not an interest in Egyptian composition, but the effects of the recently abandoned Gothic compositions in which space generally was flattened into a single plane and objects in that plane were pictured either frontally or in profile. This planar tendency was diminished considerably by the pull of the Renaissance convention, but the Classic style reflects the tension of the compositional styles that precede and follow it.

Some concepts from art history

This is not an art history text. Yet perhaps it would not be out of place to consider briefly some concepts traditionally used in the teaching of art history even if those concepts are currently rather out of vogue. These are the concepts given us by Heinrich Wölfflin (1932), the eminent art historian, nearly fifty years ago. He taught us to think of paintings as either *painterly* or *linear* (more or less) and of the techniques of spatial depiction as either *planar* or *recessional*. By linear, Wölfflin meant that the depiction of form in a painting was dependent primarily on silhouette, on clarity of line; by painterly, that form depiction was accomplished through massing of color, or of patches of light and dark. In the former, outline is dominant; in the latter, the interior masses. "Linear style sees in lines, painterly in masses". By planar composition of spatial layout, Wölfflin meant that increasing distance in the picture is ordered in strata parallel to the picture plane; by recessional composition of space, he meant that pictorial depth is created by dominating orthogonals or diagonals thrusting into the space behind the picture plane. It is useful to remember that Dürer was a very linear artist, whereas Rembrandt was very painterly; Raphael was very planar in his compositions, but Rubens was recessional. For Wölfllin, these dichotomous contrasts were intended to distinguish the Classical (fifteenth- to sixteenth-century) from the Baroque (sixteenth- to seventeenth-century) painters – Classical painters being linear and planar, Baroque painters painterly and recessional. Like almost any dichotomous categorization in its actual application, the contrast is not without numerous exceptions, yet it remains a valuable teaching device and useful entrée to unfamiliar works of art. Wölfllin's categories are useful to us in the present enterprise because they exemplify in quite traditional terms some of the options developed here and shown in Figure 9.2.

Composition and projection

The compositional technique of conceiving of the space to be depicted as a series of planes makes a number of appearances in the art of the world, but it is not properly an aspect of the *projection* system assumed by an art style. It does not touch directly on the relative orientation of object and image surfaces, nor on the distance of the station point, or on the nature of the projection lines. It is not necessary to the realization of any of the projection options. Yet planar composition is a persistent stylistic variable occurring in many cultural styles, always in conjunction with a

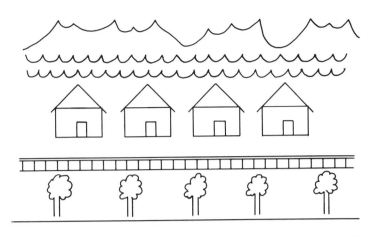

Figure 9.6. Parallel plane projection
of the naturally stratified scene.

a tendency toward frontal, Metric, object surface projection. Similarly, planar compositions tend to covary with parallel projections. Planar, rowlike, arrangements of objects do not occur often in nature. When they occur in pictures they are usually an artistic contrivance, with the planes of the scene nearly always organized parallel to the picture plane, as in Options 1, 2, 5, and 6. However, it is possible that a scene could be "naturally" stratified, usually through the hand of man, as in the case of the plowed furrows of a field. As a more extreme example, one could imagine that a long straight road could have a row of cottages beyond a fence, with rows of plowed furrows still farther, and a row of mountains in the distance, as in Figure 9.6. The closer one gets to the city, the easier it is to find such artistically uncontrived stratification of objects in space. Nature is seldom this tidy, or seldom tidy in this way. Figure 9.6 illustrates a case in which the stratification required by Options 1, 2, 5 and 6 not only occurs "naturally," but the composition also is created from a *single* station point. This is very rare. Such stratification is ordinarily a contrivance that requires a multiple-station-point assumption. Where such stratification occurs naturally, the picture plane may be placed parallel to the strata, as in Figure 9.6 , or at an oblique angle intersecting the depth planes, as in Figure 9.7.

Uniformity of object orientation relative to the picture plane (or any other plane, for that matter) is also a rare

Figure 9.7. A "naturally" stratified country scene: an oblique projection.

occurrence in nature, and thus usually would have to be contrived by the artist to occur in pictures. The simplest way to accomplish this uniformity of object orientation is through the assumption of a different, usually idealized station point for the dominant or ideal plane of each subject to be depicted – a multiple station point assumption. Options reflecting uniformity of orientation relative to the picture plane are 1, 3, 5, and 7. Options 3 and 7, uniformity of object orientation parallel to the image plane, *without* stratification, do not seem to have been embraced by any cultural style. Some Egyptian art can be seen to be similar to Option 3, but it is rather as if Option 1 were simply executed badly on occasion. There is no evidence that Option 3 was ever a viable, consistent artistic option for the Egyptians. Nor can I find any evidence that Option 7 appears anywhere as a consistent style. It may be the case that the aesthetic impulse to "frontalize" objects through depiction of the dominant plane goes hand in glove with the desire to stratify them in space. Certainly, I cannot find frontality in the absence of stratification.

I have noted that European art seldom uses parallel image and subject planes, but that Classic planar compositions approach it, giving instances of Option 6. When a composition is arranged thus in a series of planes, the appearance of two-dimensional form on those planes becomes quite striking. As I pointed out in Chapter 7, the individual forms projected to a specific place on a plane not only interact to make up the overall two-dimensional composition, but also must be comprehensible in and of themselves as figures. The outline, the cutout form, of the figure must be informative about the shape of the figure. An extreme version of informative outline form is found in friezes, a single-locus planar composition, where figures march along walls or borders in a repetitive and easily understood manner. This is common in Egyptian art, but not in European post-Renaissance or Japanese art. Classic European compositions approach this extreme, but never meet it. Figures tend to be either frontal or in profile, but are almost never purely so because in European post-Renaissance art, the image plane and the subject plane, the dominant plane of the subject, are almost never parallel; they are oblique, intersecting planes. The two-dimensional emphasis in Classic art is arresting, but mainly in contrast to the three-dimensional character of most other post-Renaissance work. Interesting as this contrast is, it should not be forgotten that the issue of degree of emphasis on two-dimensional composition is no more relevant to the geometrical classification scheme than is stratification of space into a planar layout. Within any geometrical type are many compositional degrees of freedom.

Classification and geometry

Are choice of geometry and compositional bias really independent of each other? What would a broad survey of the world's art styles reveal? Table 9.1 shows various art styles from Europe, Africa, the Middle East, the Far East and America arranged chronologically and classified in terms of station point option and geometry. Under each style is noted the option number, the geometry, the number of station points, and the compositional emphasis on two or three dimensions.

Table 9.1. *Categorization of style*

Dates	Europe	Africa	Middle East	Far East	America
★					★
30000	★ Ice Age Proj:3D (8)	★	★	★	★
3500	★	★	★	★	★
2500	★	★ Old Egypt Met:2D (1)	★	★	★
2000	★	★	★	★	★
1900	★	★ Mid Egypt Met:2D (1)	★	★	★
1800	★	★	★	★	★
1700	★	★	★	★	★
1600	★	★	★	★	★
1500	★	★	★	★	★
1400	★	★ New Egypt Met:2D (1)	★	★	★
1300	★	★	★	★	★
1200	★	★	★	★	★
1100	★	★	★	★	★
1000	★	★	★	★	★
900	★ Assyrian Met:2D (1)	★	★	★	★
800	★	★	★	★	★
700	★ Etruscan Met:2D (1)	★	★	★	★
600	★	★	★	★	★
500	★ Greek	★	★	★	★
400	★ Vases Aff:3D (4)	★	★	★	★
300	★	★	★	★	★
200	★	★	★	★	★
100	★	★	★	★	★
1	★ Roman	★	★	★	★
1	★ Murals Aff:3D (4)	★	★	★	★
100	★	★	★	★	★
200	★	★	★	★	★
300	★	★	★	★	★
400	★	★	★	★ Chinese	★
500	★ Medieval Aff:2D (9)	★	★	★ Caves Aff:3D (9)	★
600	★	★	★	★	★
700	★ Irish Met:2D (1)	★	★	★ Japanese	★
800	★	★	★	★ Aff:3D (4)	★

Table 9.1. *(cont.)*

Dates	Europe	Africa	Middle East	Far East	America
900	★	★	★	★	★
1000	★	★ Bushmen Proj:3D (8)	★	★ Chinese	★ Petroglyph (Hawaiian) Met:2D (1)
1100	★ Romanesqu Aff:2D (2)	★	★	★ Landscape	★ Inca Met:2D (1)
1200	★ Italian Aff:3D (2)	★	★	★ Scrolls Proj:3D (6)	★ Aztec Met:2D (1)
1300	★ Orthodox Aff:3D (2)	★	★	★ (mixed)	★ Mayan Met:2D (1)
1400	★ Renaissance	★	★ Persian	★	★
1500	★ Proj:3D (8)	★	★ Drawings Aff:2D (9)	★	★
1600	★ Baffin Is Met:2D (1)	★	★	★	★
1700	★	★	★	★ Indian Aff:3D (4)	★
1800	★	★	★	★ (mixed)	★ NW Indian Aff:2D (4)
1900	★	★	★	★	★ Cubism Aff:2D (4)
2000	★	★	★	★	★

Familiar styles

What kind of consistency is shown in the styles analyzed so far? Consider first the two-dimensional styles we have examined: Egyptian, Northwest Coast Indian, Romanesque manuscript painting, and Cubism. Egyptian art is the classic Option 1: The geometry is Metric, the station point number is multiple, space is stratified, and figures are in uniform orientation to the picture. Both Northwest Coast Indian art and Cubism exemplify Option 4, with Affine geometry and multiple station points. Neither style can be consider stratified in a conventional sense, nor is there any uniform orientation of surfaces to the image plane. Romanesque manuscript illuminations, while also Affine in geometry and multiple in viewpoint number, illustrate not Option 4, but Option 2. In these paintings, the scene is highly stratified in planar compositions or very

formal stage-drop settings. Pictured surfaces are not i
uniform orientation to the image plane. It is not easy t
detect any uniformity in this group of two-dimension;
styles.

What of the three-dimensional styles analyzed abovε
Western European, Japanese, Ice Age cave, and Bushme
art styles? We have seen that most post-Renaissance ar
selected Option 8, except Classic art, which falls into Op
tion 6. Both, of course, are Projective and created from
single station point. Most post-Renaissance art is not planaı
nor are depicted surfaces oriented uniformly. Europeaı
post-Renaissance art shows a surprising degree of kinshij
with the ancient Ice Age Cave art, and with the art of th
Bushmen of Africa. All three styles are Projective and il
lustrate Option 8. The primary difference is that the latte
two styles are multiple station point constructions, ofteı
created with no particular attempt to unify the several ele
ments of the composition. Of course, we really have nο
way of knowing today which elements belong together iı
which compositions because these are all cave painting
created, perhaps, over long periods of time. The fourtĥ
three-dimensional style is traditional Japanese art, whicĥ
exemplifies Option 4: Affine from a single station point
Japanese art is not rigidly stratified, nor are the depicteι
surfaces all in uniform orientation to the image plane. Therε
is, however, a certain tendency to maintain a fairly regula
arrangement of objects, particularly architectural units.

Do the four three-dimensional styles exhibit any consistency between compositional bias and geometry? Certainly the three-dimensional styles are more likely to bε
Option 8 than any other, but there is no evidence, at leasι
from these four examples, that the presence or absence oı
stratification or any other rigidly observed compositiona
technique is required.

Additional styles

If we look at a broader range of examples, can we find
patterns or trends that might illuminate the nature of the
relationship between the geometrical option selected and
other nongeometrical compositional variables – like the
number of viewpoints or stratification of planes in depth

or uniformity of orientation of pictured objects relative to the image plane? Other two-dimensional styles come from a broad range of cultures. The first chronologically is Assyrian, an Option 1 style. Assyrian art is Orthogonal and uses multiple viewpoints in a single composition. The image in Figure 9.8 is a fairly typical low relief from the ninth century B.C. The winged being is brought sharply up into one plane like a cookie cutout. The stylization of the form is both strikingly unique in character and remi-

Figure 9.8. (above) A Mayan image, c.14 A.D. (From Tulum, Yucatan. Photograph by H.L. Coffman.) (right) Assyrian low relief exemplifying Option 1: Metric multiple station point: "Winged Being Worshipping." (Courtesy, Museum of Fine Arts, Boston, Everett Statue Fund.)

Figure 9.9. Christian medieval gospel illustration exemplifying Option 9: Affine, multiple station point. (Evangelist from the Lindisfarne Gospels, British Museum.)

niscent of the formalisms in ancient Egyptian art, which shows much kinship with Assyrian art. Compare the Assyrian relief to the Mayan image in Figure 9.8. Chronologically, the next two-dimensional European style is early Christian Medieval painting – usually manuscript illustrations. Figure 9.9 shows a plate from a seventh-century gospel, an example of Option 9, a multiple station point Affine construction. The figures are highly frontalized cutouts arranged in a series of succeeding planes. The style is Affine, but is *very* close to Metric; image and object planes are oblique to each other but with a very heavy frontal emphasis. This style shares elements with Roman wall painting, but is much flatter; it appears very close in time to early Irish painting, but with important differences.

Early Irish monastic art, largely from the seventh century, exemplifies Option 1 (Fig. 9.10). This style is rigidly

Figure 9.10. Irish Monastic Art:
Metric, single-station-point.
Seventh-century gospel. (From
Bruce Arnold, A Concise History
of Irish Art, p. 25. New York,
Praeger, 1968.)

Metric, and is so extremely formal as to be only barely within the boundaries of representational art. The purpose of creations like these was largely decorative, not imagistic, so even representational elements are used almost nonrepresentationally. Celtic ornamentation, largely metalwork, was integrated into the Irish religious idiom. The style nearly always used front views and profiles – creatures in their most characteristic aspects – and the depictions are highly symbolic. Nevertheless, there is always a viewpoint and it is usually single. Another two-dimensional, single station point style, a style that shares more characteristics with European Christian medieval art than does its purportedly close Irish cousin, is Persian art. Persian drawing, like Irish art, is nonillusionistic, highly decorative, contrived, and elaborated. But, like non-Irish medieval art, Persian drawings are single station point Affine constructions, embracing Option 9. Figure 9.11, a small illustration from the fifteenth century, shows both the Affine character of the composition and its strongly stratified quality.

Of the eight strongly two-dimensional styles we have examined, how many fall into each geometrical category? There are three Metric (or Orthogonal), five Affine, and no Projective options. Compositionally, six of the eight exhibit a fairly regular stratification of successive planes in space; five of the eight styles tend to display objects in uniform orientation to the picture plane. We see then that a strongly stratified style is quite likely to be two dimensional in emphasis, but is it likely to be Affine because Affine was the most frequently selected geometrical option? Not really. Of the five two-dimensional Affine styles, only three exhibited strong stratification. We cannot be sure, however, of which compositional variables correlate with which geometrical system until we examine more three-dimensional styles in some detail.

The three-dimensional style most similar to two-dimensional Option 9, Persian drawing, is Option 9, Chinese Cave paintings. An example is shown in Figure 9.12. These paintings, created in caves by religious pilgrims, have a rather amateurish quality, but they are not without both skill and consistency of application of technique. Their representational quality is strongly mitigated by a pre-

Figure 9.11. Persian drawing. Option 9: Affine, single-station-point. Funeral Procession and Builders at Work, c.1485, probably Bihzad. (All Rights Reserved. Metropolitan Museum of Art, Fletcher Fund, 1963.)

vailing interest in their two-dimensional appearance. T▶ compositions are stratified, with the depicted objects plac◀ in uniform orientation relative to the picture. They a Affine and are usually constructed from a single statio point placed at optical infinity. These Chinese paintin◀ are very different in both feeling and style from the Chine paintings most familiar to Western observers: Chine landscape scrolls. Chinese landscape scrolls, like that pi tured in Figure 9.13, fall into Option 6, not 9, and th◀

are Projective, not Affine. The only features other than three-dimensional emphasis that they share with the cave paintings are stratification and the single station point assumption. Of course, the three-dimensional world depicted in these scrolls is not the mundane world, but the world of contemplation. They are highly stratified, like the cave drawings, but, unlike the cave pictures, are not composed so that surfaces are in uniform orientation to the image plane. The scroll paintings are unusual in that they nest Affine architectural components in compositions that are otherwise Projective across the whole expanse of the scene depicted. Chinese landscape scrolls are very similar in construction techniques to Classical European art. The major difference in feeling is due to the large difference in the expanse of space depicted: In Chinese scrolls the expanse is very great, in Classical art, the space is quite compressed.

Just as Chinese landscape painting is very similar to Classical European art, so too is Chinese cave painting very similar in some respects to pre-Renaissance Italian painting. Italian painting is also Affine and composed from a single

Figure 9.13. Chinese Landscape Scrolls. Option 6: Projective, single-station-point. "River Landscape", Yuan. c. 1349. (The Seattle Art Museum. Eugene Fuller Memorial Collection.)

station point, but it illustrates Option 2, not Option 9. The Giotto in Figure 9.14 beautifully exemplifies the hallmarks of this period. The style is Affine, but moving visibly into a Projective mode as the station point comes in closer from optical infinity. The scene is strongly stratified into depth planes, but depicted elements are not in uniform orientation to the picture plane. There is a consistent tendency to depict objects frontally or in profile, and some tendency to repeat both individual elements and their orientations. Vertical elements rest on a clearly horizontal ground plane. It is possible to detect remnants of the multiple station point medieval art that preceded this pre-Renaissance style just as it is possible to detect the seeds of the Renaissance to follow.

It is often argued that the Renaissance also had seeds, if not roots, in the pictorial efforts of the Romans. The Roman paintings referred to are the wall murals found mainly at Pompeii, Herculaneum, and the Roman Palatine. They are considered by historians to be copies of earlier Greek

Figure 9.15. Roman wall painting. Option 4: Affine, multiple-station-point. (Courtesy, Museum of Fine Arts, Boston. Richard Norton Memorial Fund.)

paintings but there is almost no visual evidence to supp⟨ort⟩ this argument. An example of a Roman mural is sho⟨wn⟩ in Figure 9.15 from Pompei. Roman murals are Aff⟨ine⟩ but they *approach* the Projective perspective of the Rena⟨is⟩sance. Projective constructions are implied, but an expli⟨cit⟩ consistent Projective application is avoided. Many, ma⟨ny⟩ pictures show only one pair of a set of parallel edges ⟨and⟩ hide the corresponding set by the framing of the segm⟨ent⟩ or by another architectural unit. It is rather as if th⟨ese⟩ multiple station point constructions were created wit⟨h⟩ conscious awareness of the problems implicit in combin⟨ing⟩ Projective perspective from several viewpoints into ⟨one⟩ picture. This is a strongly three-dimensional style, f⟨re⟩quently theatrical in the settings and framings of the cen⟨tral⟩ images. Depicted objects are not stratified, nor are th⟨ey⟩ shown in uniform orientation to the picture plane. Rom⟨an⟩ wall paintings illustrate Option 4.

The Greek paintings that purportedly served as models for many of the Roman efforts are lost, but Gr⟨eek⟩ vase paintings are abundant. Like the Roman paintin⟨gs⟩ they are multiple station point, Affine, Option 4 creatio⟨ns⟩ and they often employ theatrical elements in a manner v⟨ery⟩ similar to the mural shown in Figure 9.15. This a stron⟨g⟩

three-dimensional style, a fact that is particularly evident in the modeling and articulation of the human figures (Fig. 9.16). The individual elements of the composition are often arranged rather loosely in space, and there is no evidence of rigid stratification or of uniformity of orientation. This is not to say that Greek vase painting does not exhibit a very highly developed awareness of two-dimensional appearance on the surface of the bowl or vase painted. The fifth century B.C. krater shown in Figure 9.17 makes this point powerfully.

What have we learned from the three-dimensional styles about the relation between geometry and composition? We have looked at nine different styles. Do they tend to fall in a particular geometrical category? Is there consistency in the tendencies they exhibit to stratify their spatial layout or orient their depicted surfaces? Of the nine styles analyzed, four are Projective (compared to *no* two-dimensional Projective styles), five are Affine, and none is Metric. Four styles, including Classical post-Renaissance art, exhibit a fairly consistent tendency to stratify pictorial objects, but only one style uses a repetitively uniform orientation of objects relative to the picture plane.

ure 9.16. Greek Vase painting. 'oung Warrier and Woman king a Libation." Option 4: 'ine, multiple-station-point. ourtesy, Museum of Fine Arts, ston, H.L. Pierce Fund.)

ure 9.17. "Ganymede." (Musée Louvre, Paris.)

Conclusions

We can conclude, then, that there is some correlation tween geometry and dimensional emphasis in that Me styles occur only where two-dimensionality is emphasi over three-dimensionality, and Projective styles occur o where the emphasis is three-dimensional. Similarly, highly repetitive stratification of depth and uniform entation of objects tend to occur far more frequently compositions stressing two-dimensional appearan However, lest these apparent correlations seem more nificant than they are, it must not be forgotten that m of what goes into judging a style as two-dimensiona probably determined by just such factors as manipul spatial arrangements of depicted objects. It is proba inevitable that very formal contrived compositions appear two-dimensional – particularly to a judge wh own cultural convention pushes in the direction of p tographic realism. Analysis of entries in Table 9.1 rev far more about the varying degrees of kinship in the w domain of natural perspective than it does about the lations between geometry and design.

The categorization system is of value not because i luminates the nature of pattern elements in composit but because it elucidates the nature of representation its In the next chapter on development in art, I will consi what the understanding of representational options can us about the nature and direction of stylistic change.

10 The developmental question

"No present-day child, or adult of average ability, could produce drawings fit to compare with the art of the Stone Age, of the Bushmen, or of the Eskimos. On the other hand, it has been found that drawings collected by explorers and carried out at their request by average persons of savage peoples are crude and formal, and in many ways like those of our own children. Helga Eng, *The Psychology of Children's Drawings*, 1931.

Development in art

We know that art styles change from time to time, from one people to another. We know that the history of the painting of a people reveals regular stylistic changes with the passage of time. We know that styles change, but do they develop? A developmental change is a change of a special kind, a change in the direction up. A developmental change is a qualitative change, not just a quantitative one, and the higher or later stages must rest on the preceding ones. Even if we disregard all the criteria but that of improvement, it is probably not the case that the changes that take place in depiction style, in a culture or in an individual, reveal development toward any particular goal.

It is often argued, however, that there is development in art. The most common developmental change alleged to take place is that from painting what is known to painting what is seen. Children and "primitives" supposedly paint what they know, and sophisticated peoples paint what they see. The major support for this assertion comes from the work of Franz Boas and Heinz Werner. Boas, the anthropologist, and Werner, the psychologist, both reported

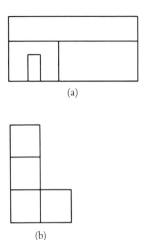

(a)

(b)

Figure 10.1. Chain style art common in the drawings of children: (a) house, (b) cube.

the existence of split-style, or chain-style, art in the w of primitive peoples and children. We have seen, in analyses of Northwest Coast Indian art, what highly st ized, technically proficient, split-style art looks like. chain-style art of children, said to be similar, is show Figure 10.1. The similarity between so-called primit work as exemplified in the Indian art and these childr pieces is that each is a multifaceted presentation of subject; each is a multiple station point composition, a Egyptian art and Cubism in its representational phase. rock art of South Africa is single station point; the p historic cave art of Altamira and Lascaux is multiple would be simpler, I think, and no less absurd, to clas the people by the art rather than the art by the people is true that multiple station point compositions occasi ally appear in the work of children; so do single stat point constructions. There is no evidence that a freque count would give evidence of the preponderance of former. We could pick either, or any one of any ot possible subdivisions, and posit a developmental cha with equal logic. Success requires only that we hold v clearly in mind what "sophisticated" or "developed" is supposed to look like.

"Developed" art

Developed art is almost invariably defined explicitly implicitly as Western post-Renaissance art, or "persp tive" art. Drawing "in perspective" is generally conside the most significant developmental change in the hist of art. It is said that art without Western perspectiv primitive art; art with some attempt at a perspective s tem, however poorly realized, is developing, and art w Western perspective is truly developed.

This argument rests on certain assumptions, the ceptance of which makes the argument sound a good c less foolish than it first appears. The assumptions are c cerned not with the nature of depiction, but with the "fac of vision. It is assumed that, despite the binocularity vision, the process of seeing any particular thing invol observation from a single station point, and that mos the things we observe are neither very close to the face nor at optical infinity. It follows, then, that the best painting style is the one that most closely conforms to these conditions, portraying the geometrical sequelae. These assumptions are by no means necessary to an understanding of vision (indeed, quite the reverse), but as we see in Appendix D knowledge of their history explains their compelling quality. They have been as compelling for Western scientific understanding of perception as for the Western history of art. The philosopher Marx Wartofsky has argued that the theory of art has determined the theory of vision, rather than vice versa. I think it more likely that the developing understanding from the time of Euclid of the formation of *images*, with the myriad ramifications of that understanding, led Western thinkers to the set of assumptions that determined the evaluation of both the experience of vision and the quality of styles which depicted that experience.

Cultural development: empirical evidence

Fortunately, we can disregard theories of development in art, both what they are and what they could be, and direct our attention in an unprejudiced manner to the evidence presented in Chapter 9. As always in art, it is better to look at what people actually do than at what they or anyone else says they do. Observation of Table 9.1 reveals no obvious developmental pattern across time or culture in terms of adoption of station point assumptions. Neither is there any clear pattern of adoption of certain geometries in sequence with advances in civilization or even in technology (a less controversial concept). It is not the case that Metric (or Orthogonal) compositions were commonplace in the earliest periods of different cultures' artistic histories. It is not even true that the earliest examples of art that we know reveal the accepted "primitive" characteristics of Orthogonality and multiplicity of station point. There is no evidence that cultures have ever moved systematically from Metric to Affine to Projective systems. Highly developed cultures have embraced each of these styles. Since these "endpoints" of development differ from culture to culture,

it seems inevitable that the patterns of change preced
the endpoints necessarily must differ also.

If we accept for a moment the often asserted superior
of the Western Projective system, it is possible to exam
the changes of style within this one, very loosely defin
cultural unit for evidence of systematic change mov
steadily in the direction of the Western post-Renaissa
mode. The evidence is not there. There are several stra
of change in Western history, but no simple dimens
that distinguishes earlier stages from later. When cert
factors were all present at once, the style called Renaissa
art came into being; when certain factors changed, anot
style was born. Rudolf Arnheim (1954) remarked so
time ago that it required only a shift of awareness to
the multiple station point creations of the moderns as
alistic in the same sense as single point projections. I
certain sense, this whole book can be seen as an interp
tation of that remark. Any composition faithful to
varieties of visual experience will look realistic to view
after a degree of exposure because what they see rep
sented in art they have seen before.

Ordinary people do not have theories of vision ab
their own visual experience of the ordinary environm
so their perceptions are not constrained by predetermi
notions of validity. We have habits of attention, cultu
and personal, that determine what we talk about in ter
of visual experience, but the extent to which they de
mine the quality of experience itself is not certain. As
learn to discriminate one wine from another, so we lea
perhaps, to see the many shades of green of the thousa
of leaves of a tree in the sun. Art, more than anything e
performs this function of directing our attention to
varieties of visual experience. This is as true for the geo
etries of spatial layout as it is for the much discussed colo
shadows of the Impressionists. But this type of devel
ment is not structured or systematic; it is qualitative o
in the most limited sense. Neither is it quantitative in
simple sense like that of the increase in vocabulary ite
with the acquisition of a new language. Stylistic chan
in art involve the loss of vocabulary items as much a
gain with time. Everything from geometry of layout

type of paint to use of color to the employment of line involves the adoption of a particular technique to the exclusion of those that have come before or will come after. Perhaps the available vocabulary grows with changes in style, but *employed* vocabulary does not seem to. It is really only in the last 100 years of Western art that we have seen the self-conscious use of the depiction styles of other times and other cultures. Perhaps this is inevitable as the world grows smaller, but it did not take place in the past.

Development in children's art

I have argued, essentially, that development in art does not take place historically or culturally, that no specifiable pattern or set of characteristics distinguishes earlier styles from later ones. Changes that have taken place within a culture will always be seen now in terms of the current mode, and there is no obvious basis for ranking the sequential modes developmentally. Even within Western art, no simple pattern of development leading to the Projective mode is apparent. But what would happen if we looked at the art of Western children whose cultural endpoint is Projective, at least in most of their exposure to depiction? I must now collapse a distinction I made earlier because modern art requires it. In the worlds of other times and places, or at least in Western commentaries on those worlds, there was no distinction between depiction in general and "Art." We speak easily of Egyptian "art," meaning tomb paintings, whose aesthetic import must have been extremely limited given the particular religious function of much of the work. Were tomb paintings more like the exhibits of current work in our galleries and museums or more like magazine illustrations of cowboys selling cigarettes? Analyses of artistic development require specification of and exposure to the artistic endpoint, but it is not at all clear to what extent modern Western children are exposed to Western *art*. They are certainly exposed to a variety of picture-book and magazine illustrations as well as to a number of the ubiquitous pictorial commercial advertisements, but not everyone will be pleased with the designation of these products as art. In this book art is

defined as the product of skilled labor, capable of evoki
an aesthetic response in the observer. Cigarette comm
cials may seldom generate much aesthetic response, b
they are certainly crafted by skilled workers. In this limi
sense, then, I shall stipulate that the average Western ch
has generous exposure to the Western projective art of
culture, however deplorable that exposure may be.

Analyses of children's art have a rather long histo
somewhat too tedious to warrant repeating here. A b
outline of the most common description of developm
will be presented to allow informed evaluation of my p
sition. Since most of the writers say the same thing, I sh
select from their writings at will to present the posit
clearly.

Traditional analyses of children's art

Lark-Horovitz and colleagues (1967) provide the simpl
synthetic model of the development of children's art. B
rowing from Rudolf Arnheim, they distinguish three m
stages through which they say all children must pass: Scr
ble, Schematic, and True-to-appearance.

A Scribble is nearly any trace left by a drawing imp
ment that is uninterpretable by anyone other than the scr
bler. There is heated and rather boring debate on whet
scribbling is primarily visual or motoric, emotional or
tellectual, representational or "abstract." I cannot see t
it makes much difference and the only moderately int
esting study on the subject that I know of is that of Jar
Gibson and Pat Yonas (1968) demonstrating that you
children are not interested in pushing a pencil around
paper unless it leaves a pigment trace. Of course not
they were, they would draw in the air as frequently as
surfaces. In any case, whatever the motivation, scribb
come first. Scribbles have excited a considerable amo
of interest in art educators because they presumably p
vide the basis upon which the child will build artistic ski
No one has ever demonstrated that such a base is necess
for later development, but this is no deterrent to spe
lation. The educator who went furthest in the analysi
the scribble is Rhoda Kellogg (1967), who has collec

thousands upon thousands of children's drawings from all over the world, but primarily from the United States. Kellogg has identified twenty kinds of Basic Scribbles produced by very young children. These are shown in Figure 10.2. Kellogg has also identified seventeen placement patterns of markings relative to the framing of the page. She has developed a system that aggregates these units into wholes she calls Gestalts, but since it is fairly simple to subsume her developmental levels into those of Lark-Horovitz et al., I shall continue with their system.

The next stage, schematic drawings, includes drawings in which outlined shapes have some degree of resemblance to actual objects. "Form is reduced and simplified. Objects or figures are represented by outlined shapes which are used consistently, again and again, to designate the same objects" (Lark-Horovitz et al., 1967:7). It is not clear to me that this stage of representational level requires a description more complex than that of outline forms more or less recognizable by adults. Kellogg in particular has done exhaustive frequency counts of the number of sun shapes, radials, rectangulars, irregulars, and such that make up the units, or "gestalts" in these efforts, but little of interest has resulted from her labor. Children can move their hands up, down, sideways, and diagonally, in straight lines and in swirls, and they do, with varying frequencies. In my opinion, the only stage of real interest for the development of picture-making skills per se is the last one, what Lark-Horovitz et al. call the True-to-appearance stage.

The true-to-appearnce stage is what Kellogg calls somewhat disdainfully "pictorialism." Lark-Horovitz et al. write:

At this stage, objects and groups of objects are drawn as the[y] are observed from a single point of vantage. Situation, positio[n,] or movement of living things is shown; bending of limbs, re[a-]sonably correct proportions among parts, and more "correc[t"] color and light. The child gives proof of his awareness of t[he] diminution of distant objects, of the line of the horizon. [He] begins to attempt perspective representation and foreshortenin[g.] Representation moves in the direction of photographic realis[m,] toward the "natural" or "real," but rarely achieves this go[al.] (1967: 10–11)

Perhaps it cannot be said too often that this particular n[o-] tion of true-to-appearance pertains only to children who[se] dominant cultural style is Western post-Renaissance a[nd,] regardless of where in the modern world they may liv[e.] An obvious research difficulty is the increasing homog[e-] nization of the world's art culture. The reader should n[ot] confuse the twentieth-century Egyptian with a counterpa[rt] 4,000 years ago, nor a modern Japanese child with one fo[ur] dynasties past. This point is obvious but often overlooke[d.]

What do so-called true-to-appearance pictures look lik[e?] It depends, of course, on the age and experience of t[he] child. Again, Rhoda Kellogg's vast collection provides [us] with numerous examples, despite her lack of interest [in] pictorialism or in the child's attempts at representatio[n.] Figure 10.3 shows drawings of buildings by children fro[m] four to seven years of age. Figure 10.4 shows drawings [of] cars by children across the same age span. The cleare[st] description of the progression evidenced in such drawin[gs] is given by Helga Eng (1931) in her engaging book on t[he] psychology of children's art. Eng writes:

The first and favorite subject that children draw is human bein[gs,] but next to that, according to my observations, the house [in] which they live. . . At first children usually draw the house fr[om] one side only, but as they know that the house has several si[des] they go on to attempt to show these as well. When they ha[ve] acquired some elementary knowledge, they only draw the t[wo] sides that they can really see, often with some sort of atten[npt] at true perspective representation. But the child very frequen[tly] draws three sides. . . both gables are then, as it were, spr[ead] out, and drawn in the same plane as the front side. (pp. 121[–)]

Observation of Figure 10.3 supports the accuracy of En[g's] description, but there is no evidence that her assumpti[on]

Buildings (four years).

Windows of varied shapes on Houses that have equally varied outlines (five to seven years).

Houses with round roofs. The majority of the windows shown are square. (five to seven years)

Buildings (five years).

Figure 10.3. Drawings of buildings by children from four to seven years of age. (From R. Kellogg, Analyzing Children's Art. Reprinted by permission of the Mayfield Publishing Company. © 1969, 1970 by Rhoda Kellogg, pp. 124–5.)

of what underlies this "progress" is correct. She assumes that children are learning to draw "the house in which they live." But most Western children do not live in the prototypical, double-gabled, single-ridged house of these drawings. Then what are they drawing? Exactly that prototype, the canonical Western house drawing. These children are learning to draw according to the drawing canons of this culture, and they need no particular subject like "the house in which they live." It is perhaps inevitable that the canonical forms for drawing should become hopelessly confused with the idea of conceptual canonical forms for objects, an idea itself in rather a great state of confusion, as I pointed out in Chapter 4.

Such descriptions of the development of particular draw-

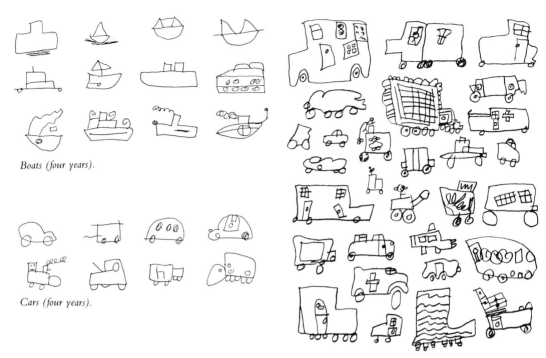

Boats (four years).

Cars (four years).

(Right). Various subjects designed for transportation (five to eight years).

Figure 10.4. Drawings of cars and other vehicles by children from four to seven years of age. (From Kellogg 1969:138–9.)

ing canons in the Western child, however interesting, a neither economical nor particularly informative about ge eral patterns of change. Purported stages of pictorialis or spatial representation are more generally described the following way: Stage 1 is the complete absence of spa or the setting of various objects alongside one anoth Stage 2 is that of conscious but unsuccessful attempts represent space, including maplike representations show ing objects turned over in the plane of the paper, unsu cessful bird's-eye views, representations from two or seve points of view, simple placing of the figures one over t other with size reduction and marking off space by simp outlines. Stage 3 is that of successful but incomplete spat representation in which the child makes use of a strip ground of some width, takes perspective foreshortenir into account, and does some masking of one figure another. These devices are deemed incomplete because t child in this stage makes no use of a horizon line. Stage "is that of the faultless pictorial representation of the who space," very rarely achieved before fifteen years of age and then only through imitation (Eng 1931: 154–5).

The absent endpoint

We really must not lose sight of the indisputable fact that this last stage of "faultless pictorial representation of the whole space" is almost *never* reached by *anyone* in *any* culture using *any* drawing system. I shall present evidence to support this statement, but for now remember that developmental promises to the contrary, most people are *not* artists. Ask ten friends to draw a house and nine will say, "I cannot draw." And they cannot. Remember too that there is no evidence to support the existence of reliable stages in children's drawing beyond the learning of canons and the increase in motor control attendant on maturation and practice wielding implements. This is odd because many people are willing to provide us with a set of quite well-defined stages. In addition to the stages already listed, Eng presents us with still another similar set: At first the child draws what it knows of a thing, without thinking of what is partially or completely invisible for perspective reasons, so he draws the four wheels of a carriage one behind the other or attached to the four corners of the body shown by a rectangle. All the sides of a house are drawn side by side, and people are placed side by side in rows. In the second stage, several planes of space are placed one above the other with more distant items drawn in the higher plane. Each plane makes a closed whole. (This reminds one inevitably of Wölfflin's analysis of the planar compositions of Classical art.) The third stage is one of establishing connections among the planes. At the fourth stage, the child finally grasps intuitively the laws of perspective, and takes pains to make use of them, although it still continues to make many mistakes.

I find this description of developmental progress fascinating but mysterious. Simply examining Figure 10.3 and 10.4 provides ample evidence of the existence of at least some components of both the first and second stages, but where is the evidence for the eventual arrival of Stages 3 and 4? Certainly they follow in theory, but do they follow in fact? Figure 10.5 shows styles of drawing a house – produced by college-educated adults from the United States. In my research, I have found numerous examples of Metric perspective, numerous Affine renderings, a couple of more or less correct Projective efforts, and even the occasional divergent excursion, but the intuitive grasp of Renaissance perspective seems to have eluded the reach of most of the adults. For objects considered alone, the Metric method clearly the preferred one. Metric projections also clearly dominate the art of children. There has been considerable speculation in the past about the reasons for this preference and even a little data on the use of different drawing systems by adults and by children.

Systems of projection in naive art

The few data that do exist on the relative frequencies drawing systems in the art of Western children have been collected primarily by John Willats (1977a,b) and Norman Freeman (1980). Figure 10.6 presents five methods drawing a square horizontal surface. This figure shows

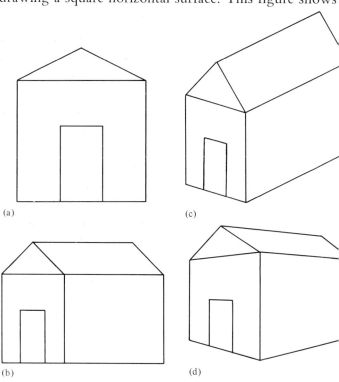

Figure 10.5. Typical drawings of a
house by present-day, college-
educated Western adults untrained in
art. (Redrawn by author.)

(a) (c)

(b) (d)

Figure 10.6. Five methods of
drawing a square horizontal surface.
(From Freeman 1980:254.)

(i)

(ii)

A   B   C   D   E

A. Two types of single supportive surface;
B. A vertical perpendicular construction;
C. An oblique projection;
D. Naive perspective;
E. "Canonical" perspective.

In terms of the geometrical projection systems, however, both A and B are Metric, C is Affine, D is a Projective projection with a distant center of projection, and E is a Projective projection with a close center. Willats examined the drawings of 108 children between the ages of five and sixteen years. All systems occurred in the drawings of the children with a clear age-related trend in the frequency of occurrence of the systems from A to E. The Affine system accounted for over 20 percent of the drawings. Willats asserted that this system does not correspond to what one ever sees and that adults do not use the style at all. Of course, neither of these assertions is correct and the reader is referred to the very fine Affine renderings in Figure 10.5.

Willats found that only a small minority of children used the Metric, or Orthogonal, methods, but this result is not supported by the findings of others. Figures 10.3 and 10.4 reveal that over half the drawings are Metric and a study cited in Norman Freeman's (1980) book on strategies of drawing in children yielded a similar finding. It may be the case that the children tested by Willats were a bit too old to be producing many Metric drawings, although the adult drawings in Figure 10.5 show that the Metric style never actually disappears from the drawings of ordinary people. Willats's children were between five and sixteen years of age, whereas most of the drawings shown above were produced by children between four and eight years.

In younger children, Orthogonality is commonplace;

from my counts, it seems to be the most frequently produced projection system. In older children Affine and Projective systems also make an appearance as reasonable solutions to the problems of representation. Individual adults, apart from artists, usually do not adopt a particular projection system as a consistently preferred style. Each object, or perhaps each class of object, seems to demand a particular style of rendering. The adults whose drawings are shown in Figure 10.5 each produced four drawings: house, car, man, and chair. Only 10 percent employed the same projection system across all four pictures. Eighty percent used two different systems, and 10 percent used three. Norman Freeman and Clara Hayton (Freeman 1980) found the same sort of thing in a study of twenty children ten to eleven years of age. The drawing system employed was a function of the object drawn. They remark: "Clearly it is too much to expect that the use of a drawing system will be independent of the object to be drawn." (1980: 258). It is not perfectly clear to me why that should be too much to expect. Certainly the artists within a culture draw most objects in the dominant geometry of their artistic zeitgeist. No art style is without its exceptions, as we have seen, but geometrical consistency is certainly the rule. However, the average adult, not to mention the average child, is not an artist. The average person drawing will try to reproduce all of the structures available to natural perspective, from Orthogonal to Projective, with the frequencies constrained somewhat by the artistic preferance of the culture. As the world becomes ever more homogeneously Western, if it does, the developmental trend observed by Willats probably will become the rule.

Canonical form

There are three interesting questions about the frequencies of drawing styles in the representational pictures of ordinary people, and two of them involve the issue of canonical form: Why are Metric projections so numerous in the art of young children? Why are Projective projections relatively rare in the drawings of the adults of a culture in which they are the accepted mode? Why do occasional examples of divergent perspective appear? The first two questions are frequently answered in terms of canonical form. It is said that Metric projections are commonplace because they are the canonical forms for many common objects, whereas Projective forms are rather rare because they do *not* show the canonical forms of many common objects. This argument becomes rather messy, as we saw in Chapter 4, as soon as one tries to specify what is meant by canonical form. Generally the concept evoked is so poorly defined as to explain very little. For example, Freeman (1980) writes: "It is as near a general purpose representation as can be achieved. The canonical representation of a triangle is most probably as an equilateral: the form which can generate the maximum number of other types of triangle with the minimum amount of transformation" (p. 17). It should be clear from Chapter 3 that in terms of any precise specification of the word "transformation," an equilateral triangle does not enjoy the special status that Freeman suggests.

The concept of canonical form is a terrific muddle. In her attempt to explain the high frequency of Orthogonal projections in children's art, Eng invokes the concept under different terminology. She writes that we have a basic tendency to hold fast to certain fundamental forms of objects, to their characteristic or "orthoscopic" forms. Eng says that the orthoscopic form of a table top is a rectangle, and, citing Katz (1906), she writes:

A square surface, in order to be seen as square, must be in a position at right angles to the line joining it to the observer, so that the lines of fixation of the eyes are symmetrical. This case therefore differs physiologically from others. It also differs psychologically, since the object is best grasped in this manner. If a rectangular surface, for example a picture, is not in this position, we move it until it is, in order to be able to see it clearly. Hence the rectangular surface is preferred in this form to all the other innumerable forms which it can assume from various points of view. (Eng 1931: 130)

This is a wonderful explanation, invoking as it does images of people rushing around to remain en face to all the rectangular surfaces in a room, bending over table tops, hunching over manuscripts being typed, and moving their heads from side to side while reading magazines held rigidly vertical. It is rather a far-fetched explanation. A less far-fetched but equally unsupported explanation for the use of canonical form in representations is offered by Freeman (1980). He believes, along with Rudolf Arnheim whom he cites frequently, that the canonical form of the human figure is a frontal projection (Orthogonal) because it preserves most of the distinctive spatial relationships, and that of a table the oblique projection shown in Figure 10.6C because it preserves the most information about the table's structure and supportive function. Freeman quotes Arnheim as saying that the oblique projection system is the "only method that unambiguously represents spatial orientation in the three dimensions" (p. 259). A great many people, including architects, engineers, artists, and myself disagree with Arnheim, and Freeman's post-hoc formulas give us no general rules to apply and evaluate.

I do not wish to conclude that canonical form is an empty concept. We do not know enough yet. We know that different projection systems preserve different numbers of invariant properties of the represented object; we know that each system allows the artist to convey somewhat different information about the subject. Despite the Freeman/Arnheim assertion, we know that Orthogonal systems preserve the most invariants and Projective systems the fewest. We know that Orthogonal projections are less tied to a specific time and place, to a particular point of view, than are Projective projections, and this suggests the reason for their popularity with children. As James Gibson argued in 1971, the momentary appearances of objects in frozen slices of time have very little to do with the perception of a changing world by a moving observer. The pickup of invariants takes place across change; we perceive the persistent properties of the world through the experience of transformations. Momentary structures are available in the light, but incidental to perception. If we believe that children represent their perceptions of the world, then the prevalence of both Orthogonality and multiplicity of station point in their work is readily understandable. So too is the relative infrequency of strictly Projective projections even in the work of adults. Gibson's argument holds as true for adults as for children. For purposes of successful representation alone, apart from the artistic conventions of a culture, Projective projections do not recommend themselves uniquely. They capture so few invariants; they are tied to a frozen moment of time. They make of the interactive world a still object, an extension of one's self. Such projections are certainly "natural" in that they occur in natural perspective all of the time, but frozen observation of a static world is hardly a commonplace occurrence in ordinary perception. To repeat the conclusion of Chapter 3, more work is needed on ecological geometry, on the geometry of the structures in the light under various naturally occurring situations, for us to reach conclusions about the existence and importance of canonical images.

Divergent perspective

The third rather interesting question that arises from observation of the drawing efforts of untutored people is: How can the occasional appearance of divergent perspective be explained? That it does indeed appear is evident in the drawings of both children and adults. Why is it a problem for the theory espoused here? Metric, Affine, and Projective projections all occur naturally. Situations and conditions of observation arise in ordinary perception of the ordinary world in which each of these three projection systems is approximated to within trivial limits in the structures of the light to the eye. However, it is not possible outside the laboratory to set up a visual situation in which the metrically parallel edges of a perceived surface would diverge in projection, be the projection parallel or central. As long as the surface remains rigid and light continues to travel in more or less straight lines, then the observer cannot experience divergent perspective retinally.

I have argued that representational art represents what actually is, that all of the different forms of perspective embraced by the art styles of the world are components of natural perspective, are structures in the light to the eye. Divergent perspective is no such thing except under contrived conditions. Why, then, does divergent perspective make an appearance in the world's art styles? The answer is that it doesn't. Various art styles have certainly flirted with use of the divergent device; it can be found in some Japanese works like *Hasadera Enji* (Fig. 7.7), in a few third-century Chinese works, in some Roman wall paintings, and most noticeably, in Gothic art. Divergent perspective is not *characteristic* of any of these styles, not even of the Gothic. It is a logical representational device to attempt for the depiction of spatial layout if only because it is the third of the pictorial possibilities for the representation of parallel edges in space: They can remain parallel, converge, or diverge. The first two make sense physically and the third does not. The first two were adopted by various cultures as enduring representational systems; the third was not. It is rather as if cultures experiment with all possible depiction modes, much as children and unartistic adults do, and adopt over time only those that make sense in terms of natural perspective. Thus we see that although divergent efforts are never very frequent, even in the drawings of young children, they become even less so in the artistic attempts of adults. It is noteworthy that the relatively recent use of divergent perspective by artists like Cézanne was never adopted with much consistency by his cultural cohorts or descendents, despite a vigorous intellectual defense of the technique for compositional purposes. Apparently, then, if a spatial layout system *cannot* look right in the ordinary world, it will not look right in a representational pictorial world.

Children and primitives

We have seen that outside of increased motor control and a growing but limited knowledge of the drawing devices and canons common in their culture, most ordinary people exhibit little if any development in their style of drawing over time. Of course, this lack of skill is apparent only in the drawings of the unartistic and untutored. It is also apparent that the art work of such people as the Northwest Coast Indians, the Bushmen, and the Stone Age people of Altamira and Lascaux could hardly be the product of artistically naive "primitives." Indeed, all this artwork very clearly shows the marks of a skilled hand, of practice and training. To argue that this is not the case demands some very complex explanations for the absence of skill in the adults of modern cultures. How then is it that comparisons between the artistic efforts of children and the artistic works of "primitive" adults were and are so common among psychologists, art educators and historians, and anthropologists?

The art of children and that of primitives are both more likely than skilled Western post-Renaissance artistic works to display multiple station points and Metric geometry. However, so too are the artistic endeavors of the average modern Western adult. This comparison is never made. For some reason, an attractive comparison frequently drawn is that between the "average savage," so to speak, and the gifted child. This comparison is made in response to the clear artistic superiority of such artists as those of Altamira, but it is a very misguided response. Its apparent intent is to acknowledge and compensate for the inferior motor skills of average children relative to adults, but the comparison creates a good many more problems than it solves. "Average savage" is a concept whose referent is extremely elusive, but without attempting definitions, I shall simply assert that the gifted child draws better than the average adult however savage or civilized. Further, it is not at all clear that it is possible to distinguish between the works of unartistic savage adults and those of unartistic civilized adults. So-called primitive art ranges from the Cave art of Altamira and Cueva del Civil (Figs. 8.19-20) to the petroglyphs from the island of Hawaii shown in Figure 10.7.

The drawings of untutored people look like the drawings of untutored people, be they children or adults, ancients or moderns, from whatever culture. There are characteristics of this body of work that distinguish it from *any* advanced artistic work and some that distinguish it only from very specific subdivisions of artistic work. Multiplicity of viewpoint and the presence of Orthogonal perspective are the most striking of the "primitive" characteristics, but they are also shared by advanced styles like that of the ancient Egyptians. Helga Eng (1931) provides us with a longer list and an explanation for the sim-

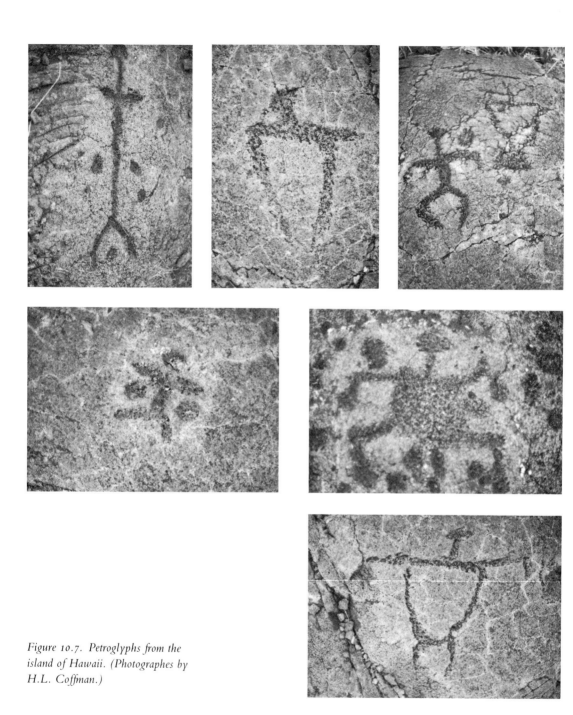

Figure 10.7. Petroglyphs from the island of Hawaii. (Photographes by H.L. Coffman.)

ilarities. She writes: "The unquestioned parallels between the drawings of primitive man and that of children – formalism, transparency, turning-over, spacelessness, want of synthesis – are based on features common to the psyche of the child and primitive man, on the want of firm voluntary attention, of penetrating analysis and higher synthesis, on the weakness of the power of abstraction and of logical and realistic thinking" (p. 213). Eng includes under the primitive man rubric even the skilled artists among the Bushmen, as well as Giotto and his contemporaries – indeed anyone not engaged in post-Renaissance painting. It is less contentious to describe the very diverse non-Renaissance artists in terms of the station-point assumptions they make than in terms of undeveloped psyche, which would condemn all of the unartistic among us modern Western adults to a very disconcerting developmental level – a level disconcerting to the theorists as well as to its assignees.

I think there is no other issue in the psychology of art subject to more prejudice and less thought than the question of development in culture and in individuals. A final example of the kind of muddled thinking that mars this area will suffice as a closing to this chapter. Helga Eng, after observing that Eskimo art is the product of highly practiced artists who use a multiple station point system, presents a study by Louise Maitland on the art of Eskimo children. Maitland writes: "Everything in these drawings is full of life and motion. At the same time, we find the mistakes characteristic of children's drawings, mixed profiles, confusion of plan and elevation, transparancy and turning over" (Eng 1931: 198). I cannot understand how it could have escaped anyone's attention that these observations apply equally well to the skilled artists of that culture. By Maitland's criteria, as the children grow more proficient in the creation of the art of the culture, they will grow ever more childlike.

Appendix A:
Affine transformations

Skew reflection

Ordinary reflection, the Metric transformation, is defined in the context of two distinct lines, x and y, perpendicular to each other in the plane. Skew reflection is similarly defined, but the axes are no longer perpendicular to each other. Then, given any point, M, of the plane, we draw the parallel to y through M, to meet x in P, and continue it to M'. Thus $MP = PM'$. So skew reflection is just reflection of points, lines, or figures through the x-axis, but in a direction parallel to the y-axis when the y-axis is not perpendicular to the x. (Visually, this is a lot clearer than it is verbally.) The examples in Figure A.1 show several skew reflections from simple to more complex. Note that distance is not preserved in all of the examples.

Skew compression

Skew compression is to compression as skew reflection is to ordinary reflection; that is, the direction of the compression is no longer perpendicular to the axis of the compression. For example, assume two lines x and y, *not* perpendicular to each other, and a positive number, k. (Fig. A.2). Then, through each point, M, of the plane, draw the line parallel to y, and let it meet x in P. Let M' be the point of PM such that $M'P = kMP$. If M lies on the line x, then $M' = M$. This transformation is called the Skew Compression onto the axis x in the direction of y and with the coefficient k. If $k < 0$, then the transformation is considered to be the product of the ordinary positive skew

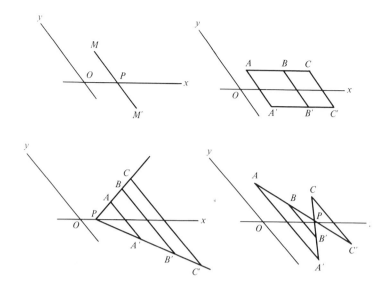

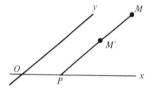

Figure A.1. Simple and complex
skew reflection.

compression with positive coefficient k and the skew reflection in x in the direction of y, in either order.

Hyperbolic rotation

Hyperbolic rotation is an exotic-looking transformation
that is really the simple product of two (skew) compressions in opposite directions. The examples in Figure A.3
illustrate hyperbolic rotation when the axes of compression
are perpendicular to each other: M' is the compression onto
Ox, parallel to y, with coefficient k; M'' is the compression
onto y, parallel to x, with coefficient $1/k$. This movement
of points is called hyperbolic rotation because on a hyperbolic curve the product of each of the point coordinate
values xy always equals a constant C, just as do the point

Figure A.2. Skew compression.

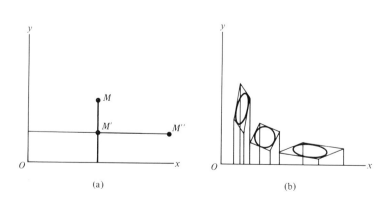

Figure A.3. Hyperbolic rotation
with perpendicular axes of
compression.

(a)   (b)

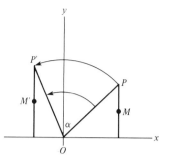

Figure A.4. Elliptic rotation.

products of this transformation, $x'y' = xy$. So, if a point, M, lies on a hyperbola $xy = C$, its image M' lies on the same hyperbola since $x'y' = xy = C$. Under hyperbolic rotation, areas of figures are preserved because all areas are multiplied first by k and then by $1/k$. In general, however, area is *not* preserved by affine transformations.

Elliptic rotation

Elliptic rotation is also the product of two compressions, but in this transformation both compressions have the same axis of compression and their product is combined with a rotation as well. In Figure A.4, A is a compression onto x with coefficient k $(k>1)$, R is a rotation about a point O of the line OP through an angle α, and A^{-1} is the reverse compression with coefficient $1/k$ following the rotation. Thus the elliptic transformation $T = ARA^{-1}$, and it takes each point, M, of the plane into M' via P and P'. It is called an elliptic rotation because it leaves invariant all of the ellipses with center O and major axis l with an ellipticity of k. (Ellipticity is the ratio between the major and minor axes of the ellipse.) That is, a circle (ellipse) is changed to an ellipse, rotated, and returned to a circle by this transformation. It should be noted that all the affine transformations can be described in terms of one or two compressions and a similarity transformation. This type of equivalence of transformations is one of the characteristics of a group of transformations.

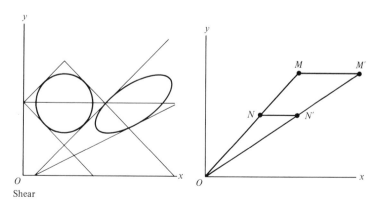

Shear

Figure A.5. Shear.

Shear

A shear transformation is a one-dimensional stretch. Assume two axes, x and y, not necessarily perpendicular to each other (Fig. A.5). A shear is a mapping of the plane that takes each point $M(x,y)$ of the plane onto the point M' (x', y') so that $x' = x + ky$ and $y' = y$. So the y values of the image points are left unchanged while each point is transferred horizontally (increasing or decreasing x) a distance proportionate to its distance from the x-axis, that is, a distance proportionate to the y value of each point.

Appendix B:
Cross-ratio of lines and the harmonic property

The cross-ratio of lines is the cross-ratio in which two lines, c and d, divide two other lines, a and b. Given four concurrent lines, a, b, c, d, with c and d between a and b, the cross-ratio is composed of two ratios of division: the ratio of division of a and b by c, and the ratio of division of a and b by d. (Fig. B.1). The first ratio of division in the figure is given by KC/JC. We say that the ratio in which the line c cuts lines a and b is the line segment (KC) between lines c and b formed when a line is drawn perpendicular to b and intersecting c at some angle, and the line segment (JC) between a and c formed when a segment is drawn from the point of intersection, C, of KC and line c to the line a, at a $90°$ angle to a. The second ratio of division, that of a and b by d, is given by LD/MD, derived in a similar manner. Then, $KC/JC = r1$, and $LD/MD = r2$, and $r1/r2$ is the cross-ratio of the lines a, b, c, d. The cross-ratio of lines, like the cross-ratio of points, is invariant for all positions of the center of projection.

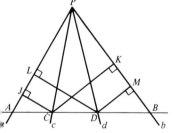

Figure B.1. *Invariant cross-ratio of lines.*

Harmonic property

Four collinear points A, B, C, D are said to be a harmonic set when the value of their cross-ratio equals -1.

Appendix C:
Trigonometric functions and the gradients

Trigonometric functions

Trigonometric functions are basically just the ratio of one side of a triangle to another. Consider Figure C.1. Here a triangle is drawn in ordinary rectangular coordinates with angle θ at the origin. The sides are called x, y, and r (for radius of a circle that could be drawn). The trigonometric functions are then all the possible ratios of x, y, and r to each other. They are

sin	=	y/r	sine
cos	=	x/r	cosine
tan	=	y/x	tangent
cot	=	x/y	cotangent
sec	=	r/x	secant
csc	=	r/y	cosecant

The trigonometric functions of similar triangles are equal. Similar triangles have the same shape, the same three angles. The lengths of the sides of two similar triangles are always proportional so the trigonometric functions, which are ratios of one side to another, must be the same.

Purdy's exposition of the gradients

In Figure C.2 from Purdy (1959), the large triangle, OPN is approximately similar to $XP'F$ when the angle a subtended by the ground unit $A \times A$ is small relative to the depression angle r. In that case, we consider angle r and angle r' to be identical, or very nearly. Since both these triangles also have a right angle, we know the third angle must be equal as well (because the three angles of a triangle

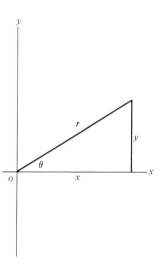

*gure C.1. The trigonometric
ctions.

add up to 180°). Three equal angles determine similar triangles, and therefore proportional sides and equal trigo-
nometric functions like $\sin r = XF/XP' = ON/OP = H/OP$. In Figure C.2, the eye of the observer is at O, the
height of the observer above the ground is $H = ON$, and
N is the nadir – the point on the ground directly under the
nodal point of the lens of the eye. The ground is marked
off in units that measure $A \times A$. OP is the direction of
the gaze and the angle r is the number of degrees down
from the horizontal of the gaze (the angle of depression).
When the observer is looking straight out at the horizon,
the angle, r, is 0 degrees; when the observer is looking
straight down, the angle r is 90° off the horizontal. When
units of texture along the ground are being considered, as
in this figure, the angle r' formed between OP and a line
running straight along the ground from N to P is the same
as the angle r above (as long as angle a is very small relative
to angle r). Angle a is the angle subtended by the near–far
dimension of the ground unit, and angle b is the angle
subtended by the width, the left–right dimension of the
ground unit. Together, angle a and b comprise the solid
angle, w, subtended by the whole square ground unit.
Purdy wrote that angle a is given approximately as follows:

$$a = F/OP = A \sin r \times \sin r/H =$$
$$(A/H) \sin^2 r \qquad\qquad (1)$$

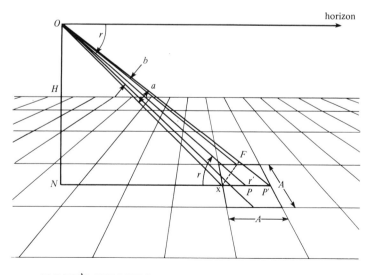

*ure C.2. An illustration of the
ivation of the texture gradients.
om Purdy 1959.)*

To get this, multiply the numerator and denominator fi▮
by A/A, then by H/H. Assuming the triangles are simila
both F/A and H/OP are equal to sin r, so simply substitu
sin r for these ratios. Angle b is given thus:

$$b = A/OP = (A/H) \sin r.$$

To get this, multiply A/H by H/H and substitute sin r f
H/OP. The solid angle $w = a \times b$, so the equation is:

$$w = a \times b = ((A/H) \sin^2 r) ((A/H) \sin r)$$
$$= (A^2/H^2) \sin^3 r.$$

A is the size of the ground texture unit and A^2 is the ar
of the unit; H is the height of the eye above the grou▮
and sin r simply equals H over OP. It is therefore qu
simple to put in actual values and solve the equations
determine the size of the solid angle w.

Of course, the main point about a gradient is that it
a measure of *change* in something. So the solid angle w th
measures the projected size of any single unit of grou
texture at whatever place on the surface is not in its▮
important here, but the change in w with distance is. Pur
defined the *gradient of texture size* as the relative rate
change of the solid angle subtended by successive textu
elements as the line of regard is swept along a radial ▮
rection. That gives us

$$G_s = \frac{dw/dr}{w}$$

where G_s is the gradient of texture size, w is the sol▮
angle size, and r is the depression angle or the angle ▮
tween the ground surface and the line of regard. Subs
tuting the solid-angle equation (3) for w, we get the absol▮
rate of change of w with respect to depression-angle r
differentiating equation # 4:

$$\frac{dw}{dr} = \frac{A^2}{H^2} 3 \sin^2 r \cos r$$

The relative rate of change of solid angular size, w, w▮
respect to the depression angle r is found by dividing t
equation (5) by w:

$$G_s = \frac{dw/dr}{w} = \frac{A^2/H^2 \; 3 \sin^2 r \cos r}{A^2/H^2 \; \sin^3 r}$$

Then,

$$G_s = 3 \cot r \qquad (6)$$

Purdy pointed out that the relative rate of change of solid angular size with depression angle is independent of the height of the station point, H, and of the size or coarseness of the physical texture. It is a function only of the depression angle, r, which, in the ordinary course of events, is simply a function of how far away one is looking, that is, the distance of the target.

Working from this function (6), Purdy developed all the other monocular gradients, which are simple variations on the same theme. Briefly, the *gradient of texture density* is

$$G_D = de/dr \;/\; e \qquad (G_D = -3 \cot r) \text{ differentiated}$$

where e is the number of texture elements per unit of solid angle, however determined. The *gradient of size perspective* is essentially the same as the gradient of texture size. The *gradient of linear perspective* is the convergence of receding parallel edges to a vanishing point on the horizon. Purdy defines it as the relative rate of change (convergence) of the angular size of the interval between the parallel edges of a surface as the line of regard is swept along a radial direction, that is,

$$G_L = db/dr \;/\; b \qquad (G_L = \cot r)$$

where b is the angular separation of the parallel lines, as defined above for the width of a unit of ground surface, and r is again the depression angle. The *gradient of texture compression*, the foreshortening that a pattern undergoes in perspective, was defined by Purdy as the ratio of angular size of the radial dimension to angular size of the tangential dimension of a texture element, that is $c = a/b$ where a and b are defined as above. Then

$$G_C = dc/dr/c \qquad (G_C = \cot r)$$

For irregular textures, mean sizes and other measures of the above are used, which is how the term "stochastically" regular came into use.

In summary then, Purdy argued that each of the gradients of the optical stimulus is related to the spatial parameters of the physical environment by the same general function, namely,

$$G = k \cot r$$

where r is the optical slant or the depression angle of t[h]e line of regard from the horizon of the surface, and k is[a] constant peculiar to the particular kind of gradient. Purd[y] argued that all of these gradients are particular cases of[a] general relationship between the physical environment a[nd] the optical stimulus, which relationship is independent [of] the position of the station point of the eye and of the patte[rn] or texture on the surface (within the class of the stochas[t]ically regular textures). Purdy defined *perceived* slant [as] distinct from *physical* optical slant:

$$r' = \text{arc cot } \frac{1}{k}G$$

and argued that perceived optical slant r' is equal to r [if] the surface texture is stochastically regular. Purdy extend[ed] this gradient analysis to a specification of the slant, di[s]tance, height, width and depth, and shape of objects, [as] well as to the effects of magnification in ways that ne[ed] not concern us here. For a modern analysis of gradien[ts] not dependent on certain of Purdy's less tenable assum[p]tions, see Sedgwick (1980).

Appendix D:
Natural perspective: a history of structure in the light

Information and appearance

The visual information for the size and shape and such characteristics of things in the environment ought to bear some relation to the way they look to the ordinary observer. So it would seem that a characterization of visual information ought to produce a fairly comprehensive description of the appearance of things in the environment. This is the approach that I have taken throughout this book, but it depends largely on the interpretation of the seemingly clear and innocuous phrase "the appearance of things" in the environment, and on what is meant by "visual information." Ten people asked to write what they mean by these terms generally produce astonishingly diverse phenomenological descriptions and psychological theories.

This terminological and conceptual muddle involving "visual perception," "visual information," "natural perspective," and "the appearance of things" can be cleared up only through an understanding of the history of the terms and issues, of their changing references and ramifications. How we know by sight alone what and where things are and what is happening to them is not a matter on which there is or ever has been much agreement, although it has long occupied the attention of many good thinkers. There is a great deal of controversy over the general *structure* of the light to the eye, and no consensus on what properties of light do and do not serve as visual *information* for the objects and events in the world. The structural question generally deals with the issue of the

relationship between the light to the eye and the obje[ct]
in the world from which it is reflected. What kind of [re-]
lationship is it? One of resemblance or of arbitrary sig[ni-]
fication? One of abstract formalisms irrelevant to percepti[on]
or of geometric correspondences informative for visi[on?]
"Natural perspective" is the general term for the struct[ure]
of the light to the eye, and "natural perspective geometr[y]"
is the mathematical description of natural perspective[,]
whatever that may be. The information question exami[nes]
the adequacy for the support of visual perception of wh[at-]
ever optical structures are deemed to exist. Historical si[gn-]
posts, like the terms and issues in visual theory, may [be]
more a matter of viewpoint than of consensus, but i[t is]
nevertheless to history that I shall turn to lay the foundat[ion]
for the modern geometrical analysis of vision. I shall be[gin]
with Euclid because he provided the foundation upon wh[ich]
modern visual theory is built.

Structure in the light to the eye:
history of visual angles

Euclid

Euclid in *Optica* (c. 300 B.C.) developed the first comp[re-]
hensive model to describe and determine the relations[hip]
between the visual world and the ordinary environme[nt.]
He bequeathed us the concept of *visual angle* as the h[eart]
of this relationship between how things appear to be [and]
how they actually are. Visual angles are formed suppose[dly]
by rays emitted from the eye in straight lines falling [on]
objects in the world; rays must fall on an object for it [to]
be seen. Euclid generated a number of visual postula[tes]
based on the two assumptions that visual rays trave[l in]
straight lines forming solid visual angles with bases at [ob-]
ject surfaces, and that *the appearance of objects is governe[d by]
the size and location of these visual angles*. The most fami[liar]
of these postulates are the ones stating that things s[een]
within a larger angle appear larger, those within a sma[ller]
angle smaller, those within equal angles appear equal; th[at]
things seen by higher or lower rays appear higher or low[er,]
respectively, and those seen by rays to the left or ri[ght]
appear to be to the left or right, respectively.

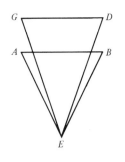

Figure D.1. "Objects of equal size unequally distant appear unequal and the one lying nearer to the eye always appears larger." (After Euclid: Fig. 5, p. 358.)

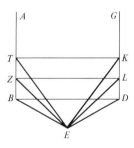

Figure D.2. "Parallel lines, when seen from a distance, appear not to be equally distant from each other." (After Euclid: Fig. 6, p. 358.)

These postulates are critical for determining the appearance of things geometrically, yet they are not in themselves demonstrated geometrically. The relationship between appearance, a perceptual property of vision, and angular structures composed of visual rays and object surface planes, the geometrical property of vision, was assumed by Euclid in his postulates, not proven in his propositions. This weakness in the theory left it vulnerable to later attack.

Euclid used the postulates, along with certain propositions dealing with the properties of triangles, to determine the appearance of things seen under a variety of conditions. For example, he worked out the rules determining apparent size and the nonparallel appearance of parallel lines at a distance. Figure D.1 illustrates Proposition 5: *Objects of equal size unequally distant appear unequal and the one lying nearer to the eye always appears larger.* In these propositions, "objects" are usually lines and points. Euclid argued that the nearer line (AB) appears longer than the farther (GD) because, with the eye at the common vertex (E), the angle (AEB) formed when the visual rays fall on the endpoints of the near line (A and B) is greater than the angle (GED) formed when the visual rays fall on the endpoints of the farther (G and D), and "things seen within greater angles appear larger." This line of reasoning gave succeeding ages what is called the "size-constancy problem." Proposition 6 uses a similar argument to describe the nonparallel appearance of parallel lines seen at a distance. The proposition states: "*Parallel lines, when seen from a distance, appear not to be equally distant from each other*" (Fig. D.2). Euclid reasoned that with the eye again at the common point (E), the angle formed with the nearest line ($<BED$) is greater than the angle formed with the middle line ($<ZEL$), which is greater than the angle formed with the farthest ($<TEK$). Thus the nearest line (BD) appears greater than the middle line (ZL), which in turn is greater than the farthest line (TK) because these three lines fall within the three angles respectively. Thus the two parallel lines, AB and GD, will appear to be closer and closer together the farther and farther they are from the eye. This proposition still has many adherents today in people who argue that railroad tracks, for instance, appear to become progressively closer with distance. How-

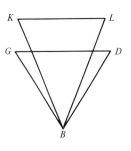

Figure D.3. *"Objects located nearby are seen more clearly than objects of equal size located at a distance." (After Euclid: Fig. 2, p. 357.*

ever, as James Gibson, the noted perceptual psycholog once remarked, railroad tracks may appear closer toget to the painter but not to the train engineer: "If the r appear even slightly convergent to an engineer, it is ti to apply the emergency brakes" (1950:38).

Not all of Euclid's propositions can be proved using o the postulates dealing with rectilinearity and visual ang Some demonstrations require the use of what might called the "perceptual" postulates, or aspects of postula dealing with the character of the visual rays themselv These postulates state that visual rays come from the e and diverge to the limits of our vision, and that obje seen within more angles appear more clear. These sumptions allow for some arguments that are, to the co temporary theorist, somewhat surprising. For examp Proposition 1 states: *"Nothing that is seen is seen at once its entirety"* and the case is made that because the vis rays are divergent from the eye they could not fall cont uously on an object. The rays of vision are shifted rapic giving the impression of continuous visibility. It is diffic to interpret this argument because nowhere does Eu indicate how great he thinks the momentary span of prehension is. If the span is only two points large, point where each of two rays strikes an object, then rays of vision must be shifted rapidly indeed to maint a stable visual experience. Looking at an object would rather like exploring a pitch-dark environment with t tiny pen lights.

Euclid's second "perceptual" proposition is Proposit 2, which states: *"Objects located nearby are seen more cle than objects of equal size located at a distance."* Using Fig D.3, Euclid argued, essentially, that all the rays that on the far line (KL) fall on the nearer (GD), but the c verse cannot be so unless the farther line was longer t the nearer, which is not the case; clearly, then, more vis rays fall on the nearer than on the farther. Thus, "GD appear more clear than KL: for objects seen within m angles appear more clear." Obviously this strange ar ment is coherent only if one accepts the perceptual p tulates. One last example will illustrate the nature consequences of the perceptual assumptions in Euclid's

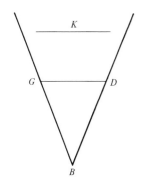

Figure D.4. "Every object seen has a certain limit of distance, and when this is reached, it is seen no longer." (After Euclid: Fig. 5, p. 357.)

tics. In Proposition 3 Euclid states: "*Every object seen has a certain limit of distance, and when this is reached it is seen no longer.*" At first hearing, this sounds as if Euclid were going to argue that objects that are too small or too far away, like a fly at 1,000 feet, cannot be seen because the visual angles they occupy are too small for vision. He is not. With reference to Figure D.4, he writes, "For let *GD* lie midway in the divergence of the rays, at the limit of which is *K*. So, none of the rays from *B* will fall upon *K*. And the thing upon which rays do not fall is not seen. Therefore, every object seen has a certain limit of distance, and, when this is reached, the object is seen no longer." This argument is not perfectly clear even if one accepts the concepts of divergent rays and the limit of vision. Euclid assumed the limit of vision to prove the limit of vision.

These propositions concerning the clarity, range of apprehension, and limit of vision, as well as related propositions, all follow from Euclid's assumption that the visual rays are *emitted from* the eyes, *not reflected to* them. In most cases, whether the visual rays come to or from the eyes is not critical for determination of appearance even in Euclid's system. The critical factor is the *rectilinearity*, the straightness, of the rays. The relative sizes, distances, and locations of objects will be determined exactly as they are for Euclid under the assumption that the visual rays travel *from* objects *to* the eye, and the proofs will be the same. But Propositions like 1, 2, and 3 about the span, clarity, and extent of vision will not necessarily be the same under the alternative intromission theory, and where they are, the proofs cannot be the same. For example, Propositions 1 and 2 stating the relationship between number of visual rays and angles and clarity and range of vision cannot be maintained if the rays are assumed to be continuous rather than discrete. This book is not the place for a review of the centuries of debate over the directionality of the visual rays, and, besides, we know who won that argument (intromission). Suffice it to say that reflected-light theory was a long time reaching ascendance because it failed to provide a satisfactory solution to the problem of determining which of the large number of rays emanating or reflecting from an object will reach the eye and effect perception. So, all the progress

made by Euclid and his followers in describing the rela
tionship between visual rays and things seen could not b
applied to the theory of reflected light.

It was Alhazen (b. 965 A.D.), an Arabic geometer, sci
entist, and philosopher, who made the postulates and proo
of the *Optica* applicable to reflected-light theory. Alhaze
argued that the cornea and lens of the eye are concentri
and that only rays striking at right angles to both will reac
the back of the eye and stimulate vision. David Lindberg
in *Theories of Vision from Al-Kindi to Kepler* (1976) explain
"By confining his attention to the perpendicular rays, A
hazen managed to appropriate the visual pyramid of Eu
clidean and Ptolemaic optics, thereby transforming th
intromission theory into a mathematical theory of visio
. . . able to accomplish mathematically everything that ha
traditionally been achievable only with the mathematic
theories of Euclid, Ptolemy, and al-Kindi" (p. 78). Thu
intromission optics gained the power to determine, as i
extromission optics, the relative sizes, distances, *and loc*
tions of objects on the bases of *visual angles* and the rect
linearity of visual rays, while avoiding the problem
occasioned by the Euclidean "perceptual" postulates dea
ing with divergent extromitted rays and the limit of visio
Additionally, Alhazen's assumption that the visual rays a
very nearly continuous, because their object sources a
punctiform, removed the problems of limited clarity ar
span of apprehension following from the Euclidean po
tulates. However, it should also be remembered that si
nificant as his achievement has proven to be in th
development of the theory of vision, Alhazen was wron
Figure D.5 is a reminder that intromission of light to th
eye is not quite as simple as he proposed. Neverthele
the geometrical specification of intromitted light followir
Alhazen's formulation is a legacy with us today. *The r*

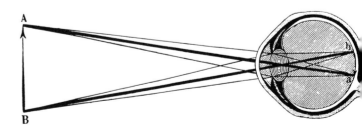

Figure D.5. The effect of the lens
on the light to the eye. (From
Pirenne 1970:3, top.)

A

B

*lationship between the visual world and the ordinary environment
as worked out by Euclid in terms of the visual-angle specification
of relative sizes, distances, and locations was thereafter an aspect
of visual theory.*

Question of resemblance

What kind of relationship was this between "the world as
seen" and "the world as it is"? *Resemblance* is not exactly
the right concept to describe this relationship; it is more
one of *mutuality of determination*, of a wholeness made out
of two parts. The base of an angle and its apex are not
separate things; they define each other mutually. The size
and the shape of the angle are determined by the spatial
relationship between the base and the apex and can be
altered by a change in either component. Moreover, Euclid
assumed that appearance was determined by *relations* between such variable angles. He thought that the appearance
of things in the world was a function of the relations between at least *two* visual angles. All of Euclid's propositions
concerning appearance turn out to be based on angular
comparison. It seems that a single object at a single point in
time could present no appearance to the viewer at all. One
must have at least two objects at one time or one object
at two different times or places. For Euclid, it was the
relative sizes, shapes, and locations of visual angles that
determined the apparent sizes, shapes, and locations of
things in the world.

Again, is this a relation of resemblance? Do the relative
sizes, shapes, and locations of visual angles actually *resemble*
the relative sizes, shapes, and locations of objects in the
world? Well, an object to the left will appear to be to the
left, and the visual angle it generates (exterior to the nodal
point of the lens) will be to the left. Certainly an object
that is small produces a visual angle that is small and the
object appears to be small as well. At least, it appears to
be smaller than a bigger object, unless the bigger object is
farther away. A smaller, nearer object is indistinguishable
from a larger, farther object. This is the perceptual problem
of *size constancy*, which, along with its cousin, *shape constancy*, we owe to the formulations of Euclid. What do the

constancy problems imply about the resemblance relatio
between visual angles and objects in the world? Certain
small angles resemble small objects in that they both a
small. But how do small angles resemble far objects? The
do not. We say that far objects appear to be small becau
they occupy small visual angles and appearance is go
erned, supposedly, by visual angle. Apparent size shoul
be governed by visual angle size. There is a direct, sp
cifiable relationship between the sizes, shapes, and loc;
tions of visual angles and the sizes, shapes, and location
of objects in the world, but it is by no means a simp
resemblance relation. Not in the simple sense that visu
angles to the left are determined by objects to the left
small visual angles by small objects or even circular sol
angles by circular objects.

This lack of a simple resemblance relationship was
major reason that visual angles became discredited as
source of information about the world. They give info
mation for what is always called *apparent* size, shape, a
location, but there is no perceptually understandable r
lationship between "appearance" in this sense and the thin
themselves. One would know very little about the tr
sizes, shapes, and locations of objects if there were
information to rely on except Euclid's visual angles. Visu
angles are infinitely ambiguous about their sources.

Problem of appearance

What does "appearance" mean, anyway? Do objects fa
ther away from you really appear to be small in the sen
that a close, truly small object does? Do people seem
grow and shrink as they walk to and fro? No. Of cour
not. So what is "appearance"? The concept could be
artifact of Euclid's formulation of visual experience, b
that wouldn't account for certain types of experience. Is
not true that sometimes, under certain circumstances, o
can be aware at least to a limited extent of the appearan
of things in Euclid's sense of the term? This is particular
true when some comparison standard is used. For examp
when the thumb is held out at a constant distance in fro
of the face, as in an old-fashioned drawing class, then it

easy to notice the angular size of objects at different distances compared to the angular size of the thumb. That is, the thumb subtends a visual angle of a certain size when it is at a certain distance and the visual angle of the thumb can be compared with the visual angle subtended by other objects. When people say, "It appears small because it is far away," they mean that the object subtends a small visual angle. They do *not* mean that the object itself appears to be small but growing in size as one approaches it. Thus, by "appearance" people generally mean two seemingly inconsistent things – how things really look, and how things would look if perception were truly governed by visual angle alone.

Euclid's formulation lands us right in the middle of the question of how we ever arrive at the higher level experience of "appearance," which we do take to be the way things really are. Again, for example, we know that parallel edges "appear" to get closer and closer together with increasing distance, while we also know that parallel edges actually "appear" parallel and different from edges not parallel to each other. What machinations (today called "processing") have to take place for us to move from the experience of visual-angle appearance to that of so-called "true" appearance? Because the relationship between surfaces in the world and visual angle is one of an infinity to one, it was assumed for a very long time that it was necessary to postulate some other source of "visual" information in order to resolve all this ambiguity.

What then is the legacy of Euclid to the understanding of the visual perception of the world?

1. "Appearance" is a concept with two rather strongly opposed meanings.
2. Reliance on visual angles alone for the determination of perceived size, shape, and location of objects engenders the theoretical and perceptual problem of the infinite ambiguity of visual angles as to world sources.
3. Since visual-angle appearance, as a source of information for "true" size, shape, and location, is unreliable in the extreme, both the theoretician and the ordinary perceiver must have access to some other, more reliable

source of information about the way things "really
are.

The Renaissance painters

The hopeless indeterminacy of visual "information" f
vision came about largely because Euclid considered on
two or three visual angles at a time, and never consider
the complex of relations among many angles simultar
ously. The outlook for the future of visual informati
became a good deal more hopeful when the Renaissan
painters came along because of two critical differences b
tween the painters' approach and Euclid's.

First, the Renaissance painters dropped a plane, the pi
ture plane, between the objects in the world and the ey
and, second, on that plane they projected not just one
two or three visual angles, but whole scenes of nested visu
angles from a myriad of world objects. With little analys
but with an impressive array of demonstrations – fillin
the art museums of the Western world – they develop
the isolated visual angle of Euclid into the set of subtend
angles, nested small into large, that we recognize as t
perspective image or scene on the picture plane. The plan
conceived of as a window, was situated in front of t
observer, cutting right through all of the solid visual a
gles. (Figure D.6). From this time on, it was not visu
angle that was touted as the source of information abo
the world, but the sections through the angles comprisin
the images on the picture plane. With this advance, it b
came much easier to talk about the two levels of appea
ance: We have the way things really are and the way the
appear in a picture.

Perceptual propositions

In addition, the painters adopted or developed a set
"perceptual" propositions considerably extending the rath
modest assumptions made by Euclid about the nature
the perceptual process. As summarized by John White
his book *The Birth and Rebirth of Pictorial Space* (1967:27
five of the main propositions of the painters were

Figure D.6. A Renaissance "picture window" (Reprinted from Dürer, 1963).

1. Visible things are not comprehended by means of the visual sense alone.
2. It is only possible to judge the distance of an object by means of an intervening, continuous series of regular bodies.
3. The visual angle alone is not sufficient for the judgment of size.
4. Knowledge of the size of an object depends upon a comparison of the base of the visual pyramid with the angle at its apex.
5. Distance is most commonly measured by the surface of the ground and the size of the human body. (See Fig. 6.1)

These propositions created what might be called *pictorial scene analysis*, which was missing in Euclid's exposition of optical information, as he dealt with a very small number of rays or angles at a time.

Of course it was still necessary to stipulate various machinations by which one moved from seeing pictures to seeing the world. To accomplish this, all the so-called "depth cues" by means of which we are said to "interpret" pictures were invented. It would seem that a newer, richer *Optica*

would have been written integrating Euclid's and the painters' insights, particularly after the discovery by Kepler of
images or pictures on the retina. His discovery paved the
way for a theory of vision based on the idea of little pictures
in the eye, but no one ever wrote the book. A "little
pictures" theory of vision was certainly developed and is
the dominant theory today, but neither its roots nor its
assumptions are often stated explicitly.

"Little pictures"

Generally, it was believed from Kepler's time to the present
that little pictures were projected onto the retina much as
if it were a canvas. Thus, all of the analysis of information
in pictures and the attendant interpretative "depth cues"
were applied, *mutatis mutandis*, to the analysis of ordinary
perception. What do a picture and the objects it pictures
have in common? Certainly, the sizes of picture images
are not the same as the sizes of the objects, and the shapes
of the images are certainly not the same as the shapes of
the objects. Color in a restricted range of wavelength and
brightness is somewhat the same in pictures and the ordinary environment if one stretches quite a few points, and
location – in terms of up, down, left, and right – is similar.
What of distance? All the picture pieces are on the same
plane, which is not quite the same thing as being at the
same distance because the shortest distance on the plane is
right in front of the viewer and all other points are farther
away, but certainly the variable distances in the real world
do not resemble the same-plane distances of objects in
pictures. Thought about in this way, the resemblances between pictures of the world and the world they picture are
not very impressive. It happens that pictures and their
subjects, projections of surfaces and the surfaces themselves, do have various things in common, but most of
those things are not easy to describe without modern geometry. And the Renaissance painters did not have the
geometry, nor did their descendants for 400 years.

   We can see from the painters' principles listed above
under "Perceptual Propositions" that greater attention was
focused on compensating for the limitations of pictures

than on extolling or exploiting the similarities between pictures and world. Perhaps for this reason, other thinkers, such as Descartes, Berkeley, and Helmhottz, in the visual perceptual realm, were not much impressed by the resemblances between visual images and objects, nor with geometrical analysis of information for vision. The rejection of resemblance between visual images and the world is largely their legacy to the theory of perception today. They concentrated their attention on the development of *extravisual* sources of information about the world. Most of their theorizing involved the role of haptic, or touch, information in the acquisition of knowledge about the world. Their approach is often tagged the "touch teaches vision" approach, where "touch" was and is interpreted broadly enough to mean the movements of the eyes, limbs, and whole body as well as the movements or activities of the hands.

"Extravisual" visual information

Descartes: physiological reductionism

Descartes rejected even considering the question of resemblance, expressing little interest in the realism of visual images. He wrote: "Now it is in this way that we must think of the images which take form in the brain, and must recognize that the only question we need raise is that of knowing how the images can supply to the mind the means of sensing all the diverse qualities of the objects to which they stand related, and not how in themselves they bear resemblance to them" (1637:147). As indicated by a remark he made about the falsity of one of the axioms of the "ancient optics," Descartes apparently felt that geometrical optics was either inapplicable or misleading for his theory of vision. Given his assumption of the lack of much resemblance between image and object, it was incumbent on Descartes to provide other, nonpictorial sources of information about what he thought of as the six principle aspects of the objects of vision: light, color, situation, distance, magnitude, and shape. He gave us an abundance of such mechanisms, many of which survive in theory today.

*Figure D.7. "As regards situation, we do not perceive it otherwise by our eyes than by our hands."
(Descartes,* La Dioptrique *[Sixth Disco..rse], p. 105.)*

To explain the perception of *light* and *color*, Descartes wrote that "we have to think of our soul as being of such a nature that the force of the movements which take place at the points in the brain at which the small fibers of the optic nerve terminate, determine it to have the sensation of light, and the sensation of color" (p. 152). Brightness is due to the quantity of light that moves the optic-nerve fibers; quantity varies as a function of the amount of light that is in the objects, the size and distance of the object from the observer, and the amount of space on the back of the eye occupied by rays from the object. Descartes wrote that "light is nothing else than a movement, or an action which tends to cause some movement . . ." and different colors are different kinds of movements of light which move the points on the retina in different ways.

Descartes argued: "As regards *situation*, i.e., the side toward which each part of the object is located relatively to our body, we do not perceive it otherwise by our eyes than by our hands." He gave the example of a blind man touching an object with the ends of two sticks held one in each hand. (Figure D.7). He argued that the nerves in the hand cause certain changes in the brain that give the mind the means of knowing the location of the hands and of all the points along the sticks held in the hands including, presumably, the point of intersection. He held that the same informative innervation of muscle is operative when the eye or head turns in a certain direction. He does not, in this case, explicitly reject geometrical argument, but neither does he accept it. In the passage on *distance* perception immediately following, the appeal to what he calls "natural geometry" is clear. Again with recourse to the blind-man analogy, Descartes argued that just as the blind man can determine the position of a point by the interval between his hands and the magnitude of the angles formed by his hands and the sticks, so also can the distance of a point be determined by the knowledge of the interocular distance and the angle of convergence of the two eyes on a point. Descartes said that this process is "a reasoning quite similar to that which surveyors make when, by means of two different stations, they measure inaccessible points." Descartes wrote that this operation can also be performed

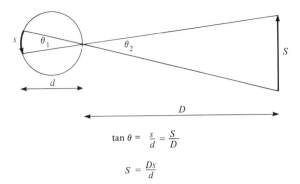

$$\tan \theta = \frac{s}{d} = \frac{S}{D}$$

$$S = \frac{Ds}{d}$$

Figure D.8. Computation of "real" size from retinal size.

by a single eye through change in its position. Note, however, that the calculation is performed on lines and angles formed by the *body*, not present in the *light*. He also proposed that *relative* distance could be perceived through the use of familiar size or shape, color, situation, or brightness in conjunction with the retinal image. Then relative size and shape could be estimated from the perceived distance plus the size of the retinal images – in a kind of chicken-and-egg perceptual process. This remains a popular theory in perception today (Figure D.8).

Descartes's theory of vision, then, rested on access of the perceiver to immediately felt tangible and proprioceptive innervations, to trigonometric tables and computation rules, and to visual images analyzed at least into patterns of varying quantities (brightnesses) and qualities (colors) of light. That is, Descartes appealed to nervous sensations, to geometry, and to images to explain vision.

A critical difference between Descartes's theory of vision and the theories of Euclid and the Renaissance painters is that Descartes did not put the burden of information on the visual rays to or from the eye, but rather on the sensory processes of the nerves and brain. Indeed, one might characterize Descartes as the father of physiological reductionism – the theoretical approach to the study of vision that reduces all questions and answers to the level of physiology, usually neurophysiology. He wrote that the soul will sense as many different qualities in objects as there are varieties in the movements caused by those objects in the brain. From this point of view, the resemblance, geometrical or otherwise, between objects and visual images, or between objects and types of movements in the light (what we call structure) is secondary. One could argue that the very postulation of types of movements in the light as the primary source of visual stimulation should have invited further analysis of that light, but for Descartes, it did not.

Berkeley's contribution

Dismissive as Descartes was of a relation of resemblance between light, or image, and object, and of geometrical analysis of images, it fell to Berkeley to completely reject the possibility that information for the world is carried in the light to the eye or in the pattern of stimulation at the eye. In *An Essay Towards A New Theory of Vision* (1709), Berkeley began by pointing out that everyone agrees that distance, of itself and immediately, cannot be seen. "For distance being a line directed end-wise to the eye, it projects only one point in the fund of the eye, which point remains invariably the same, whether the distance be longer or shorter." Therefore, since distance is by its own nature *imperceptible*, and yet perceived by sight, it follows that the perception of distance is effected by some other *perceptible* idea.

For Berkeley, it was perfectly clear that since the lines and angles of the geometers were not themselves perceivable by sight, they certainly could not be the vehicle for the perception of *distance* (Fig. D.9). Berkeley argued that it is the *sensations* that accompany the alteration of the dispositions of our eye, the lessening and widening of the distance between the pupils as the eyes are turned, that brings the ideas of greater or lesser distance into the mind. (Today, this is called "convergence.") He was swift to point out, however, that the connection between distance and disposition of the eyes is neither natural nor necessary.

But because the mind has by constant experience found the different sensations corresponding to the different dispositions of the eyes to be attended each with a different degree of distance in the object, there has grown an habitual or customary connexion between those two sorts of ideas, so that the mind no sooner perceives the sensation arising from the different turn it gives the eye, in order to bring the pupils nearer or farther

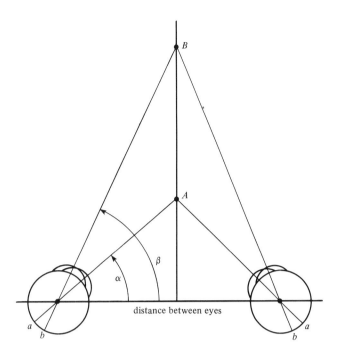

Figure D.9. The computation of relative distance with convergence information.

assunder, but it withal perceives the different idea of distance which was wont to be connected with that sensation. (p.174)

Berkeley wrote we must not think that "brutes and children" or even "grown reasonable men" perceive the varying distances of objects by virtue of geometry and demonstration.

Berkeley thus rejects any appeal to so-called "natural geometry" as information for distance whether the geometrical analysis be applied to the light to the eye or to the sensations arising from eye muscle movement. The mind does not perceive the *angles* formed by the converging eyes and the axis between them; it perceives only the *sensations* caused by the positioning of the eyes. It is these directly perceived, proprioceptive sensations that become associated through experience with different relative distances. The mind does not apply computational rules somehow involving access to trigonometric functions; the mind simply perceives and associates sensations. Berkeley has substituted the more vaguely defined "sensations" for Descartes's explicitly defined movements of nerve fibers. In a similar vein, he argues that *clarity* or *confusion* of the image or appearance is also sensation associated by long

315 EXTRAVISUAL INFORMATION

experience with varying distance. This latter idea probably had its roots in Euclid's perceptual postulates but Berkeley, following Descartes, does not say so.

Associations. Berkeley did write that it was well known since Euclid that the same size object at a near distance subtends a greater angle than at a farther distance. "And by this principle (we are told) the mind estimates the *magnitude* of an object, comparing the angle under which it is seen with its distance, and thence inferring the magnitude thereof." Berkeley rejected this geometrical approach to the perception of size (magnitude), arguing that it was a mistake of assuming a perceptual process of *inference* rather than one of simple *association*. The mistake occurs, according to Berkeley, because the same ideas that suggest distance also suggest size. That is, we judge objects to be near or far by taking into consideration the size of the retinal image (visible object), its confusion or distinctness, and its vigorousness or faintness. Visible objects that are small, faint, and confused must be far away. Judgments of size, like judgments of distance, also depend on the disposition of the eyes, and the number, figure, and situation of objects and other circumstances that have been observed to attend to great or small tangible magnitudes. Again, this involves only a simple process of association.

Tangible objects. Generally speaking, Berkeley, like Descartes before him, did not think that the nature of the projected image, the visible object, warranted much attention or analysis. He wrote that in perception "small heed" is taken of the visible figure and magnitude. Berkeley's position, like Descartes's, followed from his rejection of any objectively determined resemblance between "tangible, touchable objects" and appearance on the retina-"visible objects." Just as he rejected the use of geometry in the process of perception by the perceiver, so he rejected its utility in the matter of perception. For Berkeley, core percepts or ideas are of *tangible* bodies "operating on our organs by an immediate application." These objects are "adapted to benefit or injure our own bodies, and thereby produce in our minds the sensations of pleasure or pain."

That is, *all* tangible bodies when touched must produce immediate sensations in the mind, because all tangible bodies operate on the body for benefit or injury on immediate application. Things felt either hurt or they do not. Berkeley seemed to include in tangible ideas the proprioceptive sensations of muscle and joint position and movement as well as directly apprehended "clarity" or "confusion" of the image on the retina. Clarity seems to be the only aspect of *visual* stimulation that is directly sensed: All other aspects of visible ideas or objects require interpretation.

Visible objects enable the perceiver to foresee the benefit or damage likely to ensue upon application of the body to this or that body at a distance, *after* the visible ideas have become associated with the tangible ideas *empirically*, through experience. In and of themselves, visible ideas, "retinal images," are uninformative about the world and "the objects that environ us." Touch teaches vision.

This position, that visual images in and of themselves are uninformative for the world they represent, that they acquire meaning only through association with the tangible effects of experience, became a fundamental tenet of all perceptual theorizing for the next 200 years. Most people believe it today.

Hermann von Helmholtz

Hermann von Helmholtz (1821–1894), perhaps the greatest of the old perceptionists, accepted this Empiricist theory as true, along with the "fact" of nonresemblance between objects and events in the world and the sensations they produce in the organism.

Functional correspondence. Helmholtz argued that the only defensible position on the relationship between world and observer was one of correspondence between regular arrangements and sequences in each. As long as a regular arrangement or sequence in the world corresponds with a regular arrangement or sequence of sensations, then the latter serves as a sufficient "sign" for the other. He argued that signs sometimes have image quality, when they are in part "similar in kind" to what they signify, but it is the *fact of signification*, not imaging, that is critical for *functional correspondence*. Helmholtz regretted that it was not only uneducated persons, but even educated ones who "are inclined to demur to so complete a want of any closer correspondence in kind between actual objects and the sensations they produce" than the law of regular correspondence.

Helmholtz followed Berkeley in his acceptance of the tenet that "touch teaches vision" and of the position that there is no necessary connection between tangible and untangible (visual) experience. He accepted both sensations as the units of perception and association as the fundamental process. Yet Helmholtz followed Descartes in his involvement of computational rules in his analysis of distance perception and binocular vision, and assumed the experience of coherent visual images in even the youngest child. It is interesting to follow his reasoning as he reconciles the associative and inferential approaches to perceptual processing.

Tangible experience. The primacy of tangible and kinetic experience, of touching and handling objects and of moving through space, was reiterated by Helmholtz many times and in many places. He wrote that the only theory that does not lead to contradiction is one "which regards all of our perceptions of space as depending upon experience, and not only the qualities, but even the local signs of the sense of sight as nothing more than signs, the meaning of which we have to learn by experience" (1868: 174). In explaining what he meant by experience, Helmholtz formulated a *theory of perceptual learning* that remains the dominant theory today. He explained that we become acquainted with the meaning of the signs of the sense of sight by comparing them with the results of our own *movements*, that is, with the changes produced in the visual world by our movements. He wrote than in the beginning an infant does not know how to turn his eyes or hands to an object that attracts his attention by its brightness or color. At first, the infant plays with his hands. Then, a little older, the child seizes "whatever is presented to it, turns it over and over again, looks at it, touches it, and puts it in his mouth." The child will spend weeks in this way with a single toy, learning all of its perspective images, then throw the toy away and go on to another.

By this means the child learns to recognize the different views which the same object can afford in connection with the movements which he is constantly giving it. The conception of the shape of any object, gained in this manner, is the result of *associating* all these visual images. When we have obtained an accurate conception of the form of any object, we are then able to imagine what appearance it would present if we looked at it from some other point of view. All these different views are combined in the judgment we form as to the dimensions and shape of an object. (1868: 175; italics mine)

Helmholtz went on to say that, as a consequence of such experiences, we can anticipate the various images an object would present when seen from different points of view, as well as the various movements we would have to perform on it to obtain those successive images. This description of development may sound quite reasonable, but it certainly does not apply to human infants. Perhaps it is not necessary to note that the infant who will spend weeks playing with a single toy probably has not yet been born. The closest example that I can think of to what Helmholtz had in mind is the fascination for the computer exhibited by many older children. His description has nothing to do with babies.

It is noteworthy that despite the fact that Helmholtz himself was a geometer, in his perceptual theory he argued that the perspective views of an object are linked only by *association,* not formally through geometrical structures. Although perfectly aware of the geometrical structure of the light to the eye, he never made the case that that structure is, in and of itself, informative for vision.

Unconscious inference. In his treatment of the perception of *distance* of objects from the eye, Helmholtz wrote that we have two sources of information for this type of perception. One source is based on experience and previous acquaintance with the special nature of the object, and the other derives from sensation. The former is ideational or conceptual; the latter is perceptual, although also dependent on experience. Of the conceptual method of apprehending distance Helmholtz writes:

> The same object seen at different distances will be depicted on the retina by images of different sizes and will subtend different visual angles. The farther it is away, the less its apparent size will be. Thus, just as astronomers can compute the variations of the distances of the sun and moon from the changes in the apparent sizes of these bodies, so, knowing the size of an object, a human being, for instance, we can estimate the distance from us by means of the visual angle subtended or, what amounts to the same thing, by means of the size of the image on the retina. (1868: 282) Thus, an apparent size-distance relationship as determined by Euclid's visual angles is augmented mentally to produce a "true" perception of size-at-a-distance.

Formally such an unconscious computation would be trigonometric, but I do not think the case can be made that this is what Helmholtz meant by this kind of *unconscious inference*. Although he explicitly and frequently drew the parallel between such unconscious computations and conscious logical thought, it is important to realize that Helmholtz regarded logical deduction itself as essentially inductive. He not only explicitly stated that the premises in logical reasoning are inductively reached, but he implied as well that even the *logic* of deduction is primarily associative. In any case, he did not see such computations as really perceptual.

The *perceptual* experience of distance, for Helmholtz, as for Berkeley and Descartes, was based on the *sensations* (or innervations) accompanying such activities as the accommodation of the lens and the varying convergence of the eyes with distance. He even argued that the complex retinal changes that accompany movement are informative only by virtue of the associated sensations they produce and not through any process of computation or logical inference. These changes are of three types:

1. Change in *perspective* views of the same object as seen from different points
2. Differential apparent angular *velocities* of objects in the field of view, inversely proportional to distance
3. Relative *displacement* of objects at different distances with respect to each other.

(The first and third today are generally classed as motion perspective effects, and the second as motion parallax.)

It is not completely clear why Helmholtz regarded these sources of information for distance as noncomputational. Presumably it was because they do not involve the kind of knowledge that can be verbalized easily. Rather they involve the kind of geometrical "knowledge" never thought of by those unskillful in optics, as Berkeley would have put it. For Helmholtz, as for Berkeley, it is the *sensations* that accompany these geometrical alterations in optic structures, and *not* the geometrical relations themselves, that serve as the basis of perception. A sensation is a meaningless unit of experience of brightness or color, unlocalized in space. This emphasis on sensation, on the development of meaning in perception through associated sensations, rather than geometric computation, even underlies Helmholtz's extensive quasi-geometrical treatment of binocular vision. His predictions of relative and absolute distances perceived binocularly are clearly and explicitly based on a visual-angle analysis, as was Descartes's treatment of distance, but his geometrical approach is not extended either to the perceptual process or to the information on which it is based.

One could make the case that Helmholtz's visual-angle analyses apply to the distal *stimulus,* to the structure of the light "out there," but not to the proximal stimulus out of which percepts are made. From this point of view, then, it could be argued that Helmholtz's theory of perception was geometrical in the tradition established by Euclid for the *analysis of visual rays.*

Primacy of Association. However, this approach really does not do justice to Helmholtz's unequivocal commitment to Empiricist theory. Helmholtz believed that meaningless sensations of brightness and color, not complex angular structures, were the building blocks of perception, and that the only process of perception was one of association of sensations and of memories of sensations. Helmholtz argued that the *only* relationship between regularities in the world and regularities of experience was one of indeterminate correspondence, so formal geometric analyses of the properties of the visual field, of changing patterns of retinal images, were never carried out despite his obvious awareness of them. From Helmholtz's point of view, such formal analyses might describe certain regularities in the world, in the light to the eye, but could never describe corresponding regularities of experience. The far-reaching consequences of this epistemological position are nowhere more obvious than in Helmholtz's description of the development of the perception of constant shape. Although he certainly had the mathematical tools as an accomplished geometer, Helmholtz declined to apply a geometrical description to the family of views of an object created by movement relative to it (Fig. 2.10). Indeed, he wrote that the only perceptually relevant relation among the different views is one of association; that we anticipate or imagine particular perspective views in the set through association alone. Just as he rejected the importance of image quality in a single retinal stimulus, so too did he reject the importance of describing similarities among many different images. If the quality of a single image has no importance, then the quality of the many has none either. Helmholtz's knowledge of the geometrical structures of visual angles in reflected light was vast, but he did not see that these structures could possibly serve as information for perception. So he did not apply his geometrical knowledge to extend the theoretical analysis of vision based on visual angles begun with Euclid. It was not until the work of James Gibson in the middle of this century that visual-angle analysis of vision was lifted out of the Empiricist doldrums.

James Gibson: theory of ecological optics

Gibson initially retained the concept of visual angle derived from Euclid and the pictorial post-Renaissance approach to visual information. At the same time, he avoided both the assumptions and consequences of adoption of Euclid's laws of appearance – including the necessity of postulating "depth cues" and/or "extra-optical" sources of information to effect perception of the "real world." At least, that was Gibson's approach in the beginning. He ended by adopting a different level of analysis of optical information altogether, a level in which appearance in the sense of "the way things are" is directly given in visual information, not inferred or added. He built on the work of all of his predecessors, extending the best of their theories and learning from their mistakes. It has been my intention in this book to extend his analysis of ecological information to the world of pictures in ways he did not consider (and probably would not have approved).

References

Abbate, F. 1972. *Egyptian Art*. London: Octopus Books.

Alberti, L.B. (1436), 1966. *On Painting*, rev. ed. Translated, with introduction and notes by John R. Spencer. New Haven: Yale University Press.

Arnheim, R. 1967. *Toward a Psychology of Art*. Berkeley: University of California.

　1969. *Visual Thinking*. London: Faber & Faber.

　1954, 1974. *Art and Visual Perception: A Psychology of the Creative Eye*, rev. ed. Berkeley: University of California.

　1977. Perception of perspective pictorial space from different viewing points. *Leonardo 10*: 283–8.

Arthur, J., Canaday, J. 1979. *Richard Estes: The Urban Landscape*. Essay by J. Canaday, Catalogue and Interview by J. Arthur. Boston: Museum of Fine Arts and New York Graphic Society.

Benson, C., Yonas, A. 1973. Development of sensitivity to static pictorial depth information. *Perception and Psychophysics 13*: 361–6.

Berkeley, G. 1948. An essay towards a new theory of vision, 1709, in A.A. Luce and T.E. Jessop, eds.: *The Works of George Berkeley, Bishop of Cloyne*. London: Nelson and Sons.

Beveridge, W.M. 1940. Some racial differences in perception. *British Journal of Psychology 30*: 57–64.

Bleek, D.F. 1930. *Rock Paintings in South Africa*. London: Methuen.

Boas, F. 1955. *Primitive Art*. New York: Dover.

Bower, T.G.R. 1974. *Development in Infancy*. San Francisco: Freeman.

Bower, T.G.R., Broughten, J.M., and Moore, M.K., 1971. Infant responses to approaching objects: An indicator of response to distal variables. *Perception and Psychophysics*. 1971, Vol. IX, p. 193–96.

Briguet, M.F. 1962. *Etruscan Art: Tarquinia Frescoes*. New York: Tudor.

Bunim, M.S. 1970. *Space in Medieval Painting and the Forerunners of Perspective*. New York: AMS Press.

Butzer, K.W., Fock, G.J., Scott, L., Stuckenrath, R. 1979. Dating and context of rock engravings in Southern Africa. *Science 203*: 1201–14.

Capart, J. 1923. *Lectures on Egyptian Art*. Chapel Hill: University of North Carolina.

Cassirer, E. 1944. The concept of group and the theory of perception. *Philosophy and Phenomenological Research* 5: 1–35.

1953. *Substance and Function*. New York: Dover.

Coffman, H.L. 1980. Pictorial perception: hemispheric specialization and developmental regression in the neurologically impaired, in M.A. Hagen, ed: *The Perception of Pictures*, Vol. II. New York Academic Press.

Cooper, R.G. 1977. Development of sensitivity to geometric information for viewing shapes and sizes in pictures, in R.N. Haber ed: *Proceedings of the Tenth Symposium of the Center for Visual Sciences*. Rochester, N.Y.: University of Rochester.

Deregowski, J.B. 1972. Pictorial perception and culture. *Scientific American* 227: 82–8.

Muldrow, E.S., Muldrow, W.F. 1972. Pictorial recognition in a remote Ethiopian population. *Perception* 1: 417–25.

Descartes, R. (1637), 1965. *La Dioptrique*. Translated by P.J. Olscamp in *Discourse on Method, Optics, Geometry and Meteorology: René Descartes*, New York: Bobbs Merrill.

Dürer, A. 1963. *Complete Woodcuts of Albrecht Dürer*. W. Kurth, ed New York: Dover.

Edgerton, S.Y. 1975. *The Renaissance Rediscovery of Linear Perspective* New York: Basic Books, Inc.,

Ellis, W.D. 1969. *A Source Book of Gestalt Psychology*. London: Routledge & Kegan Paul.

Eng, H., 1931. *The Psychology of Children's Drawings*. London: Routledge & Kegan Paul.

Euclid, *Optics*. 1945. Translated by H.E. Burton. *Journal of the Optical Society of America* 35: 357–72.

Fairservis, W. 1955. *Cave Paintings of the Great Hunters*. New York Profile Press.

Farber, J. 1972. The effects of angular magnification on the perception of rigid motion. Doctoral dissertation, Cornell University, Ann Arbor, Michigan: University Microfilms, no. 73–7134.

Francastel, P. 1967. *Medieval Painting*, vol. II. Translated by R.E. Wolf New York: Dell.

Freeman, N.H. 1980. *Strategies of Representation in Young Children*. London: Academic Press.

Fry, E.F. 1966. *Cubism*. New York: Oxford University Press.

Gans, D. 1969. *Transformations and Geometries*. New York: Appleton-Century-Crofts.

Gibson, E.J. 1969. *Principles of Perceptual Learning and Development*. New York: Appleton-Century-Crofts.

Gibson, J.J. 1947. *Motion Picture Testing and Research*. Aviation Psychology Research Reports, No. 7. Washington: U.S. Government Printing Office, pp. 181–95. (Reprinted (1958) in D. Beardslee and

M. Wertheimer, eds. *Readings in Perception*. Princeton, N.J.: Van Nostrand.)

1950a. Perception of visual surfaces. *American Journal of Psychology* 63: 367–84.

1950b. *The Perception of the Visual World*. Boston: Houghton Mifflin.

1951. What is a form? *Psychological Review* 58: 403–12.

1954. A theory of pictorial perception. *Audio-visual Communication Review* 1: 3–23.

1960. Pictures, perspective and perception. *Daedalus* 89: 216–27.

1966. *The Senses Considered as Perceptual Systems*. Boston: Houghton Mifflin.

1971. The information available in pictures. *Leonardo* 4: 27–35.

1973. On the concept of formless invariants in visual perception. *Leonardo* 6: 43–5.

1974. Visualizing conceived as visual apprehending without any particular point of observation. *Leonardo* 7: 41–2.

1979. *The Ecological Approach to Visual Perception*. Boston: Houghton Mifflin.

Gibson, J.J., Cornsweet, J. 1952. The perceived slant of visual surfaces: optical and geographical. *Journal of Experimental Psychology* 44:11–15.

Gibson, J.J., Olum, P., Rosenblatt, F. 1955. Parallax and perspective during aircraft landings. *American Journal of Psychology* 372–85.

Gibson, J.J., Yonas, P. 1968. A new theory of scribbling and drawing in children, in *The Analysis of Reading Skill*. Final report, project no. 5-1213. Cornell University and the U.S. Office of Education.

Gleizes, A., Metzinger, J. 1960. Cubism 1912, in E.F. Fry: *Cubism*. London: Thames and Hudson.

Gombrich, E.H. 1972a. *The Story of Art*. London: Phaidon.

1972b. *Art and Illusion: A Study in the Psychology of Pictorial Representation*. Princeton University Press.

1975. Mirror and map: theories of pictorial representation. *Philosophical Transactions of the Royal Society*, London 270: 119–49.

Gombrich, E.H., Hochberg, J., Black, M. 1972. *Art, Perception and Reality*. Baltimore: Johns Hopkins University.

Goodman, N. 1968. *Languages of Art*. Indianapolis: Bobbs-Merrill.

Gregory, R.L. 1970. *The Intelligent Eye*. New York: McGraw-Hill.

1971. *Eye and Brain*. New York: McGraw-Hill.

Groenewegen-Frankfort, H. A. 1951. *Arrest and Movement: An Essay on Space and Time in the Representational Art of the Ancient Near East*. London: Faber & Faber.

Haber, R.N. 1980. Perceiving space from pictures: A theoretical analysis, in M.A. Hagen, ed: *The Perception of Pictures*, Vol. I. New York: Academic Press.

Hagen, M.A. 1974. Pictorial perception: toward a theoretical model. *Psychological Bulletin* 81: 471–97.

1976a. The development of sensitivity to cast and attached shadows

in pictures as information for the direction of the source of illu
mination. *Perception and Psychophysics* 20: 25–8.

1976b. The influence of picture surface and station point on the abilit
to compensate for oblique view in pictorial perception. *Develop
mental Psychology* 12, 57–63.

1976c. The development of the ability to perceive and produce tl
pictorial depth cue of overlapping. *Perceptual and Motor Skills* 4
1007–14.

1978. An outline of an investigation into the special character
pictures, in H.L. Pick, Jr. and E. Saltzman, eds: *Modes of Perceivir
and Processing Information.* Hillsdale, N.J.: Erlbaum.

1979. A new theory of representational art, in C. Nodine and I
Fisher, eds: *Perception and Pictorial Representation.* New York: Praeger

1980a. Cultural and historical options in the forms of depiction,
J. Fisher, ed: *Perceiving Artworks.* Philadelphia: Temple Universi
Press.

1980b. Generative theory: a descriptively adequate perceptual theor
of pictorial representation, in M.A. Hagen, ed: *The Perception
Pictures*, Vol. II. New York: Academic Press.

Hagen, M.A., ed. 1980c. *The Perception of Pictures*, vols. I, II. Ne
York: Academic Press.

1985. James J. Gibson's ecological approach to visual perception,
S. Koch, ed: *A Century of Psychology as Science.* New York: McGraw
Hill.

Hagen, M.A., Elliott, H.B. 1976. An investigation of the relationsh
between viewing condition and preference for true and modifie
linear perspective with adults. *Journal of Experimental Psycholog
Human Perception and Performance* 2: 479–90.

Hagen, M.A., Elliott, H.B., Jones, R.K. 1978. A distinctive chara
teristic of pictorial perception: the zoom effect. *Perception* 1: 62
33.

Hagen, M.A., Glick, R. 1977. Pictorial perspective; perception of siz
linear, and texture perspective in children and adults. *Perception*
675–84.

Hagen, M.A., Glick, R., Morse, B. 1978. The role of two-dimensio
characteristics in pictorial depth perception. *Perceptual and Mo
Skills* 46: 875–81.

Hagen, M.A., Jones, R.K. 1978. Differential patterns of preference f
modified linear perspective in children and adults. *Journal of E
perimental Child Psychology* 26: 205–15.

1978. Cultural effects on pictorial perception: how many words
one picture really worth? in R.D. Walk and H.L. Pick, eds.: *Pe
ception and Experience.* New York: Plenum.

1982. The perception of distance in real scenes and pictures, in
Baddeley and J. Long, eds: *Attention and Performance* IX. Hillsdal
N.J.: Erlbaum.

Hagen, M.A., Jones, R.K., Reed, E.S. 1978. On a neglected variab in theories of pictorial perception: truncation of the visual field. *Perception and Psychophysics* 23: 326–30.

Hagen, M.A., Teghtsoonian, M. 1981. The effects of binocular and motion-generated information on the perception of depth and height. *Perception and Psychophysics* 30: 257–65.

Hay, J.C. 1966. Optical motions and space perceptions: An extension of Gibson's analysis. *Psychological Review* 73: 550–565.

Helmholtz, H. von. (1868), 1962. *Treatise on Physiological Optics*. J.P.C. Southall, ed. New York: Dover.

Hochberg, J. 1962. The psychophysics of pictorial perception. *Audio-Visual Communications Review*.

　1978. *Perception*. Englewood Cliffs, N.J.: Prentice-Hall.

　1978. Visual arts and the structures of the mind. In S.S. Madeja, ed:*The Arts, Cognition and Basic Skills*. St Louis: CEMREL.

Holm, B. 1974. *Northwest Coast Indian Art: An Analysis of Form*. Seattle: University of Washington Press.

Holm, B., Reid, B. 1978, *Indian Art of the Northwest Coast: A Dialogue on Craftsmanship and Aesthetics*. Seattle: University of Washington.

Ienaga, S. 1978. *Japanese Art: A Cultural Appreciation*. Translated by R.L. Gage. New York: Weatherhill/Heibonsha.

Inverarity, R.B. 1950. *Art of the Northwest Coast Indians*. Berkeley: University of California.

Ivins, W.M. 1964. *Art and Geometry: A Study in Space Intuitions*. New York: Dover.

Jacobs, H. 1974. *Geometry*. San Francisco: Freeman.

Jahoda, G., McGurk, H. 1974. Pictorial depth perception: A developmental study. *British Journal of Psychology* 65: 141–9.

Johansson, G. 1975. Visual motion perception. *Scientific American* 232 (6): 76–88

　1978. About the geometry underlying spontaneous visual decoding of the optical message, in E.L.J. Leeuwenberg and H.F.J. Buffart, eds: *Formal Theories of Visual Perception*. New York: Wiley.

Jones, R.K., Hagen, M.A. 1978. The perceptual constraints on choosing a pictorial station point. *Leonardo* 11: 191–6.

　1980. A perspective on cross-cultural picture perception, in M.A. Hagen, ed.: *The Perception of Pictures* Vol. I. New York: Academic Press.

Kahane, P.P. 1968. *Ancient and Classical Art*, edited by H.L.C. Jaffe, translated by R.E. Wolf. New York: Dell.

Kaplan, G. 1969. Kinetic disruption of optical texture: the perception of depth at an edge. *Perception and Psychophysics* 6: 193–8.

Katz, D. 1906. Ein Beitrag zur Kenntnis der Kinderzeichnungen. *Zeitschrift fur Psychologie* 41: 241–56.

Kellogg, R. 1969. *Analyzing Children's Art*. Palo Alto, Calif.: National Press Books.

Kellogg, R., O'Dell, S. 1967. *The Psychology of Children's Art*. New York: CRM-Random House.

Kennedy, J.M. 1974. *A Psychology of Picture Perception*. San Francis Jossey-Bass.

Klein, F. 1872. Vergleichende Betrachtungen uber neuere geometris Forschungen. Erlangen.

Kline, M. 1956. Projective Geometry, in James R. Newman, ed.: *World of Mathematics*, Vol. 1.

Koffka, K. (1935), 1963. *Principles of Gestalt Psychology*. New Yc Harcourt Brace Jovanovich.

Kubler, G. 1962. *The Shape of Time: Remarks on the History of Thi* New Haven: Yale University Press.

Kohler, W. 1940. *Dynamics in Psychology*. New York: Liveright.
1947. *Gestalt Psychology: An Introduction to New Concepts in Moc Psychology*. New York: Liveright.

Land, E. 1978. *Harvard Magazine*.

Lark-Horowitz, B., Lewis, H.P., Luca, M. 1967. *Understanding C dren's Art for Better Teaching*. Columbus, Ohio: Merrill.

Lee, D.N. 1974. Visual information during locomotion, in R.B. MacL and H.L. Pick, Jr., eds.: *Perception: Essays in Honor of Jame Gibson*. Ithaca: Cornell University.

Leonardo da Vinci. 1970. *Notebooks* I, II. Compiled and edited by Richter, New York: Dover.

Lindberg, D.C. 1976. *Theories of Vision from al-Kindi to Kepler*. L versity of Chicago Press.

Loran, E. 1963. *Cézanne's Composition*. Berkeley: University California.

Lumsden, E.A. 1980. Problems of magnification and minification explanation of the distortions of distance, slant, shape and veloc in M.A. Hagen, ed: *The Perception of Pictures*, Vol. I. New Yc Academic Press.

Mace, W.M., Shaw, R.E. 1975. Simple kinetic information for tr parent depth. *Perception and Psychophysics* 15: 209–10.

McGurk, H., Jahoda, G. 1974. The development of pictorial de perception: the role of figural elevation. *British Journal of Psycho* 65: 367–76.

Mark, L.A. 1979. A transformational approach toward understanc the perception of growing faces, doctoral dissertation, Univer of Connecticut.

Miller, R.J. 1973. Cross-cultural research in the perception of pictc materials. *Psychological Bulletin* 80: 135–50.

Modenov, P.S., Parkhomenko, A.S. 1965. *Geometric Transformati* Translated by M.B.P. Slater. New York: Academic Press.

Monet's Years at Giverny: Beyond Impressionism. 1978. The Metropol Museum of Art. Published on the occasion of the exhibition. N York: Abrams.

Newman, J.R. 1956. *The World of Mathematics*, Vols. I–IV. New Y Simon & Schuster.

Nodine, C.F., Fisher, D.F., eds. 1979. *Perception and Pictorial Representation*. New York: Praeger.

Olson, R., Yonas, A., Cooper, R. 1980. Development of pictorial perception, in M.A. Hagen, ed.: *The Perception of Pictures*, Vol. II. New York: Academic Press.

Panofsky, E. 1955. *Meaning in the Visual Arts*. New York: Doubleday.

Pastore, N. 1971. *Selective History of Theories of Visual Perception: 1650–1950*. New York: Oxford University Press.

Perkins, D.N. 1973a. Visual discrimination between rectangular and nonrectangular parallelopipeds. *Perception and Psychophysics* 12: 396–400.

1973b. Compensating for distortion in viewing pictures obliquely. *Perception and Psychophysics* 14: 13–18.

Perkins, D.N., Cooper, R.G. 1980. How the eye makes up what the light leaves out, in M.A. Hagen, ed.: *The Perception of Pictures*, Vol. II. New York: Academic Press.

Perkins, D.N., Hagen, M.A. 1980. Convention, context and caricature, in M.A. Hagen, ed.: *The Perception of Pictures*, Vol. I. New York: Academic Press.

Picard, G. 1968. *Roman Painting*. Greenwich, Conn.: New York Graphic Society.

Pirenne, M.H. 1970. *Optics, Painting and Photography*. Cambridge University Press.

Pittenger, J.B., Shaw, R.E. 1975a. Aging faces as visual-elastic events: Implications for a theory of non-rigid shape perception. *Journal of Experimental Psychology: Human Perception and Performance* 4: 374–82.

1975b. Perception of relative and absolute age in facial photographs. *Perception and Psychophysics* 18: 137–43.

Purdy, J., Gibson, E.J. 1955. Distance judgment by the method of fractionation. *Journal of Experimental Psychology* 50: 374–80.

Purdy, W.C. 1959. The hypothesis of psychophysical correspondence in space perception, doctoral dissertation, Cornell University. Ann Arbor, Michigan: University Microfilms, no. 58-5594. Reproduced in part as Report No. R60ELC56 of the General Electric Technical Information Series.

Reed, E.S., Jones, R.K. 1978. Gibson's theory of perception: A case of hasty epistemologizing? *Philosophy of Science* 45: 519–30.

Reed, E., Jones, R.K., eds. 1982. *Reasons for Realism: Selected Essays of James J. Gibson*. Hillsdale, N.J.: Erlbaum.

Reggini, H.C. 1975. Perspective using curved projection rays and its computer application. *Leonardo* 8: 307–12.

Robertson, M. 1979. *Greek Painting*. New York: Rizzoli International Publications.

Robinson, B.W. 1965. *Persian Drawings*. Boston: Little, Brown.

Rosinski, R.R., Farber, J. 1980. Compensation for viewing point in the perception of pictured space, in M.A. Hagen, ed: *The Perception of Pictures*, Vol. I. New York: Academic Press.

Rubin, W., ed. 1977. *Cezanne: The Late Work.* New York: The Muse
of Modern Art.

Ryan, T., Schwartz, C. 1956. Speed of perception as a function of me
of representation. *American Journal of Psychology* 69: 60–9.

Sedgwick, H.A. 1973. The visible horizon: a potential source of vis
information for the perception of size and distance. Doctoral c
sertation, Cornell University. Ann Arbor: University Microfil
no. 73-22,530.

Sedgwick, H.A. 1980. The geometry of spatial layout in pictorial r
resentation, in M.A. Hagen, ed: *The Perception of Pictures*, Vol
New York: Academic Press.

    1980. Perceiving spatial layout: the ecological approach. Paper de
ered at symposium, "The Contributions of James J. Gibson
Perception": Annual convention of the American Psycholog
Association, Montreal, September 1–5.

    1983. Environmental-centered representation of spatial layout: av
able visual information from texture and perspective, in Jacob Be
Barbara Hope, and Azriel Rosenfeld, eds: *Human and Machine*
sion. New York: Academic Press.

Shaw, R.E., McIntyre, M., Mace, W.M. 1974. The role of symme
in event perception, in R.B. MacLeod and H.L. Pick, Jr., e
Perception: Essays in Honor of James J. Gibson. Ithaca: Cornell U
versity Press.

Shaw, R.E., Pittenger, J.B. 1977. Perceiving the face of change
changing faces: implications for a theory of object perception
R. Shaw and J. Bransford, eds: *Perceiving, Acting, and Know*
Toward An Ecological Psychology. Hillsdale, N.J.: Erlbaum.

    1978. Perceiving change, in H.L. Pick, Jr. and E. Salzman, eds: *M*
of Perceiving and Processing Information. Hillsdale, N.J.: Erlbaum

Shepherd, R.N., Metzler, J. 1971. Mental rotation of three-dimensic
objects. *Science* 171: 701–3.

Shikibu, M. 1979. *The Tales of Genji.* Translated by E.G. Seidenstic
New York: Knopf.

de Silva, A. 1967. *The Art of Chinese Landscape Painting.* New Yc
Crown.

Smart, A. 1978. *The Dawn of Italian Painting: 1250–1400.* Ithaca: Cor
University Press.

Smith, R. 1974. Natural versus scientific vision: the foreshortened fig
in the Renaissance. *Gazette des Beaux-arts* 84: 239–48.

Spencer, J.R. 1966. *Leon Battista Alberti On Painting.* New Haven: Y
University Press.

Thompson, D. (1917), 1977. *On Growth and Form*, rev. ed. Cambri
University Press.

Vredeman, Jan de Vries. 1968. *Perspective.* New York: Dover.

Wallach, H., O'Connell, D.N. 1953. The kinetic depth effect. *Jou*
of Experimental Psychology 45: 205–7.

Wartofsky, M. 1980. Visual scenarios: the role of representation in vi

perception, in M.A. Hagen, ed.: *The Perception of Pictures, Vol. II.*
New York: Academic Press.

Werner, H. 1948 (rev. ed.). *Comparative Psychology of Mental Development.* New York: International University Press.

Weyl, H. (1940), 1956. The mathematical way of thinking, in J.R. Newman, ed: *The World of Mathematics*, Vol. III. New York: Simon & Schuster.

White, J. 1967. *The Birth and Rebirth of Pictorial Space.* Boston: Boston Book and Art Shop.

Willats, J. 1977a. How children learn to draw realistic pictures. *Quarterly Journal of Experimental Psychology* 29: 367–82.

   1977b. How children learn to represent three-dimensional space in drawings, in G.E. Butterworth, ed: The Child's Representation of the World. New York: Plenum.

Willcox, A.R. 1963. *The Rock Art of South Africa.* Johannesburg: Nelson.

Wölfflin, H. (1932), 1950. *Principles of Art History: The Problem of Development of Style in Later Art.* Translated by M.D. Hottinger. New York: Dover.

Name index

Subject index

Adoration of the Magi, 216
Adoration of the Shepherds, 228
affine invariants: in Japanese art, 112–13, 188–95; in Northwest Coast Indian Art, 195–8
affinities, 42–52; and compression, 43–4; definition of, 42–3; equivalence classes in, 45–7; and growth and aging, 49–51; and parallelism, 44; and parallel projection, 43; in perception, 47–52
affordances, 6
aging: and classes of events, 20
Allegory of Sowing and Reaping, 216
Altamira, 232, 268, 284
analysis of style: utility of, 117–8
animate events: and stretchy events, 51; and topology, 51
animate objects: in Egyptian depictions, 169–170
appearance: in Euclid, 300–6; geometrically determined, 18; and resemblance, 305–6
architectural units: drawings of, 188; in Japanese art, 189–90, 256
art: children's, 3; definition of, 2–3, 204; geometrical kinship in, 8; nonperspective, 1; primitive, 1
art styles: Egyptian, 1, 285; Eskimo, 287; Gothic, 5, 284; Greek vases, 264–5; Ice Age, 3, 256; Irish, 259; Italian, 236; Japanese, 5, 256, 284; Mayan, 258; Northwest Coast Indian, 1; Persian, 259; rock art of South Africa, 1, 15; Romanesque, 255; Roman mural, 5, 258, 264, 284; Western post-Renaissance, 256
artist: definition of, 81
artistic vision: truths of, 80–82
associations: and Berkeley, 316; and Helmholtz, 321
associativity: definition of, 29

Assyrian art, 257
"average savage", 285

Bakemono no Soshi, 189
Baroque compositions: Japanese, 150; Western, 137
Battle of Naked Men, 243
binocularity, 61–2; and distance perception, 61–2
Birth and Rebirth of Pictorial Space, 308–9
borders in the light, 11
Burning of Sanjo Palace, 194
Bushmen art, 235–8, 256, 284, 287

camera: and artists, 111; and eye, 88–9; fixed lens, 107–9, 111; movie, 17; obscura, 136; view, 148
canonical form, 245; in affine geometry, 281–2; analysis of, 281–2; and conic sections, 45–6; and cultural conventions, 72; and "good" pictures, 72–3; in house drawing, 275; new definition of, 72; traditional definition of, 71
categorization system: list of options, 112–13; statement of principle, 112; and style, 6
Celtic ornamentation, 259
center of projection, 123–4
Cézanne, 202, 207–8
Characteristic aspects: and recognizability, 245; of various objects, 242–6
Chilkat blankets, 195–6
Chinese painting: in caves, 259–60; landscape scrolls, 260–1; third century, 284
clarity of vision: in Berkeley, 315–16; in Euclid, 302
closure, 29, 34
color, 7; and Descartes, 311–12; in painting, 203

commutativity, 29
composition, 205–6
concept of group: Cassirer's exposition of, 76–7; and generativity, 76–7
congruent figures, 34; in perception 35
constraints, 100–1
construction rules: tacit knowledge of, 84–5
constructivism: and Cassirer, 77–8
conventionalism, 86–7
convergence, 314; correction of, 10⬤ 110; and distortion, 106–7; in photos, 88; in real world, 302; o⬤ retina, 88
coordinate system, 23
cross-ration: of lines, 293; of points 293
Crows, 244
Cubism, 255
Cueva del Civil, 234–5, 285
cultural convention: and theory of vision, 83

Dead Christ, 137
deformations, 19
degree: of an equation, 26; of degree similarity between object and image 247
Deir el Bersheh coffin, 181, 183, 212⬤
development: theories of, 272–8; tra⬤ ditional formulation of, 267–8
distance, 7, 9, 20; and Berkeley, 31⬤ 15; and Descartes, 312–14; poin⬤ 123–4
distortion: in Western perspective, 106–7, 137; Dürer, 140–1

Ecological Approach to Visual Perception, 6, 18, 97
ecological optics, 11
ecological validity: in pictures, 92–

elliptic rotation, 291
empiricism: and Helmholtz, 321–2
environment: cluttered, 36; and the
    organism, 6; and perception, 6–7
Epiphany, 263
equivalence class: definition of, 34–5;
    direct perception of, 66
*An Essay Towards a New Theory of
    Vision*, 314
Euclid, 12, 15, 18, 19, 181, 299–324
events, types of, 21–2

fidelity of representation, 197–8
figure and ground: in Romanesque
    painting, 217
foreshortening, 137–8; lack of inter-
    est in, 196–7
format: and cave art, 234; and com-
    position, 207–8; in Egyptian art,
    212; in Romanesque painting, 217
*Foundation Ceremonies of a Buddhist
    Temple*, 142–3
frontal-parallel angle assumption: in
    Egyptian art, 175–6
function: graphable, 25; as mapping,
    26–7; mathematical, 23–4; straight
    line, 25
functional correspondence: in Helm-
    holtz' theory, 317–18
*Funeral Procession and Builders at
    Work*, 260

Ganymede, 265
generative concept: of perceptual
    form, 246
Genji Monogatari, 142–3, 148, 189
geometrical concepts: and structure
    in perception, 77
geometry: and nonperspective art, 2;
    and the "real world," 73–4
Gestalt psychology: in art, 205–6;
    and art criticism, 208–210; princi-
    ples of, 205–6; the revolt against
    sensationists, 77
gestalts: in children's art, 273
gradients: of compression, 120; and
    cross-ratio, 56–9; and informa-
    tion, 59–62; of line, 17; motion
    generated, 62; Purdy's exposition
    of, 294–98; of size, 17; and slant,
    61; of texture, 17; of texture
    flow, 15; in Western art, 199
groups, 2: characteristics of, 28–30;
    definition of, 29–30; utility of
    concept, 29
growth, 19, 22; and aging, 49–52;
    and cardioidal strain, 50

habitat, 11
harmonic property, 293
Hasadera Enji, 147–8, 190, 194, 284
Heiji monogatari Emaki, 229–230
Herculaneum, 263
heuristic function of pictures, 82
hierarchy of geometries: and Klein,
    27–8; of transformations, 31–2
history of geometry and art, 1
horizon: and horizon-ratio relation,
    32; and size information, 40–2
house drawing: in children's art,
    274–5; by adults, 277–8
hyperbolic rotation, 290–1

identity, definition of, 20
illumination, changing, 19
Impressionism, 84
inference; and Berkeley, 316; uncon-
    scious (Helmholtz), 319–20
information, potential, 20
intromission theory, 303–4
invariants, 2; Affine, 31; conclusions
    about, 64; definition of, 27; Met-
    ric, 31; Projective, 31; in each
    projection type, 99–100; Similar-
    ity, 31; and transformations, 27–
    8; texture gradient, 56–60; types
    of 19–20

Kane, Art, 137
Kibi Daijin Nitto E-kotoba, 189
kinship networks, 178
krater, 265

Lascaux, 268, 284
Les Desmoiselles d'Avignon, 219
lifelikeness: definition of, 81–2, 84; in
    Western pictures, 201
light: ambient, 11; and Descartes,
    312–13; radiant, 11
limit of vision: in Euclid, 303
"little pictures" theory, 87–90, 310

Madonna and Child, 226
magnitude: *see* size
Mantagna, 137
mappings, 19–20; and functions, 23–
    7; pictures as types of, 98–100
meaning: in the context of behavior,
    68; of visual stimulation, 18
metric geometry: definition of, 33–4;
    invariants of, in Egyptian art,
    180; transformations of, in per-
    ception, 35–7
moderate distance assumption: and
    Alberti, 133; and Einstein, 134;

and Leonardo, 134; limits of,
    136–9
modifications of perspective, 89–94;
    limitations on, 89–94
momentary appearance, 282
monocular vision, 61–2
"most characteristic aspects," 172–3
motion parallax, 15
motor control, 273, 277, 284
movements of observer, 17; and con-
    gruence, 35–6; and invariants,
    104; and types of events, 21
multiple station point: in children's
    art, 268; in Egyptian art, 168–76,
    184–5; in Northwest Coast Indian
    art, 160–3; in primitive art, 285
mutuality of determination, 6–7, 65,
    305

natural geometry: and Berkeley, 315;
    in Descartes, 312; and Helmholtz,
    321–22
negative space, 207–8
non-Euclidean geometry, 27
Northwest Coast Indian art, 158–9,
    255, 284

oblique angle assumption: in Euro-
    pean art, 140–1; in Japanese art,
    154–6; in Northwest Coast Indian
    art, 166–8
occlusion of texture, 15, 17
Optica, 173–76, 180, 300–6, 310
optical flow, 62
optical infinity distance assumption:
    in Japanese art, 145–8; in Egyp-
    tian art, 174–5; in Northwest
    Coast Indian art, 163–5
optic array, 12, 19
Optics, Painting and Photography, 88
options, 1, 113
ordinary environment, 73
orthogonality: in children's art, 279–
    80

painterly, 250
parallelism: in Euclid, 301, in North-
    west Coast Indian art, 196
"passage," 222
perception: definition, 6–7
Perception of the Visual World, 61
perceptual learning, 318–19
perspective: artificial, 8, 95–6; axono-
    metric, 91; and development, 268;
    divergent, 147–8, 189–90, 284;
    and gradient information, 199;
    linear, 14, 95, 118–25; motion,
    15; natural, 8, 11–15, 78, 95–6; in